question by the reader will render any resulting actions solely under their purview. There are no scenarios in which the publisher or the original author of this work can be in any fashion deemed liable for any hardship or damages that may befall them after undertaking information described herein.

Additionally, the information in the following pages is intended only for informational purposes and should thus be thought of as universal. As befitting its nature, it is presented without assurance regarding its prolonged validity or interim quality. Trademarks that are mentioned are done without written consent and can in no way be considered an endorsement from the trademark holder.

Table of Content

Facebook

Introduction

Are you starting out with Facebook Marketing? This book is for you.

So you have probably heard that you have to be on Facebook. It is the largest social network in the world, with 2.27 billion active users, of which nearly 1.5 billion are active every day.

Welcome to the great world of Facebook, where you can connect with long-lost friends with relative ease and promote your business with just 10 - 20 minutes a day as your investment.

Facebook is far from that simple online student directory for students of the University of Harvard we all heard of. As mentioned before, it now has 2.27 billion users around the world: a vast market of potential customers and customers that businesses of all sizes can turn to.

As an entrepreneur, have you considered adding Facebook marketing to your overall marketing strategy? If you have, then you're on the right track.

After all, according to a Syncapse study, "85% of brand fans on Facebook recommend brands to others." Imagine all this free promotion to a wider audience!

You will find your best marketing opportunities on the world's largest social network and that won't change anytime soon. Spending time learning Facebook marketing is worth the investment.

Are you still convinced now? The next big question you must be asking yourself now is "How do I get started?" I have the answer for you.

In this guide, I'll show you the basics of using Facebook to your advantage. This guide is intended for the beginner who wants an introduction to marketing their business on the world's largest social network.

Chapter 1: Facebook Marketing Basics

Facebook marketing is the central part of social media marketing for many brands.

This means, in a nutshell, Facebook marketing is a central part of marketing for most brands.

Regardless of the natur of your industry (B2C or B2B), and regardless of the size of your actual business, you need Facebook Marketing.

But Facebook marketing is changing a lot. It's almost unrecognizable since it crossed college campuses in 2004, with over 1.47 billion users per day.

To put it in perspective, approximately 1.42 million people live in Hawaii, Facebook has more users than many states have.

Instead of being intimidated by the changes taking place on Facebook, it's best to embrace them and adapt to them.

In this chapter, we'll take a look at everything you must know about Facebook marketing now, and what you are expected to see in the future.

Starting Personal

I still remember that time when Facebook was starting out. There I was, refusing to do a Facebook and a Myspace.

I didn't see the point; why create a completely different profile, especially when they were so similar? They had the same information, you could write on people's walls, and all without the ferocity that comes with choosing your best friends.

Pages did not exist at the moment. Instead, there were "fan pages" you might like. Anyone can open these pages, whether or not they are affiliated with the company.

We all know the rest is history. Facebook has become something completely different from what Myspace once was. It is now a vital part of online marketing.

In the rest of this chapter, we'll take a look at the present and future of Facebook marketing, giving you an idea of how it should be used now and what to expect (and how to adapt!).

Facebook Marketing: What It Looks Like Now

Facebook had made great strides from when it was just another competitor to Myspace and has become a much more lucrative marketing tool than any other social media site that came before it ... and that's even if we do not talk about the Facebook Ads.

Initially, Facebook marketing was just trying to get as many likes as possible to deliver content to its audience. After all, nothing like a complex algorithm, that slashed away at reach.

Now the attention is more on building relationships with the audience, as follower count doesn't matter if engagement rates are in the toilet and relationships matter more than shouting messages at your audience anyways.

Today, there are five trends in Facebook usage that have defined Facebook marketing as it is today and will continue to do so.

Let's discuss a little about each of them.

1. Personalization

As a user, you have certainly seen "We have been friends for eight years!" videos that look exceptionally personalized.

You've probably also noticed that your feed is showing content from the people and brands you interact with most often.

Both are examples of how personalization is taking hold of Facebook and Facebook Marketing.

Brands should take this into account when creating strategies and content for Facebook.

It doesn't matter if you want to send an endless stream of promotions for your products and services, or even for your blog; Chances are, this isn't what your audience wants to see, which will cost you engagement.

Instead, find out the different types of content your target audience responds best to and create something from that.

2. Communication

Some users trust Facebook Messenger as their primary method of communicating with their friends and businesses they want to chat with.

Friends, I text; some, I speak almost exclusively with Messenger.

I think this is applicabl to most people; this is an evolving trend and many customers are more likely to message brands on Facebook than to call or even send emails. It's instantaneous and gives people the immediate answer they want and expect, whether they have a problem that needs to be resolved or they are shopping and need an answer to a question.

You can use brands to their advantage, being ready to process incoming messages as quickly as possible.

This increases your response rate, which is public on Facebook, and also makes your customers happy.

This is a significant part of marketing because it helps build your reputation, especially on Facebook.

3. Dynamic Marketing

Facebook took a lot of steps to make the platform as interactive and dynamic as possible for users.

Some popular examples include:

- Polls, especially in groups
- Different reaction buttons that go beyond simple likes
- 360 videos, which viewers can interact with to see a full scene
- Live video, in which users can comment in real-time to interact with the brand hosting the video

If you'd like to take advantage of Facebook marketing, you need to use dynamic marketing strategies and resources to do it.

This is what most users are most likely to interact with and watch. This will not only assist you get results on the single post, but it will also improve your reach in the algorithm.

Remember to mix it up, use these resources whenever possible to add lots of native videos to Facebook.

4. Community Building

Relationship building now takes the center of Facebook marketing internships, so building a community on the platform is the best way to go.

You will find that this will happen most often in the form of brand-managed groups, which are designed to fortify the relationship between your followers and the brand .

The goal is to build a community so valuable that it becomes a resource, providing users with the experience that will keep them close and loyal to your brand.

5. Omnichannel Selling

Did you know you can sell products and services directly from Facebook? Because you can, not just one way, but two different ways.

The first is through Facebook Shops, which allows you to create virtual storefronts on Facebook tabs.

Users can buy directly from your online store or you can send them to your website for purchase. You can sell services and products through the store.

You can also sell through Messenger chatbots, which cut customer service costs and provides another method to encourage sales.

These chatbots can be a bit expensive and/or time-consuming to set up, but once properly programmed, you will not only have a robotic customer service representative, but a sales representative as well.

Stores like DSW have chatbots that give customers with shoe suggestions based on their style, so that customers can purchase in the app. And if they don't want shoes, they can order pizza from the Dominos chatbot.

Omnichannel selling is something we see more of in general (and not just on Facebook), so agree here if or when it's ideal for your business, that should be something to consider.

Notice here that I say "consider." I want to stress that actual selling on Facebook may not be ideal for all businesses.

Having a store on Facebook can cost you clicks to your website, where you have lead magnets, pop-ups, and discounts to better attract customers, along with robbing you of better retargeting.

And chatbots aren't the right choice for every business.

Okay, and keep an eye out for best practices to see what new options are available to you. You can even integrate omnichannel sales by posting offers and nurturing leads on Facebook Marketing using contests, offers, and more.

The Future of Facebook Marketing

Every few months, an article is posted stating that Facebook is DEAD. Death, death, death. Sometimes they say this on the advertising side of the platform, but they usually refer to the marketing.

I don't know if we'll reach a point in our lives when Facebook marketing is dead, at least not with major changes.

The number of users increases on a daily basis and activity levels are still high. Facebook isn't complacent either, so it keeps coming up with new features to evolve with users' wishes and needs.

Going forward, I would put some money in to keep all these awesome captions are going to stay important and define the future of Facebook marketing.

More personalization, more attention to the community, more transparency and more interactivity will be the way that Facebook goes, because that's what today's (and tomorrow's) audience wants.

In addition to seeing these trends continue, there are currently indications that we will see some of the following in the future:

More virtual reality (VR) and augmented reality (AR) on Facebook.

Facebook already possess its own virtual reality platform available to VR headset users and a growing number of brands are using their mobile apps or website features to enable potential customers to use AR to see how the products would work for them. As this technology becomes more available to businesses and consumers this trend is increasing, so be prepared.

Consumers and brands connect on Facebook Messenger.

Users will increase the use of messaging applications on social networks (including and in particular the Facebook Messenger application) to reach brands. Marketing is likely to play a bigger role in Messenger than it currently does, and customer service in Messenger will remain important.

Increasing omnichannel selling can become a priority.

Brands can now sell on Facebook in a number of ways, as we saw above; which may continue to become more and more popular, especially if they start to embrace easier payment options or more brands start using the features.

Greater use as a search engine.

Many users already use Facebook to search for local businesses. Along with the recent local Facebook feature, they are encouraging users to make more use of this feature. Facebook has also acquired Wit.ai, which will help with speech recognition. This can be used to potentially increase voice searches, compete more with Google, or even tools like Alexa, so keep an eye on it to see how it develops.

Facebook Marketing Formats

Facebook is not only a leader in social media, but also a growing business, with half a million new accounts created every day. Over time, Facebook developers create new ad formats to meet the modern requirements of Facebook Ads funnel building, optimizing time-proven advertisements. Here is a list of Facebook marketing formats:

Video ad

It's a great way to show the features of your product in action. Facebook allows you do different types of videos to accomplish specific goals: short videos and GIFs for quick attention-grabbing on the go, or streaming videos for longer TV viewing.

Picture ads

If your budget is very limited to create a video, an image ad is a good idea for creating a high-quality ad quickly and easily. This format will help you educate and guide people to your site.

Carousel ads

This format allows you to display up to ten images or videos in a single ad, each with a link to a particular product page. It offers a wide field of creativity and interactivity, because it is possible to present a product in detail, or a few several products, or to tell a story, independently of the papers on the carousel.

Collection ads

It's like a little catalog of your own products in a post on your Facebook feed. A collection ad consists of one original video or image and four smaller images at the bottom in the form of a grid.

Slideshow ads

It is a video format that displays well even if the internet connection speed is slow. You can create this ad using a variety of images, useful video editing tools, and even music.

Lead Generation Ads

This format was developed to help generate leads, especially for mobile users. When a user touches the image in such an ad, a registration form is displayed directly on the ad, making a few clicks enough to opt-in to your newsletter.

There are also three types of ads to increase engagement: Post engagement, Event responses, and Page Likes which will be covered in a later chapter of this book.

Some Things to Understand Before Delving Into Facebook Marketing

Word of mouth has demonstrated to be one of the most powerful marketing tools for any business, and this same principle is essentially the essence of the Facebook Like button. This is certainly a vote of confidence for visitors attracted by your Facebook posts, an online word of mouth compliment can go viral in seconds - with your brand or company reaping the benefits. Your business should also take advantage of the marketing power of Facebook, and the following provides an overview of the basics that will put you on the right track to social media success.

1) Understand Facebook's rules of engagement

Before delving into the technical aspects when creating your Facebook marketing campaign, it is essential that entrepreneurs know the basic rules for engaging Facebook users. As mentioned earlier, Facebook is a platform for engagement and requires social interaction to function. People should not just join the discussion and start advertising or selling their products or services. Individuals tend to interact only with other users who can value them or meet their needs. This commitment is necessary for your business to build trust, and once that is established, your followers will definitely have interest in what you have to offer.

2) Choose a good personalized URL for your Facebook page and your groups

There are three different channels where you can create a good presence on Facebook: your personal profile, the company's Facebook page and the Facebook group. The best thing about creating these channels is that Facebook allows you to use your custom URL, as long as it hasn't been used yet or hasn't broken any Facebook rules. This custom URL can be used as a subdomain that will draw people directly to your Page or group, just like the pages or subdomains of your main site. In doing so, choose one that is simple, easy to remember and relevant to your brand, product or service.

3) Use of Facebook pages

Facebook pages are an amazing marketing tool that companies, brands and professionals can use to create their own social media brand and build followers. The most exciting thing here is that this tool is completely free, but it has more functionality to publish content, share links and interact with subscribers - all of your brand's potential customers - than traditional web pages.

Personalization can also be done to a certain extent, helping your Page to create its own stand that can establish your social media brand. There are third-party apps and tools that can help you create a welcome page that can be set up as your default landing page, not your main Facebook calendar. This can be your first point of interaction with visitors, where engagement with visitors can turn them into fans and potential customers.

4) Use of Facebook groups

The Facebook group is like an evolution of discussion groups or traditional forums, but it still works within the social media limits and boundaries of Facebook. One of the most interesting features of groups is that it can be set to Open to the public or to Private. But what has made groups an effective tool for Facebook marketing is that you not only interact with one person, but with a whole network of like-minded people and also with friends of your Facebook friends.

5) Selection of the best content to publish on your Page or in your groups

The next thing to do after creating your Facebook pages and groups is to determine the specific content that you want to publish and share with your audience. Remember the rules of engagement and don't "sell" anything. Post something: an article, a video, an image, or an external link that your audience may find useful, entertaining, and informative - something they'll like.

6) Some ways to build followers for your brand

The main objective of participating in a Facebook marketing campaign is to build strong followers for your products and services, brands, among Facebook users. Having a fan and group page can be a good start, but to build strong and loyal followers, you need to be:

- Consistent with the quality and frequency of your posts.
- Your content must be relevant to the interest of your audience.
- Your content conveys a level of enthusiasm that your audience will deem worthy enough to share and create a viral impact.
- Meet the needs of the public to be engaged and entertained.

7) Turning your Facebook engagement into sales

Again, it's important to reiterate that people don't necessarily use Facebook to buy something. Many people make use of Facebook to connect with friends and family, find information about something that is entertaining them, or interact with real people in healthy chats. This is where you build trust, an important aspect of online business. But, during your engagement with the public, you can develop a strong level of follow-up that will build trust for your brand enough to ultimately seek more information and possibly make a purchase.

8) Integrate Facebook with your website

There are several ways to integrate Facebook into your site, and Facebook social plug-ins are very useful tools for creating even greater engagement with your users. In a study, a leader in social infrastructure technology, it was determined that Internet users want to register with their social media accounts and access sites, and that the most popular social site than people used as a social connection is nothing more than Facebook! The study also explained that Facebook is still the dominant network on which most users share their content. Based on this study, we can deduce that offering users the ability to use their social media account to sign up for your website and put Facebook share and like button on all pages of your website would be a useful strategy.

9) Use the Facebook page Insight

Among other important things about Facebook is the availability of metrics, statistics and other useful information via Facebook Insights. The goal of Facebook Insight is to help you understand how to respond to your audience and how to market it properly. Facebook can provide this powerful information:

- What type of specific post solicits the greatest response from your audience?
- Information and engagement activities on your Page.
- Total weekly reach.
- Where does your page likes come from?
- Main countries and cities of your fans.
- And more

10) Using Facebook ads

Finally, to create an even greater reach for your brand, you can use Facebook Ads to promote a page or publication. You can have absolute control over the budget of these ads. The best thing is that you can specify specific Facebook users who can see your ads, ensuring that your paid ads only reach the most targeted audience for your business, attracting even more potential customers who are likely to become high-paying customers.

Facebook has revolutionized the way individuals interact with each other, bringing together people with similar interests or old friends separated by distances to connect again and share their daily experiences in a fun and engaging way. This has confirmed to be very valuable for companies who want to extend their reach and interact more with their potential customers.

Facebook As A Powerful Online Marketing Tool

With around a billion users active on Facebook every day, this social media platform remains a treasure for businesses and brands. In addition to finding friends and relatives, Facebook can also be used to advertise and promote your products and services to a greater audience. Some of the features that make Facebook a powerful online marketing tool include:

Popularity

In fact, no other social network is as popular as Facebook. About one billion people visit Facebook daily. You can simply take advantage of the countless number of Facebook users and increase your brand awareness.

Larger Demographics

Another reason that makes Facebook an influential online marketing tool is its wider demographics. Teenagers, adults and even the elderly use Facebook. As a result, Facebook is helping to create a larger demographic of individuals to market your product.

Rapid growth

In addition to Facebook's dominance over other social media platforms, the platform is also growing rapidly. This implies that lot of people are joining every day. Several pages, groups and online communities are created. Even your business can take advantage of it to connect with the right audience.

Users spend more time

Recent statistics have let us know that Facebook users spend around 40 minutes a day on Facebook, on average. Spending more time on the platform means that customers will have more time to interact with your brand.

Highly targeted Facebook ads

Finally, Facebook ads are highly targeted. You can target a specific audience using factors such as gender, age, job title, interests, jobs, etc. Companies can make use of to promote their products and services to the target audience. Apart from that, Facebook Ads come in very handy. Facebook also gives users the possibility to define and control their advertising budget so that they do not exceed their reserved budget.

Chapter 2: Becoming a Top and Successful Influencer In 2021

If you search through the internet, you will find a growing number of articles on how to become a major influencer. But there is a more basic question you must consider before thinking about participating in influencer marketing.

What Is an Influencer?

An influencer is someone who has:

- the ability to influence others' purchasing decisions based on their authority, knowledge, position or relationship with their audience.
- A sequence in a separate niche, with which he actively engages. The size of the following solely relies on the size of your niche topic.

It's important to note that these people are not just marketing tools, but social relationship assets that brands or companies can collaborate with to accomplish their marketing goals.

Social media influencers are people who already built a reputation for their knowledge and skills on a specific topic. They regularly post about this topic on their favorite social media channels and generate great followers from enthusiastic and engaged people who pay close attention to their opinions.

Social media influencers are loved by brands because they can set trends and encourage their followers to buy the products they are promoting.

What Is a Facebook Influencer?

Over the past decade, we've seen Facebook rise to prominence quickly. Facebook is the world's largest social network, with 2.27 billion active users, of which almost 1.5 billion are active every day.

Inevitably, these people are looking for influencers to guide them in decision making.

One of the Facebook influencers is a Facebook user who has established credibility in a specific area. A Facebook influencer has access to a large audience and can convince others with its authenticity and reach.

What Is a Facebook Influencer?

At a fundamental level, influencer marketing is a type of social media marketing that uses product mentions and endorsements from influencers - people who have dedicated social followers and are seen as experts in their niche. Influencer marketing is always effective because of the great trust influencers have created with their followers and the recommendations they provide are a form of social proof for potential customers of your brand.

Types of Influencers

There are several ways you can separate different types of influencers. Some of the more common methods are the number of subscribers, types of content, and level of influence. You can also group influencers based on the niche in which they operate. This implies that influencers who may appear in a lower category of a metric may appear more influential when viewed differently. For example, many mega-influencers are also celebrities. However, these two groups tend to have a less real influence on the audience as they have no experience in a dedicated and narrow niche. Many micro and even nano-influencers may have a huge impact on subscribers in their specialized niche. They can be a huge advantage for a business selling a product aimed at this industry.

By Follower Numbers

Mega-influencers

Mega influencers are people who have a large number of followers on their social networks. While there are no fixed rules on the limits between the different types of followers, a common opinion is that mega-influencers have more than a million followers on at least one social platform.

Many mega-influencers are celebrities who have gained fame offline - movie stars, sportsmen, musicians, and even reality TV stars. Some mega-influencers have won over their many followers through their social and online activities.

However, only big brands will turn to mega-influencers for influencer marketing. Their services will be expensive, up to $1 million per mail, and will likely be extremely demanding on those they choose to collaborate. In virtually all cases, mega-influencers will have agents working on their behalf to close marketing deals.

Macro-influencers

Macro influencers are a step behind mega influencers and can be more accessible as influencer marketers. You consider people with between 40,000 and 1 million subscribers on a social network to be macro-influencers.

This group tends to include two types of people. Or they're B-level celebs, who haven't made it to the top yet. Or they are successful online professionals who have created more followers than typical micro-influencers. This latter type of macro-influencer is likely to be more useful for companies involved in influencer marketing.

Macro influencers usually have a high profile and can be great at raising awareness. Since there are more macro-influencers than mega influencers, it must be easier for a brand to find a macro influencer willing to work with them. These people have the probability of working with brands than with micro-influencers, which makes communication easier.

However, you must be careful with this level of influence. This is the category most likely to commit frauds from influencers: some only reached their position thanks to the followers they bought.

Micro-influencers

Micro-influencers are ordinary people who have become famous for their knowledge of a specialized niche. As such, they've generally gained a considerable following on social media among followers in that niche. Of course, it's not just the total number of followers that shows a level of influence; it is the interaction and relationship that a micro-influencer has with his followers.

Although opinions are different, it is possible to consider micro-influencers with a number of followers between 1000 and 40,000 on a single social platform.

A micro-influencer may not be aware of a business's existence before trying to contact them. In this case, the company will first have to convince the influencer of its value. Micro-influencers have created expert followers and won't want to hurt their relationship with fans if they are seen to promote a lemon.

This requirement to align the relationship between micro-influencers and brands with the target audience means that influencers are often demanding with whom they work. Many micro-influencers are happy to promote a brand for free. Others are waiting for some form of payment. Irrespective of the price, an influencer is unlikely to want to hire a brand that is "inappropriate" for their audience.

The nature of the influence is changing. Micro-influencers are more and more common and famous. Some have gone from virtual obscurity to being almost as famous as traditional celebrities. This is specifically true for Generation Z, who spend more time on the internet than watching TV or playing sports or movies.

To be candid, micro-influencers are the future influencers. The Internet has led to media fragmentation into a lot of small niche topics. Even if you like something relatively obscure, you'll likely find a Facebook group or Pinterest panel dedicated to it. And it is in these niche and advisory groups that micro-influencers establish themselves as true influencers.

Nano-influencers

The last type of influencer to be recognized is nano-influencer. These people only have a limited number of followers, but they tend to be experts in an obscure or highly specialized field. You can think of nano-influencers like the proverbial big fish in a small pond. In many cases, they have less than 1000 followers, but they will be passionate and interested followers, ready to interact with the nano-influencer and listen to their opinions.

While many brands view nano-influencers as irrelevant, they can be extremely important to companies that make highly specialized and niche products.

For most businesses, however, nano-influencers are unlikely to have enough influence to be of much use. They can be cheap and have a huge influence on a small number of people, but in most niches, you will need to reach hundreds of nano-influencers to reach a large audience.

By Type Of Content

Currently, most influencer marketing takes place on social media, primarily with micro-influencers and blogs. With an increasing interest in videos, YouTubers are also becoming more and more important.

Bloggers

Social media bloggers and influencers (especially micro-bloggers) have the most authentic and active relationships with their fans. Brands are recognizing this and encouraging this now.

Blogging has been linked to influencer marketing for some time. There are many very influential blogs on the Internet. If a popular blogger mentions your product positively in an article, the blogger's lawyers may want to try your product.

Many bloggers have made considerable followings in a specific sector. For example, there are highly influential blogs about personal development, finance, health, childrearing, music, and many other topics, including blogging itself. The main thing that successful blogs have in common is respect for readers.

A variation of having a blogger write something that recommends your product is to participate in the guest post. If you can capture a guest post on a large blog, you can check out the content and generally be able to link your site in the author bio.

If a blog is big enough and influential enough, you can purchase a sponsored post on the site. This allows you to write an article yourself or strongly influence the blogger to write an article on your behalf. Unlike a random mention in a blogger or guest post you wrote, you'll have to pay for a sponsored post (and will likely be tagged as such). However, this did not hurt the results of many companies who have sponsored blog posts. Gen Z, in particular, seems to be immune to the Sponsored Post tag, and as long as the product is aligned with the blog's primary audience, there won't be any issues.

YouTube

Obviously, a blog is not the only type of popular content on the internet. Another favorite type of content is video. In this case, instead of any video producers with their own website, most create a YouTube channel. Brands often align with the most popular creators on YouTube.

Podcasters

Podcasting is a relatively new form of online content that is growing in popularity. Now it has made quite a few household names.

Social post only

Obviously, bloggers, podcasters, and YouTubers rarely trust their existing audience to show up on their website, waiting for new content. They usually promote new articles or videos on social media, which makes most of these bloggers and content creators micro-influencers.

In fact, the vast majority of influencers are now making their names on social media. Even though you will find influencers on all the major social channels, the leading network in past years has been Instagram and Facebook, where many influencers create their posts around an extraordinary image.

By Level Of Influence

Celebrity

Celebrities were the original influencers and still have a role to play, although their importance as influencers is declining.

Influencer marketing has grown thanks to the endorsement of celebrities. Companies have discovered for many years that their sales usually increase when a celebrity promotes or supports their product. There are still many cases of companies, especially big brands, making use of celebrities as influencers.

The challenge for most brands is that there are so many mainstream celebrities keen to participate in this type of influencer campaign, and they're unlikely to be cheap. The exception will be if a company makes a product that a celebrity already likes and uses. In this situation, the celebrity may be ready to use her influence to say how good she thinks the product is. I am sure that many musical instrument makers benefit from musicians that plays their instruments by choice.

One downside with using celebrities as influencers is whether they may lack credibility with a product's target audience. Justin Bieber could be very influential if he recommended one type of acne cream, but he would be unlikely to influence the buying habits of those looking for a retirement village.

Celebrities can have many huge fans and followers on social media. However, one wonders what real influence they exert on those who follow them.

Key opinion leader

thought leaders and industry experts, such as journalists, can also be seen as influencers and hold an important place for brands.

Industry leaders and thought leaders earn respect because of their qualifications, position or experience in the field. Often, this respect has earned more through the reputation of the place where they work. For example, a reporter for a major newspaper is probably not an expert on the subjects for which he writes a story, but is respected for being a writer good enough to work as a prestigious publication.

These experts include:

- Academics
- Journalists
- Professional advisors
- Industry experts

If you can get a journalist's attention to a national newspaper that, in turn, speaks positively about your business in an article, you will use it as an influencer in the same way you would a blogger or an influencer on social networks. There is an advantage in this situation where the journalist is likely to write his report for free.

Bloggers and creators of content generally work with leaders and thinkers in the industry, and it is not uncommon to see them mentioned in blog posts and even utilized in social media campaigns. The gap between traditional and social media is obscuring.

One thing to keep in mind when working with top thought leaders is that many have built their reputations in an offline environment and may not have active or significant social followers.

People with above-average influence in your audience

In some ways, the most effective influencers have built their reputation online for being experts in a specific niche. They look like the main thought leaders, but they usually gain a more informal reputation through their online activities. And they've created that reputation for the quality of the social posts they post, the podcasts they speak, the posts they write, and the videos they create and post on their YouTube channels.

These influencers have the best skills in communication and engagement with their audience. They have attracted their followers and have been recognized as experts in their field.

The number of followers depends a lot on your knowledge. However, you will discover that these individuals have incredibly high subscribers compared to other people in your niche.

Why Become an Influencer?

Being an influencer gives you a voice in your field. It helps you connect with other people who share your worldview and expand your horizons in your niche. Plus, you can build your brand, get cheap or free products, services, and experiences from brands that want you to promote them.

In the end, you can make thousands of dollars, depending on the domain, reach and the number of followers.

Guides to Become A Successful Influencer In 2021

If you're one of those people who wish to become an influencer to success in 2021, you are at the right place. Here, we will learn about the step by step process to becoming a successful influencer. So read on and start your journey to becoming an influencer in 2021.

1. Select your niche

Before you start your path to becoming an influencer, you must first select your niche. You need to select a niche that interests you and where you can consistently create content. You also need to have some level of skill in the industry to be able to establish yourself as an influencer.

As an influencer, you will need to research and post content in your chosen area of interest. Therefore, it is essential to choose something that you are passionate about and have fun spending time on.

If you have passion for cooking and try new recipes or are interested in DIY, you have to find your calling. You can also select a combination of 2 to 3 points of interest, but don't make it too wide.

2. Optimize your social media profiles

After selecting your niche, the next thing to do is to select your favorite social media platforms and create/optimize your profiles. Most influencers are only popular on one or two social media platforms. Therefore, it is better to focus your efforts on only 1 to 2 channels.

After selecting your channels, you need to create new profiles or optimize existing profiles.

Here are part of the actions you can take to optimize your Facebook profiles:

Switch to a business account

Before you can become an influencer, you will need to upgrade to a business account as this opens up a lot more options. Most platforms, like Instagram, Twitter, and Facebook, can create a business account in profile settings.

Create an engaging biography

Your bio is the first thing people sees when they visit your profile and therefore is an essential part of ensuring a good first impression. Your bio should be able to say a lot about you in an engaging way. It should also provide all relevant information about you, such as your full name, title, contact details, and areas of expertise.

Add a profile photo and cover photo

You should also add a profile photo and a cover photo to your profile as these are also important parts of your brand's personal identity. People usually recognize a social media profile from their profile picture, so you need to carefully select an image. Similarly ensure that the image quality is good and that your face is clearly visible.

3. Understand your audience

Before you can create and publish content on social media, you need to understand your target audience. Influencers have influenced their audience and have strong ties to them. This is because they don't satisfy everyone, but only those with similar interests in the same niche.

To become an influencer, it is important to know who you are targeting and therefore to succeed in retaining your followers. To understand your audience, you can start by analyzing your current subscriber base for information on interests and demographics.

Most social media platforms posseses a built-in analytics tool that delivers this information to today's audience. Facebook Analytics, for example, provides information on interests, genders, locations, and more of your current subscribers.

Once you know what your audience likes, you're ready to give it to them.

4. Create and publish relevant content

The next phase in becoming an influencer is to post useful and relevant content for your followers. The more you are able to interact with your audience, the more people will be influenced by your opinions and recommendations.

This is the most significant condition for being an influencer, that your followers really listen to you.

You must develop a content strategy and use a mix of content types, preferably those that will appeal to your audience.

Some influencers keep their feeds all in the chosen area of interest, like food, travel, fashion, beauty etc. These influencers don't mix their personal life posts with niche posts and keep the content focused only on the niche.

This means that food influencers can post recipes, photos of restaurant visits, reviews, and even brand promotions.

Some influencers prefer to mix content from their personal lives to better connect with their audience. Adding posts about your everyday life helps influencers appear more authentic and recognizable. It strengthens your bond with the audience.

Whatever content strategy you choose, be sure to make it broad enough to allow for future collaborations with brands. Your sponsored posts should be able to adapt naturally to the rest of the content you post. You can add comments as a regular feature to your feed, to make room for paid review opportunities you might receive later.

Overall, make sure your content strategy is focused on your niche, but not too rigid. Think long-term and start preparing to be an influencer from the start.

5. Be regular and consistent

After deciding the kind of content you will post, you will need to finalize a posting schedule and frequency. Most social media platform algorithms give preference to accounts that post regularly. This is especially true on Facebook, which requires a regular posting frequency for greater visibility. It is also the largest influencer marketing platform.

You may wish to post daily, weekly, or as often as you like. You should also consider the platform before you decide. Some other platforms, like Twitter, are more dynamic in nature and necessitate a higher posting frequency before you can become an influencer on that platform.

You are allowed to post edits once or twice a week on other platforms like Instagram and Facebook. However, select the days and times to post and be consistent.

Research has found that there are days and times of the week when you can get the most out of your posts. For most platforms, the highest rates of engagement can be seen in the late morning and mid-week. Wednesday is the most effective day to post on most platforms. You should check the best times to publish your articles on the chosen platform and create your publishing schedule accordingly.

6. Interact with your audience

Once you begin to post content on social media, you usually get likes and comments on your posts. For an influencer, it's important to connect with your followers, so you can't ignore these comments.

It's a good idea to respond to comments and answer questions posed by your followers. You can also "like" their comments to show your gratitude.

Another way you can interact with your audience is to ask a question and start a conversation about a topic of common interest. Interactions like this help build personal connections with the public and strengthen the position of an influencer.

7. Let other brands be aware that you are open to partnerships

The last step in your quest to become an influencer is to spread the word to the world. You have to go out and declare yourself an influencer interested in collaborating with brands.

This can be done by writing in your bio that you are an influencer and that you are interested in partnerships. You can also give out contact details for potential customers, providing them with an easy way to contact you.

Another way is to take your own break and send messages to relevant brands in a tone about what you can offer. It is best to create a marketing template that you can use to reach different brands as it will prevent you a from lot of stress.

There are several influencer platforms on which brands and influencers are located. You can also use them to find brands in your niche looking for partnerships.

These are some of the more direct ways to find brand partnership. An indirect way is to tag brands and mention them when you talk about their products in your posts.

It's imperative to make a name for yourself and engage with your niche brands. This may not produce immediate results, but it will help you form long-term brand associations that can lead to future collaborations.

Chapter 3: Setting Up A Facebook Business Page

Creating a Facebook business page shouldn't pose a problem. You probably already have all the photos, texts and ideas you need to create your Facebook business page. Just sit back, relax and follow a few simple steps to get your Page up and running.

Do you need motivation to get started? Remember that 2.5 billion people make use of Facebook every month and over 140 million other brands already use Facebook to connect with this large audience.

So let's see how to create a Facebook account for a business. Follow these steps to start your Page by the end of the day.

But before diving in:

4 Facebook Business Page Faqs

Here are the ideal answers to four frequently asked questions on Facebook business pages.

1. What is a Facebook business page?

A Facebook business page allows you to manage your brand's presence on the world's largest social network. Your page enable you to connect with your customers and nurture potential customers by doing the following:

- Respond to customer service requests
- Share content
- Have personal conversations with subscribers
- Collaborate with clients and other brands
- And more ...

2. Can I make use of a personal Facebook profile for my business?

There are many well-meaning entrepreneurs who use personal Facebook profiles for their brands, instead of a real Facebook business page.

It's a bad idea.

If you create a personal profile, you lose a whole set of tools for the creation of content, analysis and paying promotional opportunities provided by a Facebook Business page. Also, users need to submit a friend request for you to engage with your brand.

And you don't want to make it harder for your customers to interact with you on social media. So utilize the power of Facebook business pages.

I've already created a personal profile for my brand ... "Don't worry, I've got you covered:

3. How can I convert my personal profile to a Facebook business page?

Facebook allows you to easily create a new business page based on your profile. You will then have a profile and a page.

Facebook will copy your information, profile photo and cover image. Additionally, you can select friends, followers, photos and videos to upload to your new Facebook business page.

Additionally, if you convert a verified profile, the verified status will also be moved to the new page.

There is a downside: All video views or other metrics will remain on your profile and cannot be transferred to your new Facebook business page.

To convert your profile to a Facebook Business page:

- Go to "facebook.com/pages/create/migrate."
- Click on "Get Started" and proceed with the on-screen instructions.
- Your new Facebook business page will be published at the end of the conversion process!

Note: If you manage other Facebook pages or groups, you will need to add multiple people as administrators of those properties. It's just to make sure that those pages and groups aren't left without an admin, in case something goes wrong while converting the profile to a Business page.

4. How much does a Facebook business page cost?

Like Facebook profiles and groups, you can create and use a Facebook business page for free, no matter the total number of likes or followers you have.

Even if you are spending money on the ads Facebook, organic aspects of your business Facebook page are always free.

Plus, Facebook doesn't even charge a commission for adding a storefront to your page!

So why doesn't a Facebook business page cost anything? Well no, it doesn't.

In return for using the platform and engaging your customers, you are helping Facebook gain even more attention from your audience.

Facebook therefore turns this attention to advertisers in the form of Facebook ads.

Now let's create a killer Facebook business page!

Create A Facebook Business Page

Before registering for your Facebook business page, you must log in to your personal Facebook account. But don't worry: your personal account information will not be visible publicly on your business page.

So, if you have not already logged into your personal account, log in now and dive into the creation of the Page.

Step 1: Sign up

- Visit www.facebook.com/pages/create.
- Select the Page type you want to create business/brand or community/public figure. In this book, let's say you are creating a page for a company or brand, then click the **Get Started** button for the option.
- Then enter information about your business. For the name of your Page, you can use the name of your business or the name individual are likely to search for when they try to find you.
- For category, type one or two words that describe your business and Facebook will offer you a few options. If your brand belongs to more than one category option, choose the one that your customers will probably think of when they think of your business.
- Once the category has been chosen, the box expands to ask for more details, such as address and telephone number. You can decide to make this

information public or display only your city and state.

- When you are ready, click **Continue**. Please note that this indicates your acceptance of the policies relating to Facebook pages, groups and events, so you can check them before continuing.

Step 2. Add images

Next, you will download the profile and cover images on your Facebook page. It is always better to make a good first visual impression, so choose wisely here. Make sure the images you choose are aligned with your brand and easily identifiable with your business.

You will first upload your profile photo. This image accompanies your company name in search results and when you interact with users. It can also be seen in the upper left corner of your Facebook page.

If you own a recognizable brand, making use of your logo is probably a safe way. Whether you are a celebrity or a public figure, a picture of your face will definitely be effective. And if you're one local business, try a well-designed image of your subscription offer. The important thing is to help a subscriber or potential customer recognize your Page immediately.

Remember that your Facebook profile image is displayed at 170 x 170 pixels on the desktop and 128 x 128 pixels on the mobile device. It will be cut in a circle, so don't put critical details in the corners.

After choosing a great photo, click **Upload Profile Photo.**

The next thing to do now is setting your cover image, your cover image is your Facebook business page's most important image.

Ensure that you convey the personality of your brand and capture the essence of your brand through this image. It will be shown at 640 x 360 pixels on the mobile device and 820 x 312 pixels on the desktop. The image must possess a width of at least 400 pixels and a height of 150 pixels, but the recommended download size is 720 x 315 pixels.

After selecting an appropriate image, click **Upload Cover Photo.**

Ta-da! You have a corporate Facebook page, even if it is extremely sparse. Obviously, while the skeleton of your company's Facebook page is now active, you still have some work to do before sharing it with your audience. Don't worry: your Page is not yet visible to the public. (We will do this later in this book.) What you see now is a preview.

Step 3: Create your Username

Your Username, also known as a custom URL, is how you tell everyone where to find you on Facebook.

Your Username may be up to 50 characters long, but don't use extra characters just because you can. You want it to be easy to write and remember. The name of your company or an obvious variation is a sure bet.

- Click **Create a page @ Username** in the left menu to define the custom URL.
- Click **Create Username** when you are done. A window will appear showing the links that people can use to connect to your business on Facebook and Messenger.

Step 4: Add your business details

Although you may be tempted to leave the details for later, it is important to fill in all the fields in the Information section of your Facebook page from the start.

Since Facebook is often the first place a customer gets information about you, it's important to have everything that matters. For example, if someone searches for business open until the 9th, they want to confirm this information on your Page. If they can't find it, they will definitely keep looking until they find another, more imminent place.

To start entering your business details, click **Edit Page Info** from the top menu. On this screen you can share all the important information about your business.

Description

This is a brief description that shows in the search results. There should only be a few sentences (255 characters maximum), so there is no need to be too elaborate here. We'll let you know where to add a longer description later.

Categories

Here you will find the category entered in step 1. If you like, you may add extra categories here to make sure that Facebook shows your Page to all the right people.

Contact

Add any contact information you want to make public, including phone number, website, and email.

Location

If you own a storefront or physical office, make sure your location is correctly marked on the map. You may also add details about your service area, so people know, for instance, which area you deliver to.

Operation Hours

If you are open to the public at specific times, enter them here. This information appears in the search results.

Additional options

If applicable, insert your Impressum, your price range and a link to the privacy policy. An Impressum is a legal declaration of ownership and is not usually required in some European countries.

Make a click on **Save changes** in each section to carry out the changes you go.

Step 5. Tell your story

You've entered all the simple details about your business, but there is still not much to tell people why they should interact with your business on Facebook.

Fortunately, there is a section on your Facebook business page which gives you the ability to add a longer description of your business. To have access to this, click on **See more** in the left menu, click on **About,** then click on **Our Story** on the right side.

Here, you can add a full description of what your business offers customers and why they should follow or like your Page. It's a great place to set expectations. How will you relate with fans through your Facebook page? Give them a compelling reason to stay.

Enter a title and text for your story and upload a relevant photo. When you're done, click **Publish**.

Step 6. Create your first post

Before you start inviting people to enjoy your company's Facebook page, you need to post some valuable content. You can create some of your articles or share relevant content from your industry leaders.

You can also create a specific type of publication, such as an event or a product offer: click on one of the options in the Create area at the top of the Page.

Make sure everything you post offers value to your visitors when they get to your Facebook page, so they'll be inclined to stay

Step 7: Invite an audience while you publish your Page

Your Facebook business page now represents a solid online presence that will make potential customers and fans interact with you. It is time to click on the big green **Publish page** button on the left menu.

That's all! Your Page is active and visible to the world. Now you must have fans!

Start by sending invitations to your existing Facebook friends to enjoy your Page. Use your other channels, such as your website and Twitter, to promote it. Add "Follow Us" logos to promotional materials and the electronic signature. If you feel contented doing so, ask your customers to check it out on Facebook.

How To Verify Your Page

Have you ever noticed a small gray check or blue mark next to the names of certain companies and brands?

Depending on the ranking of your Page, you may be eligible for a verification badge. A blue badge indicates that Facebook has confirmed an authentic page for a public figure, media company or brand. A gray seal indicates that Facebook has confirmed an authentic page for a business or organization.

A verification stamp is not absolutely necessary, but it does add a sense of authority to your Page and your business. This can be specifically important for businesses in the e-commerce or online services sector who want to build trust with potential buyers and initiate online transactions.

To qualify, make sure your Page has a profile photo and a cover photo. Go to "Settings"> "General". Here you will find the "Page Verification," where you can enter your phone number, country and language. You will receive a verification code through a call.

The blue checkered badge is only available for certain public figures, celebrities and brands. Unfortunately, it is impossible to request a blue badge.

Chapter 4: Getting Million Real Likes and Fans In 2021

Okay, before I start, I want to distinguish between purchased followers and real Facebook followers. You can do any kind of Google search and find hundreds of sites that will get their bot and spam account subscribers to like your Facebook Page within hours. And you'll ruin your Facebook Page if you do this. See, Facebook has an algorithm that searches for this type of activity. And if they think your page provides a quick fix, they'll penalize you. Going forward, your organic coverage will suffer and your page will never have the potential it could have made if you build the legal way.

Now, while we're talking about real followers, there are two different ways to this – paid and free. As regards the paid method, you will not be purchasing likes but instead, you'll be paying Facebook. Because Facebook has become a pay-to-pay network for business. They only want to ensure that you are paying them and not someone else. And when I say you're going to pay them, I mean you're spending promotional dollars to attract them.

Well, is it possible for a quarter of a million people to like your page in less than a month and a million people in four months? Yes, actually, it's pretty easy when you follow a set plan. I have done this several times alone on the pages my agency owns and manages.

You will need time and money to achieve this. If you hope you can do it for free, it's still possible, but it's ridiculously unlikely that you can do it on time (More on that later).

A brief note before we begin. There is an opportunity to "boost" your Facebook page, which will attract people who will like and follow your page. People will like your page, on average, from 50 cents to $ 5 per subscriber. This is not that strategy. Instead, we're going to move to a cost per new follower well below 5 cents.

Step one

You will first need to identify an audience that has a significant number associated with it. By that I mean you want to choose who the fans of your Facebook page will be. And you want to make sure there is enough to secure a 1,000,000 follower count. Therefore, if you are creating a Facebook page for dog owners, choose dog owners. Don't choose hairless Chihuahua owners who live in Arizona. This second audience is very small and you will never get the sequence you want.

After identifying them, we recommend that you create a registered audience on the Facebook advertising platform for this group. I recommend creating half a dozen target audience versions and targeting them in different ways. For example, you can choose people who like dog pages. You can also target individuals who follow other popular dog pages. There are also ways to target people based on their buying habits. So, create different ways to target dog owners (again, the audience we are using as an example).

Step two

Configure your Facebook page and enter all the relevant information. I also advice creating an Instagram page at the same time since you can enjoy a lot of Instagram side benefits from your Facebook activities. For example, one of the pages I created on Facebook reached the 1,000,000-follower mark and the Instagram page reached 120,000 followers at the same time, with almost no extra effort.

Step three

Now you want to know what your audience is interacting with. Go to the pages that speak to your target audience and study the articles they publish. Find out which ones get the most likes and shares. Then create a posting schedule for your page and emulate those posts. For example, if you notice that people are interacting with funny pictures of dogs (which they are doing) at a high rate, then you will want to source as many posts like this as possible. They can also engage with training tips (which they do), so we recommend that you work on articles on this topic as well.

On average, we recommend that you post at least 4-6 times per day. And ensure to spend a few days populating your page with posts before you start any kind of promotion. Thus, the page appears to have been around for some time. People are more likely to follow your page if they see a bit of history.

Step four

Now you will want to improve each article you publish. I recommend using a small amount per post. It usually costs between $ 5 and $ 10. And you will want to boost them for just one day.

As a quick tip sheet, images will have more engagement in terms of reactions (likes, love, laughs), shares and comments. The videos will get many views, but fewer shares. Updates are in third place and link shares are dead last in the number of people you can reach for the same amount. So, firstly, I spent most of my time on image posts.

Step five

The reason you improve every post is because you look for variances in cost per engagement. Some posts may cost 10 cents per engagement and others may have over $ 1 per engagement (a terrible post if applicable). But there are the lucky ones that will get less than two cents per engagement and still others less than a cent. These are the posts you are looking for. As you go through the data, find posts that have performed very well based on cost per engagement, come back to those posts and scale them up with more budgets.

You can spend as much as you like but watch out for diminishing returns. Eventually they start to cost more because of the commitment over time. And it varies in the extent to which each post can be improved. I had articles that I spent thousands of dollars on and I also have others that lost effectiveness after $50.

Step six

Now you need to start increasing your followers. People will like and follow your page based on some of your promotions. But the fastest way to get new followers is to check out the posts that get reactions, click on the people who reacted, and now you can invite those people to "like" your page for free. You have limits to the total number of people you can invite per day and it varies by account.

I recommend adding admins to your page to increase the number of invitations you can send. For example, when I started doing this, I would add my wife's Facebook account as admin on my pages and then I would have her go through and invite her daily limit after I was done. If you have co-workers, friends or family, I recommend you use them.

This will let you gain thousands of subscribers at an extremely affordable price as you have managed to get them to react to your page for pennies or even less and you can invite them for free which has reduced your costs to almost nothing for a new follower.

Step seven

Continue this process every day for an entire month. Towards the period of two weeks you will now begin to "boost" your page, like I said. If you have great, engaging and follower content, you should now be able to reduce your paid followers to below 20 cents if you target your audience correctly. If you can't, don't activate this campaign. It's not worth the shot.

And that's how you can reach over 250,000 followers in just under a month, continue this strategy for four months to have 1,000,000 followers. Like I said, this has been done a few times by my team and me. It takes hard work and your budget will probably end up being about $10,000 to $15,000 in paid advertising on Facebook.

And if you are still wondering if it is worth it. The answer is a resounding yes. If I just promote a post to an audience on Facebook, I can reach 1,000 people for every $5 to $20 spent. With an audience of 1,000,000, my average post reaches over 750,000 each time I post. If I post 4-10 times a day, I can recoup my costs in a matter of weeks.

Free Method to Get More Likes On Facebook

To make it a little bit easier for you, we've put together another in-depth guide on how to get more likes on your Facebook page for free so that you can get the most out of your posts.

What Facebook can do for you

The fact that you are here implies that you probably understand the power of Facebook as a social platform.

Many brands and businesses - large and small - have experienced the power to go viral and build a loyal fan base on Facebook.

With more than 5 million followers, they have a large audience that allows their content to gain tons of traffic and go viral.

Although very few marketing methods outperform email marketing, Facebook, if done right, can be one of the most effective methods to build your brand and take your business to a whole new level. And combined with email marketing to get even better results.

Obviously, every business has different needs and things that will work better for them than for others, but Facebook is not something to ignore.

While increasing the popularity of the business page can be long and tiring, it is a space that can be beneficial in the long run.

Ways to Acquire More Likes On Your Page Using Your Blog

Before you go out and start implementing any kind of strategy, you need to clean up the foundation first.

In other words: you must start with your blog and go from there.

Add a like box to the sidebar

It is becoming more obvious that in the internet age, sidebars tend to be completely ignored by the average viewer.

However, it has a potential that should not be overlooked. Something as easy as this Easy Facebook Like Box can assist you to easily capture likes on your Facebook page.

Many of these Like Box plugins are simple enough to be easily configured and integrated as a sidebar or footer widget. They tend to stand out because they look different from your average widget and just a click of a mouse makes them a done deal.

Plus, readers of your blog might not even know you have a Facebook page; therefore, having something there makes it much easier to follow up.

But it's essential to note that these boxes can show the number of people who like your page. If this number is low enough, it may discourage you from liking your page. Also known as "negative social proof."

In other hand, a large number of likes will convey a feeling of positive social proof.

Use calls to action

Calls to Action are available on the web in a number of ways, but they are effective.

To convince your readers to follow you on Facebook, let them know that's what you want from them.

Use pop-up windows and notification bars

There are ways here to use pop-ups and notification bars which isn't super annoying and which can add a warmth touch to your website.

If you like to know how to do it, you will have to keep reading until the end of this point to learn an ingenious trick.

The main way people use pop-ups and notification bars is by collecting emails to create their own signature list.

It is important and should not be missed. But you can use it to increase the likes of your Facebook page.

Here's how to do it:

Step 1: Create a thank you page. On this page, create a call-to-action to like your Facebook page. Make it big, make it stand out.

Step 2: Create a notification bar to display on your website that collects email subscriptions. (e.g., WP notification bar, HelloBar, etc.)

Step 3: Link the notification bar to bring your user to the thank you page after signing up for your list.

To encourage an incentive to like your page, you can use the SocialLocker plugin to mask another PDF or video that encourages them to like your page (I'll explain in more detail this plug-in in a moment). With a single stone, you will be killing two birds.

Now, I mentioned earlier a way to use notification bars and pop-ups in a less annoying than average way that further improved the conversion.

As promised, here is how:

You can do this via a method called **web personalization.**

This is where you personalize your website content to suit your user.

A typical example here is creating something like a pop-up or notification bar enabled to appear based on an event.

For example:

Suppose a reader of your blog arrives on your site three times in a row in a month. The third time they reach your blog, you can activate a notification bar that displays something like this:

Haooy to see you here again. Have you seen our Facebook page? Let's connect!

Something like this adds another layer to the raport you're trying to build with your followers and convince them to want to click the link to your FB page and follow you.

Here is another example:

Someone is coming to your site from Facebook, perhaps through an ad or a friend's post.

You can enable a pop-up so that it only appears to people who visit your website from Facebook and can say something like this:

Hey there fellow Facebook enthusiast. Thanks for coming! Don' forget to like us on Facebook to stay up to date with our promotions and freebies.

It's the little things with the most impact.

In the past, this and other customization tricks were difficult to achieve, but there are WP plugins that make it a lot easier.

The MyThemeShop's Notification bar is a free plug-in that can be used for this.

Install OnePress Social Locker

Okay, it is not compulsory, but you should, because it's fantastic. I mentioned it above, but I thought it would be a good thing to talk about it a bit more.

This plugin locks content on posts and pages using a passcode that forces people to either like you on Google Plus, Twitter, or Facebook to unlock the rest of the content or download something special to from your website.

It's something to be used sparingly, but if you have the knack for making people want your content, placing a content block right when your post is about to get good is a great way to get some social attraction in exchange for giving your readers something very cool.

Don't be boring when using this tool, but don't be afraid to try it either.

Smart Tactics to Acquire More Likes On Your Facebook Page In 2021

You will notice that we have included the word "smart" in the title. This is because there are many tips on this topic that work to get more likes.

As stated earlier, we never give advice like buying from a no-face brand that promises 1,000 likes on your Facebook page for $200 because it's bad advice, and that's not what we do. (Also, you won't find it as a suggestion on our list.)

It's understandable that you want to see the results of your efforts to expand your Facebook network, but the truth is, it takes time.

It's all part of the overall picture of building your brand, business, income, authority, and all the other happy things that come with building an income online.

However, you still need to be smart and recognize that time and effort pays off - but not always overnight.

Saying that, here is a list of smart tactics you can use to start getting likes on your Facebook page.

Start with who you know

After creating your Facebook page, you have the option to always invite your Facebook friends to like your page.

If you have a lot of individuals you know on Facebook, but haven't made an effort to follow them, start doing so now.

Most people who know you will follow him. After that, you can invite them to like your page.

In many cases, your friends will do it out of courtesy, and you can easily increase your likes from there.

Although your Facebook friends may not be your ideal target audience for your Page, however, the fact that they are familiar with you and the Page is yours means that they are likely to repost the things you post there.

This will definitely expand your reach and help you launch a larger network in the long run.

Include a link in your emails

If you're like me, you probably send a lot of emails every day. I know for myself that on average I send 5 to 15 per day.

Too many emails in a month!

One way to acquire more likes on your page is to simply add a link to your FB page in your email signature.

My favorite method is to use Wisestamp.

It's easy to set up, free, and the call to action for following a page stands out a lot better than anything I've found so far.

Include shareable images in your posts

It might sound a little senseless to say, as I'm sure you've done it before, but it's worth mentioning.

Captivating, relevant and even fun images make it easy for people to share your images.

Obviously, you should make it easier for people by including a social media plug-in like Social Snap or Monarch on your website, so sharing these images is as easy as hovering and clicking.

So how do you create an image that people can't help but share?

Well, there's really no way to do this, but you can copy a method that many do that does a great job of getting likes.

How is it exactly?

Creation of your Someecard. You've probably seen them on Facebook anywhere.

When done right, these things get likes and shares like no other. You can create them for free right on their website, save them and use them in your social media posts.

Alternatively, you can use Canva: they have several fantastic templates that you can use for free.

Grab a surfboard and ride this wave!

Comment on other pages that are in a similar niche

Here's one you might not have considered: commenting on other pages in your niche.

Don't play with it yet. Think for a moment who manages these pages.

In most cases, the person moderating this page is the influencer you want to connect with. The connection and promotion of relationships with influencers in your niche is critical to your online efforts.

By commenting on their page, liking their posts, and interacting with other followers, you will be noticed.

And if you do this using Facebook as your page, it will increase your chances of getting clicks on your page, so I like that.

It is important to add conversions to the pages of other influencers. It will grab their attention and that of their followers - which is a good thing for you.

Take advantage of other social media platforms

Lest we not forget to mention the other social media platforms. Twitter, Pinterest, Instagram and any other platform on which you are active. Probably the simplest way to promote your Facebook page and see results is Instagram.

Instagram tends to get maximum involvement from all social platforms, so if you have a decent size following there, start posting your Facebook page.

Let people know it exists. Ask people to follow you.

Use the calls to action in your images or description to like your page and edit your bio link to ensure that clicking over it is a simple procedure.

The 80/20 rule

No one likes an individual who only talks about himself. These types of showboating really make people want to kick them in the shins.

Even if you are probably not that kind of person, the content you post can make you feel that way.

If all or a lot of what you post is promotional, you can irritate others and slow your growth.

The 80/20 rule is an effective rule to adopt. 80% of what you post should be non-promotional or promoting other people's content, so the other 20% can be all of you.

Hashtags are still relevan

I am also a social media manager, so trust me - I know what you think of hashtags. At the same time, hashtags are a vital part of any social media strategy. This includes posts on Facebook.

Unlike Instagram, where posts with more than 10 hashtags get the most engagement, Facebook does best with 1 or 2 hashtags per post.

PostPlanner has noted that if 1-2 hashtag has brought in maximum engagement, by adding two more to a post there was a significant drop in participation, so less is more in this platform.

The approach, therefore, when using hashtags must be relevant. So you don't want to overdo it.

There isn't an exact science for this, but it's definitely worth a try. Your best bet is to do hashtag research, use a relevant hashtag on certain posts, and gauge your commitment to them.

Try Facebook Ads

Okay. Let's have a real love for a second. With recent updates from Facebook, the organic reach within the platform is almost stable.

This means that in general anything that you are trying to do to get likes on your page will be much more difficult than if you are paying for advertising on Facebook.

Facebook ads aren't the easiest thing in the world, but they can be worth your money if you use them correctly.

If you have a budget for advertising campaigns, this may be an area to explore. If you're not an expert in this area, but want to do it and do it right, why not consider hiring a growth hacker who specializes in this area?

GrowthGeeks has a large database of individuals who know how to use Facebook Ads. You can pay someone for a month or for how long you want to do it. Plus, you can find someone worth keeping on your team.

And the cool thing is that there are many types of ads on Facebook. Lead Ads can be used to build your email list or directly advertise your page to acquire more likes. You can also build a custom audience to promote your most recent posts.

Make use of YouTube ads

When we talk of paying for ads, YouTube is one of the cheapest options. If your budget is fixed for your marketing efforts, why not give it a try?

Of course, a lot of people might not be using YouTube ads to get likes on Facebook, but that doesn't mean there isn't any potential for it. Obviously, you shouldn't waste a lot of money on this business.

Everything is done through Google AdWords and therefore a strategy is needed for this.

As far as I know, YouTube ads work the same as Google ads in terms of rankings.

In this case, you'll want that click-through in your call-to-action of the video to connect to a relevant landing page for the keyword you're targeting. The idea of it all might be a good marketing ploy and it's definitely something I plan to explore.

Give gifts (and a word of warning)

Running a giveaway on Facebook is an effective way to generate buzz about your brand and get more people to your page.

However, there are wrong and also right ways to do it, and if you do it wrong you can get kicked out of Facebook ...

In the past (like a year ago), people could run a contest on their blogs, which allowed them to take advantage of a Facebook page as part of their contest entry.

Facebook has changed its policy in this regard and no longer allows it. While you can really work around this and do it anyway, I wouldn't support it. Facebook can simply shut you down and kick you out for life.

You can still run giveaways and contests to build buzz, but you can't make liking your page a compulsory part of the contest brief. However, it looks like a simple call-to-action to like your page can be okay as long as it's not a requirement to enter.

Always embed a link in your page in your guest posts

Another great way to get the most out of your Page is to use your guests posts to your advantage. Most blogs let you add your social profiles to your author biography.

If getting more likes on your FB page is your goal, use a CTA (call to action) to follow your page to get more content.

If you've had access to blogs using WordPress in the past, but haven't added this CTA yet, you can ask if you can add it to your bio in posts you've previously posted for them. Most of the time, they are happy to do it for you.

Don't be afraid to be funny

When it comes to posting to Facebook, it's easy to get into the same routine of sharing relevant content with your readers.

However, the fun stuff usually gets the most shares and likes. Grammarly is a nice example of a brand that doesn't take grammar lightly, but also knows how to make a joke of it.

You can do something like this by sharing funny images that your audience refers to that can tickle your funny bones.

Use the news to your advantage

Why is this a great idea? Because present events are what will be on most people's minds; they are most relevant to them.

Posting on Facebook mentioning the news is a way to grab attention, stay current, and not be too promotional.

Obviously, this suggestion addresses the subject of the current event in a general sense. You will also need to use common sense when talking about current affairs.

Some topics may be too sensitive to be a subject for your post.

Essentially:

Stay up to date and use current events to your advantage where appropriate.

There really isn't cutting and drying method to do this, so be as innovative as possible.

Why You Must Never Buy Likes On Facebook

Some brands are buying likes on Facebook in an attempt to increase their visibility on the world's largest social media platform.

However, what they should do is increase Facebook's organic coverage. Is it a good practice to buy likes on Facebook? What are the consequences?

I don't recommend anyone to buy tastes. Here are my reasons:

1. False likes do not translate into exposure

Organic reach has become harder to reach on Facebook in recent years. Marketing experts adopt creative ways to get people to like their pages and posts.

Usually, people liking your updates mean more people will see it which is different when you buy likes?

This makes exposure almost impossible. Where these false likes come from do nothing on Facebook. They don't browse and share messages like real human beings.

You can't expect anything from these false likes. It's a waste of time.

2. Fake accounts do not engage with other Facebook users

Engagement is an essential part of any Facebook marketing strategy. If a strategy doesn't involve people engaging with your updates, it's not something you should do.

One of my favorite marketing strategies on Facebook is posting lots of photo updates. Photo posts undergo 84% more link clicks than text posts and links.

Imagine taking the time to create a photo post, just to ruin your opportunities for engagement by purchasing likes.

You wouldn't want to post quality updates and fail as a result of your desperation to increase the number. Fake likes are not good.

When a fake user who likes your page doesn't engage with your post, it's a signal to Facebook that you are cheating their algorithms.

3. Fake users reduce your organic reach

Above I said fake likes don't lead to exposure because they're not real human beings. They can't purchase your product.

But fake likes can do more harm than that. They also reduce your organic feed.

Let's say 10 people liked your Facebook update. Half of this number is real and the other half is fake.

Even the real ones wouldn't impact as positive as they should if you hadn't purchased fake likes.

4. Purchasing fake likes is a total waste of money

There are countless ways to spend money wisely. Buying fake likes is not one of them.

Every potential customer is crucial to your brand. As an alternative to wasting money on something that won't produce a positive result, you can spend on the real Facebook marketing strategy that works.

For instance, advertising on Facebook is still cost effective. Facebook ads are also effective. You can reach thousands of users for less than $ 100. Unsurprisingly, 92% of marketers advertise on Facebook.

As an alternative to unnecessarily spending money on a tactic that doesn't work, why not advertise on Facebook? Facebook ad likes come from real people interested in your brand.

5. Facebook finds and bans fake accounts

Like many online communities and social platforms, Facebook finds and bans fake users.

There is no possible explanation for those who pretend to be someone they are not.

Facebook has guidelines and expects all users to follow the rules. If Facebook suspect that you are using fake accounts, you could be kicked from Facebook.

If your account is banned you will lose a reputation on Facebook and maybe the rest of the web, consumers will find it hard to believe you. This can be disastrous for your brand.

6. Facebook removes fake likes

When Facebook deletes a user, most of the time all of their fake likes follow it. Facebook has hundreds of thousands of employees who are always looking for fake accounts and erasing them immediately.

Unreal likes that are no longer valid is a big setback for you if you have a lot of them. For instance, this imples that if you have a Facebook post with 5000 likes and only 5 are real, you will have five. It's literally bad to see your post go from 5000 likes to just 5 likes, right?

Over the course of their existence, those 500 fake likes may have reduced the chances of your update getting more real likes.

7. Facebook hates fake likes

Facebook's algorithm is complex. There are many factors. Any digital marketer would expect it.

Having too many likes alone isn't enough to rank at the top of the feed. There are several things you must do well. Users must share the link to their content on Messenger.

The message must have multiple replies. People should spend time on it. It is not possible for a fake account to spend time on your Facebook post.

When Facebook considers these factors, it's easy for them to spot fake likes. And when they find out that the content has a lot of fake likes, you can be sure they won't let your users see it again.

You definitely do not want this when buying fake likes.

8. Real users are careful to interact with posts with fake likes

Detecting fake updates on Facebook is not that difficult. When you see a Facebook post with thousands of likes and no comments, it indicates that something is wrong.

The web is no longer new. Most Internet users now have the knowledge on how to spot fakes everywhere online.

There are many scammers out there. You don't want people to think your brand is one of them, as that would be extremely damaging to your reputation.

The engagement in your post should never seem real. They must be real. This means you must not try to fool Facebook's algorithm.

9. False likes will reduce the quality of information on your Facebook page

If there are fake likes on your post, the detailed Facebook data will be distorted. This means that your data can not be trusted because it is fake.

Your Facebook data is very important for making strategic marketing decisions on Facebook. You can't do anything great with fake data from fake users.

10. False likes worsen your reputation on Facebook's advertising platform

I am a huge fan of Facebook ads. The option to retarget people on Facebook is my favorite.

You can use Facebook to deepen your relationship with potential customers who have visited your site. But when you buy likes, not only do you make it difficult to retarget and build relationships with the prospect, but it also costs you money to post ads on the Facebook platform.

You will have a bad reputation in the minds of Facebook users and it will be more difficult for them to like and follow you. So why invest in buying Facebook likes if you are struggling to advertise on Facebook? It just doesn't make sense for your business.

11. Real users know fake users

It is not that hard to spot fake Facebook users when you find their profiles.

They have few or no friends. And when they have friends, most of the time their friends are like them.

They have very few photos. They have little or no messages in their accounts. In fact, they do not interact with other users of the platform.

If you're like me, sometimes you check out a commenter's profile on a Facebook post.

When you find out that the commenter was a fake, you won't feel pressured into the discussion because you know you will be responding to a bot.

Lots of fakes in your posts are something you should avoid. It will only harm your reputation on the Facebook platform.

12. False Likes Damage Your Facebook Page

A Facebook page that is constantly liked by fake users is not the place where you want to get information.

Maybe a lot of pages have bot likes. But a page that gets most of its likes from bots means it's unreliable. Buying likes on Facebook simply stops people from visiting your page.

13. False Likes Make Marketing and Converting Real Users to Facebook Difficult

No individual will ever give you their email after knowing that most of your likes are fake.

This is a sign that you will not be using their email addresses correctly. They would be afraid to receive spam from you.

This obviously makes the conversion more difficult and almost impossible.

14. You cannot remove fake likes

It's easy to buy likes on Facebook to improve your posts and expect them to have some attraction on Facebook.

Once you understand how fake it is, you won't be able to remove these fake likes.

These false tastes came from false accounts. Sometimes it can be thousands. You will better utilized your time and money creating advertisements that draw people to your business.

But these fake likes will always be tied to your business. This means that your reputation on the platform can be tarnished for a long time.

15. Fake likes do not click on links

It is not possible for a fake account to click on a link, subscribe to your email list, and purchase your product. Why buying fake like if they are not contributing to your profits?

Facebook pays attention to link clicks when measuring engagement. If a post is engaged in terms of link clicks, it can be exposed to fans who have shown that they value clicking links.

16. Fake users do not buy products and services

False users are not real. Getting likes from a fake user will not translate into sales for your business in any way.

You need real people to buy your products. You can attract these people by creating more content on your website and promoting it on social media.

A tool like GrowthFunnel will help you build strong and loyal Facebook followers.

Some tools allow you to direct visitors who have provided you with their email address and ask them to follow you on Facebook.

It may be required to offer an incentive to these visitors as a reward for following you. You can start using GrowthFunnel for free today.

17. Blackhat Facebook likes sellers won't refund your money

No Facebook Like seller can give your money back, because the service itself is obscure.

There are a lot of them there. I will not mention these sites because I think it does not contribute positively to this book.

18. Buying fake likes makes you vulnerable to hackers

Most of the fake Facebook likes sellers are hackers. They know what they are doing is illegal.

Providing payment information is risky. This exposes you to many web vulnerabilities. It is not a positive risk for your business.

You don't want information about your business to end up in the wrong hands.

19. Fake accounts will send spam to your Facebook page

You might think it was all over after dealing with a blackhat Facebook seller. The hacker can do more than you ask. And most of the time, it can be a bad experience for your business.

For example, after having had to deal with a blackhat merchant who sells Facebook Like, they may want you to continue to buy their services.

When you stop, they can threaten to spam your Facebook page if you don't send them money. Believe me, this kind of experience is not what you want.

20. Real users will not interact with your page

It's simple, real Facebook users will avoid commenting, liking or sharing your updates because they know your page has been polluted.

Real users interact with real people. Not robots.

Chapter 5: Understanding Facebook Post Types

When we talk about Facebook marketing, posting content is the job's primary function. Without a consistent content flow, your Page only exists as a source of information for people who already know your brand.

In other words, this is not different from the most basics of sites.

However, when you use Facebook to post and share quality content, it expands your reach into the big blue ocean of Facebook users. Users discover your content and can choose to take advantage of your Page to continue the relationship. Over time, their confidence in your brand increases, hopefully enough to make a purchase. It is the recipe for inbound marketing, after all.

How to Post to Your Facebook Page

To post to your Facebook page, look for the white box under the cover photo that says "**Write something** ..." and start typing. When the update is ready to run (after a review, of course), click "**Share now.**" In this field, you can also add a photo or a video, label a product or a position, carry out a search or plan or update your publication if you wish.

Facebook Images

Publishing an image is always a great option, mainly because Facebook posts with images show are 2.3 times more engaged than those posts without visuals and account for 87% of total interactions.

To publish an image, click on the "Photo / Video" prompt at the bottom, where it says "Write a post..."

Facebook image sizes

If you've ever done any type of social media marketing, understand the need to keep the size of the images handy.

There are a few types of images that you can upload to Facebook, each with its own dimensional characteristics:

- Profile picture: 180 x 180
- Cover photo: 820 x 312
- Timeline image: 1200 x 630 (aspect ratio is more important than size. Maintain aspect ratio of 1.9:1).

It's not a secret that the best Facebook images are very visual. Try to keep a consistent style on all the images you publish and don't be afraid to show your personality.

Facebook link

One of the easiest ways to start filling out your Facebook page with the content is to share your blog posts. You shouldn't be sharing every blog post you create, but rather choose the ones you know that will resonate with your Facebook audience and hopefully be shared by your subscribers.

To post a link, start the same way you would create a text message. Write a sentence or two and paste your link. Instead of summarizing blog posts in your copy, make an understandable or witty statement (as long as it matches your brand voice) that would intrigue someone to find out more.

Before posting, go ahead and remove the link to make your post cleaner and more professional. At this point, the blog post should be automatically populated below the white box with the title, meta description and image. Press **"Publish."**

In addition, be sure to include a compelling meta description in every blog post you write. Facebook automatically inserts it to describe your link.

Facebook Video

If you want to tell a story on Facebook, video is probably the best option. Recently there has been a lot of interest in videos, especially since Facebook's algorithm now prioritizes live and longer videos, with high completion rates in user news feeds. In fact, a Facebook executive predicted that the social media platform would be fully video by 2021.

To send a pre-produced video to Facebook, click on "Photos/Videos," click on the "Photos/Videos" prompt at the bottom, where it says "Write an article ..." and select "Send photos/videos." Select the file on your computer. We recommend downloading videos in MP4 or MOV format.

You will then be asked to include a title, tag and text to your message. You can also include it in a playlist. Like Facebook links, use this text to entice your audience to watch the video.

Click along with the navigation on the right to choose the thumbnail of your video and add captions and subtitles. Since Facebook automatically plays videos without audio (and almost 90% of videos are viewed without audio), SRT files are a smart choice to ensure that video is understood by those who stream their news feeds on a device mobile.

Facebook also allows you to search for your video (if it lasts at least 10 seconds), define tags for tracking and activate 360° mode (which allows users to view the video in the form of a panorama).

Since Facebook plays videos automatically, the first 5 to 10 seconds are preferred properties. When brainstorming videos for Facebook, start as convincingly as possible to encourage the user to watch the full video.

Facebook Live

In addition to pre-produced videos, Facebook Live is another option for exploring multimedia content. Facebook Live is a feature that let users stream live to their desktop or smartphone. It is available to any Facebook user, but it is particularly attractive to brands who want to capture the culture of their business and establish authentic relationships with their followers.

To test it on the desktop, go to your Page and click on "Live" below, where it says "Write a post..."

If you have never tried Facebook Live before, you will be asked to provide Facebook with access to your camera and microphone. Press the blue **"Continue"** button. Don't worry: you won't start recording yet.

You will see a dialog box on the right, where you can choose where you want to broadcast (on your Page or in your personal profile), write a description, share the screen, the title and mark your video. In the "Interactive" tab, you can also search during the playback of your live video. After clicking on "Go Live," the live video will start.

On your smartphone, open the Facebook app. Go to your Page and click on "Post" as if you were writing a fresh content and select the "Live Video" option. Before entering information, go ahead and check your privacy settings. Below the description, you will see an option to broadcast to the public, just to your friends, or just to yourself. If you are trying Facebook Live for the first time, we recommend that you use "alone" to make sure that your live stream does not show up in your news feed.

Before you start, write an engaging title that will be shown with your live video. Then make use of the two arrows in the upper right corner to determine whether you want the camera in a selfie view or vice versa. Finally, decide whether to hold the phone vertically or rotate it horizontally. As you would on the desktop, press the blue " **Go live** " button to start the broadcast.

When you go live, engage your viewers by asking questions and encouraging them to respond in the comments. Every few minutes, reappear and explain the purpose of the video, if new viewers are participating.

When you are done recording, click "Finish" to complete the transmission. The video will automatically stay glued to your Page like any other video message. You will also be provided with the choice to save the video on the filmstrip to have a backup copy.

Instant Facebook Articles

Instant Facebook Articles is a feature that allows publishers to publish text and photo content in a loaded format to their phone without leaving the Facebook app. If you've already called and clicked on an interesting title just to completely block the Facebook app, you know how infuriating it can be to download mobile content.

This is the main advantage of instant Facebook articles. They dramatically minimize the time it takes to download content to mobile devices, providing a perfect user experience. You know that you have found an instant article if there is a small gray ray in the title of the message.

When the instant articles were published, they were only available to certain publishers. From now on, any publisher can use them if they register on **https://instantarticles.fb.com/**. Facebook will guide you through submitting your first sample article and requesting approval from the Instant Articles team. Once approved, you can automatically publish it in the new format.

While instant articles are certainly not intended for all businesses, they have helped some large publishers take advantage of native advertising. Since users are 20% more likely to click on instant articles and 70% less dropout than bad user experience, publishers have more opportunities to generate revenue from native ads. However, the format has received a response, because the publishers are not responsible for the will lysis.

Facebook virtual reality

Last but not least, there is a virtual reality for Facebook. At least for now, Facebook's main virtual reality offering is **360-degree video**. Facebook 360 allows publishers to tell interesting stories that share experiences and places with their fans.

The 360-degree video experience functions well on a mobile device, as viewers are able to tilt and turn their mobile phone to reveal video content all around them. On a desktop, users are allowed to click and drag. The format is likewise compatible with VR headsets like Samsung Gear VR or Oculus Rift.

The most effective way to make a Facebook 360 video is to use a 360- degree cameras like **Allie** or **RICOH THETA**. THETA, for example, has two lenses that capture the appearance of 360 degrees together. Since there's no viewfinder, you'll need to make use of a tripod to keep the camera steady and the corresponding mobile application to set the shot. The application allows you to is share directly with Facebook.

How to Pin A Facebook Post?

Now that we have talked about all the different types of Facebook posts, it's time to customize how they appear on your Page. By "pinning" a post, you can determine what content is at the top of the Page. All other articles will appear below, even if they were published more recently than the pinned article.

To add an article to your Page, click the small down arrow in the upper right corner of a published article. Then click on "Add at the top of the page." This message will remain blocked until you choose to add another and replace it.

Facebook Engagement Strategies for Your Business Page

Do you want to gain more organic visibility in the Facebook newsfeed? Wondering what types of posts and content work for other people?

In this section, you'll find 13 ways to create Facebook posts that generate meaningful interactions and improve organic feed visibility. First, we will talk about why Facebook engagement is important.

Importance of Facebook Engagement

First, let's recap the reason behind the importance of engagement to Facebook marketing success. Engagement in a Facebook post occurs when the post has enough impact on people (and usually causes emotional involvement) that they feel compelled to respond to. Regular moments of impact and emotional engagement with a target audience are clearly at the heart of successful social media marketing.

Human nature being what it is, seeing comments and reactions in a post will activate curiosity and therefore more impact and attention.

However, for most businesses, the ultimate goal is to share their posts, as the content (and company name) will reach a whole new audience and the sharing itself will add social support or proof to the post. .

Attracting engagement is also essential for the visibility of your posts on the Facebook news feed. In January 2018, Facebook announced major changes to the News Feed algorithm, prioritizing posts from friends and family. Facebook explained that "posts that inspire discussion in comments and posts you can share and react to" would now gain visibility in the News Feed.

To rate your business's content in the News Feed, you should create posts that attract long comments and / or encourage sharing or discussion. Therefore, building engagement is essential for successful Facebook marketing.

Note that Facebook continues to downgrade posts that use engagement baits as a way to beat the algorithm. These messages encourage you to reply with a single word or emoji or ask people to tag friends in the comments.

So how can you ensure your posts attract engagement? The first thing is to do a little research on what works for you and for others.

What is working for you now?

Facebook offers a detailed analysis of all your Facebook Page activity in the Page Insights tab. **Go to posts** in the left navigation bar and check what time your target audience is likely to be online. Use this information to help plan your publishing schedule.

Scroll down to the Post tab and make sure you are:

- Consistently posting (to follow the audience and allow you to get the most out of the algorithm)
- Share a mix of several types of content, both in subject matter and media content (even your most avid fans will get bored if you always share the same things)

Then, take a look at your recent posts to see which ones have generated the most engagement. Concentrate on the number of comments and shares received, as these interactions will have a greater impact on Facebook's algorithm and Facebook's marketing results.

You can also find out which posts have reached people who are not yet fans of your Page.

In the People tab of Facebook Insights, you'll find information about your audience and the people involved in your Facebook posts. Review these details regularly to make sure your content is optimized to attract the right people to your business.

What works for other businesses?

To find inspiration for new message types, see the pages of other companies that attract an audience - similar target and see what items are interesting. Pay particular attention to the type of medium (images, videos), the format of the medium (multiple images, images with text, duration of the video, with or without subtitles), type and duration of the copy, tone of voice and frequency of publication.

You can also make use of a tool like BuzzSumo to research the competition on Facebook. If you have the intention to test BuzzSumo of large size ($ 299 / month, paid monthly, available for free for 7 days), you can use Facebook Analyzer Tool to search for publications that attract involvement. Filter the search results with regards to the type involved to obtain detailed information on what works to other pages.

Depending on the type of engagement you're targeting, you can also see the best times to post content related to a specific keyword.

It also provides information on what type of media to use and how much text to include in your posts for maximum engagement.

You can also check out the perfect time of day to share your post and attract specific types of engagement.

Although each audience is different and you find it just the best publication, testing the content of your page, the insights BuzzSumo offers a good starting point to work.

Based on the information that you have acquired from your research, below we have put together 13 tactics to write Facebook posts that generate meaningful interactions that you can adopt.

1. Collecting questions via the comments of your followers for an AMA

Allowing your audience to ask questions is a great way to get engagement and responses. This strategy works best if you designate a subject or topic for questions, I will set a time limit and explain when questions will be answered and by whom.

Be creative about who you have chosen to answer the questions. It could be your team, your suppliers, the specialists you work with, the colleagues you have met at an event, or others with whom you have collaborated. You can share the answers on your Page as a video or document or answer the questions through Facebook Live to generate even more engagement.

If resources allow, consider hosting a regular Q&A session so fans can connect with your brand and gain valuable information on a consistent basis.

2. share an offer on the news feed to generate connections on Messenger

Facebook Messenger bots are a more and more popular way for businesses to amplify the results of their Facebook marketing. Many solutions of robots designed for small businesses, as ManyChat allows you to provide automatic response to comments added to a publication. You can ask individuals to comment on your post and explain that they will receive a gift in their Messenger inbox when they receive it.

This tactic is preferable if you have a primary magnet based on value to offer and want to build a list on Messenger. You may also use it to share an offer or receipt and create a list. Once the bot tool is created, the voucher will be delivered to the Messenger mailbox with all comments on the post.

3. Illustrate the feeling with emojis

Posts that include emojis typically have higher like, comment, and share rates than those that don't. Using emojis also helps describe your business as user-friendly and makes your content more memorable.

4. Share a shout out for content created by your fans and customers

Sharing photos or content uploaded or posted by fans is a great way to show how important your community and customers are. Remember to ask for permission before sharing such photo and credit the creator.

This sense of goodwill can lead to greater involvement overall, as well as individual Facebook posts.

5. Host a comment contest

An effective and quick way to increase engagement is to run a contest or offer on your Facebook page and tell people to comment on a post to participate.

If you ask participants to share a photo as well, your contest may provide a stack of user-generated content to share, as long as you make it clear that you intend to do so.

Remember that you can only ask participants of a Facebook contest to like or comment on a post, post on your Page, or post on your Page. You should also specify that "the promotion is in no way sponsored, endorsed, administered or associated with Facebook."

6. Ask for Audience Feedback

People like to be included and feel important. What better way to make the most of this human characteristic than to ask the public for advice or help make choices in your business? This tactic can work wonders in increasing engagement.

7. Anticipate and meet the needs of your community with content

Providing the information your target audience wants and finds useful not only attracts shares and comments, but it's also another common reason consumer decide to purchase from a business. (And that is the reason we're all here, isn't it?)

The better the understanding of the people you want to attract and interact with, the easier it is to share the information they value.

And don't think you should be creating all of this information. You can also get great engagement by sharing content created by others!

8. Ask open-ended questions

Is there another way to get people to talk than to ask a question? While you want to avoid bait-engagement tactics, asking a question on your Facebook post is a quick and easy way to get responses.

Or make use of it as an opportunity to share your business details behind the scenes.

If you feel brave, dive in and ask for a topic you know is a little controversial. The questions that arouse strong feelings may very well: make sure only that the following discussion remains polite!

9. Touch the subject

Sharing Facebook posts that talk about what's going on in the world to your audience is a great way to encourage responses. It allows you to contribute to the conversations people are already having, so that your presence is more like a friend than an entity trying to sell. And human beings respond much better to friends than to salespeople.

All companies talk about the seasons and the main times of each marketing calendar. To really stand out, create articles that relate to the news you know and that interest your audience.

For local businesses, you may want to discuss events and issues that are affecting your community. Another approach is to talk about TV shows the audience will be watching.

10. Talk about community engagement and impact beyond business

People love businesses that don't just make money. On your Facebook page, share updates about the nonprofits you support, fundraising activities you are involved in as a business, or any community project you are working on.

Sharing information about the positive impact you have beyond your business (even on a small scale) will generally attract more engagement than other types of posts.

11. Invite the world to laugh with you

Share a human moment or something a little frustrating and turn it into a fun article to catch responses from anyone who can relate. Knowing your audience well to understand your pets is very important.

People like to connect with other people and feel understood. When you publish a post that your target audience identifies with, your engagement can break the roof.

We encounter funny things on a daily basis in business, so there are several ways to make people laugh even if you are not a professional comedian. We can attract a lot of comments and shares by merely telling stories.

12. Use Scroll-Stopping Media to grab attention

The first step in building engagement is to get attention to your Facebook feed posts. Using images and videos that stand out without being flashy and without speaking to your target audience is essential.

However, not all images and videos are created the same. Abused bank photos won't attract attention to your posts, so it's best to use the photos you've taken.

13. Tell a meaningful story with emotional context

We all know marketing and storytelling is a match made in heaven, but sharing a story on your Facebook page, preferably one that pulls strings from your heart, can also be a great way to engage and share.

It doesn't have to be an elaborate, long story to be effective. Only a simple story that is relevant to your customers or your community can work.

Chapter 6: Facebook Marketing Strategy in 2021

Facebook is undoubtedly one of the commonly-used online platforms by adults. And the vast majority use it on a daily basis, which continues to offer brands and businesses the opportunity to gain maximum visibility when implementing a Facebook marketing strategy.

Most times, the most difficult part is how to get started, but we're here to provide you with the steps that will help you get started with your Facebook marketing business.

Keep reading to ensure you get the most out of this increasingly powerful social media platform.

1. Set goals for Facebook

The first stage in any marketing strategy is to define the right goals. This roadmap will be an important reference to evaluate to ensure the success of your Facebook strategy. But for setting goals, we recommend that you do a little research to make sure your plan is achievable through the platform.

So if you don't already have goals on Facebook, search results are a great place to start. Also, if your business has broad goals already set, see how they overlap with your Facebook marketing plans.

Addressing Your Goals

Here are some common annual goals for businesses and how an effective Facebook strategy can help:

Increased sales quality: Improving sales quality begins with better targeting. With a well-planned Facebook marketing strategy, you reach your target audience more effectively. Just because the lake is bigger doesn't mean you'll have bigger fish. Work on the things you know best and use Facebook as a source to improve your coverage.

Add more value to your organization: Facebook can better nurture customers, increase knowledge, and provide more resources to your audience. Make Facebook your favorite news source.

Better pulse on your competitors: Are your competitors still one step ahead? By using monitoring tools of social networks, you can watch, listen and report on all social conversations that revolve around you, your competitors or industry. Always try to increase your listening skills before speaking.

More efficient recruiting: No one said that social recruiting is easy, but it is growing in popularity. Social media can be a great source to increase the efforts of recruitment and more quickly reach the best talent. Working on your employees' social networks to achieve greater social reach increases your chances of recruiting senior employees.

Smarter Growth: Reducing dropouts, limiting spending, and increasing acquisitions are all part of a successful business, but Facebook can help you in any of these areas. Whether it's ad spend, increased targeting, or increased social sales, approaching your Facebook marketing strategy can help get you closer to those goals.

Tracking Progress: Of course, ensuring you're on course to achieve these goals is essential. You should monitor all reports on your Facebook.

2. Know your audience on Facebook

Understanding the people on Facebook and what your current audience distribution looks like will be important in determining which and how Facebook marketing strategies you should use.

After you research this, take some time to familiarize yourself with Facebook demographics using Facebook Page Insights.

3. Interact proactively with your audience

Like most social media channels, they are created as networks for discussing, chatting, and sharing content. As a brand, you should not forget the basic idea of what makes up a social media network. This implies that conversation and engagement should always be remembered.

Instead, try to your audience community. Facebook is the best place to organize chats or industry discussions, with a different audience and with your customers. Although Twitter is often the center of attention for being the Mecca of services to customers, you should also remember Facebook.

You can help drive engagement on Facebook by asking people to get involved first. However, you can't relax and expect your followers to interact. You can't possibly reach everyone, but there are ways to increase engagement.

Post at the best time on Facebook

Facebook remains one of the most difficult social networks to use for organic content. Again, the algorithms make this a challenge for companies looking to find the fastest time to publish.

- Wednesday is the best day to post
- Wednesday, 11am in the morning and 1 pm in the afternoon is the busiest time on Facebook

- You can post during the days of the week between 9:00 a.m. and 3:00 p.m.
- Most people are always free on Sunday
- Less recommended times include early morning and afternoon

4. Plan your Facebook content

Creating and managing your content is an essential part of any social media strategy. On Facebook, you have a lot more options on what types of posts you can use. It ranges from stories to status and group posts.

Along with the selection of options come the specific types of content that are of interest to your audience, which should also be remembered when evaluating which Facebook marketing techniques will work best for you. Thirty percent said they wanted to link to more information and 18% wanted more images. Videos come in third place, with 17% of respondents.

For content planning, free and paid options are available. Facebook page controls allow you to schedule your posts right from your page.

Planning and scheduling your schedule makes it easier for you to see where the gaps are in your posts. By utilizing a tool like this will definitely save you time in the long run.

5. Determine your Facebook advertising strategy

If you've started on Facebook or have been working for a while, it's hard to escape the need to pay for brand exposure. Our Complete Guide to Building Your Facebook Advertising Strategy is the perfect place to start learning about Facebook Ads.

However, increasing the audience and brand loyalty doesn't happen overnight. You have to earn this.

But there is a shortcut to getting there a little faster: advertising on social media. Specifically on Facebook, there are over four million advertisers with an average click-through rate of 9%. Advertising on Facebook is easier, but not easier. You are still required to build your brand effectively and show it off perfectly with advertisements.

Seek greater brand recognition

Facebook ad campaigns should always focus on two things:

- Cheap
- Relevant

For starters, you want to keep your weekly or monthly spending allocated to Facebook to avoid overexposure and unnecessary clicks. Ad spend can increase quickly when targeting isn't effective or is set up correctly, which brings us to the next step.

Your Facebook ad should be relevant. Targeting a large audience is not a bad thing. At the beginning you really want to see what works best for raising awareness. However, relevance is crucial for large Facebook ads.

Try to create a personalized audience and target the customers who best match your Facebook content. If this is a redirect measure, make sure the content provides something recognizable, but also something new.

Decide on creative content

Earlier in this book, we took an in-depth look at the types of content on Facebook. Now is the time to choose the content that you think the advertisement is worth for a much larger audience.

Some of the best aspects of your advertising content should include:

Identity: Does it refer to your brand and does it effectively present your product/service? The logo and colors company are displayed correctly?

Reward: what do viewers get? Is this a deal, promotion, offer code, white paper, or industry guide?

Tone: Does your content keep the same tone throughout your Facebook page or your business in general?

Action: Your content should guide an action, which links to your goals on Facebook. A clear and precise plan of action is the best.

Keep Facebook ad content up to date

Facebook ad content is accurately squeezed between your family and the friends feed, which means it's seen a lot. Have you ever deemed a TV commercial as worse ever and seen it replayed forever through your program favorite? It's the same thing.

Don't allow your content to get stale with viewers. Update and reuse your ad content every week or two weeks. The goal here is directing users to a specific website or shopping page. So don't allow old content toruin your Facebook remarketing or retargeting efforts.

Create a spreadsheet and document your key metrics. Each statistic provides unique information about what you specifically want to achieve with your ad:

- **Click-through rate:** If traffic is critical, track your CTR and see where you can improve.
- **Impressions:** Do you have visibility problems? Take a look at your image or content and find out what can drive more impressions.

- **Acquisition cost:** If your goal is to limit spending and budgeting more effectively, track purchase costs and set weekly or monthly goals.

6. Encourage employee advocacy

Your employees have to be your greatest cheerleaders. According to reports, 72% of people said they felt more connected to a brand when some information about such brand is shared by their employees on social media. Employees look at brands, making them more related to consumers.

While you can try and challenge employee lawyers using company announcement emails, a solution like Bambu has been specifically intended to simplify the process and make it easier for employees to turn into brand ambassadors.

Your employees are an invaluable resource for message amplification, social sales, and genuine engagement. And, unlike industry influencers, their social services are free.

Use Bambu to easily organize employee content and track the performance of your referral program.

7. Drive traffic from your site to your Facebook page

Facebook is much more useful and powerful when you have an active website that is receiving decent traffic.

In a developed nation like the US, there are 10 Internet users for every 12 people.

The Internet is used by customers to search for the products and services they need. Having an active site will help your business gain the credibility to convert web users into customers.

According to a research carried out by research firm Inter Clutch, nearly half of small businesses in America do not yet have a website.

You can drive traffic from your site to your Facebook page. Individuals who visit your site use Facebook.

By giving them the ability to connect even more with their business on Facebook, you can turn them into customers through this.

8. Integrate social media sharing everywhere

The most powerful method of marketing the world has ever seen is the social media.

You can't possibly talk about social media today without mentioning Facebook. It has an 18% market share. That's 7% more than its closest competitor, WhatsApp, which is owned by Facebook.

By adding the market shares of Facebook, WhatsApp, Facebook Messenger, and Instagram, this makes Facebook virtually unbeatable.

To truly be successful on Facebook, you need to integrate social media wherever your business appears.

Facebook dominates social media. When you share your social profiles everywhere, you are likely to get more leads from Facebook.

9. Interact with your Facebook community

If you own an animal care business, people are talking about animals on Facebook. There are several communities for pet lovers and owners.

Since someone is sharing their sweet experience with their pet and living in New York City, that doesn't mean they can't recommend a friend who lives closest to their pet care business in Los Angeles.

Facebook is the largest social platform and information travels very fast these days.

Anyone can become your customer. Start interacting with people on Facebook. The more you do this with potential customers, the more customers will flood your business.

10. Interact with other Facebook pages

Even when you have a professional Facebook page, Facebook allows you to enjoy and interact with other pages. It doesn't matter if they are associated to your industry or not.

You need to start being on the radar of other Facebook page owners. You can build a strong raport with them. This can open up the possibility of collaborating on content creation or even collaborating with them.

11. Create or join Facebook groups

Today there are millions of active Facebook groups. There is a group for all interests or topics in the sun.

Facebook groups can be used to build your business and increase your influence.

Join Facebook groups related to your products. This will help you connect with colleagues for possible partnerships and potential clients.

If you can't find any active Facebook groups related to your brand, you can create a new one. Creating a subscription for a new group will only take a while.

Be sincere and available in Facebook groups. People will know if you fake it. Helping people sincerely will lead to a strong reputation and relationships. Nothing can beat you.

When you have a good reputation and meet a lot of people, promoting your product and getting people to buy becomes a lot easier.

Having an active group can drive a lot of traffic to your Facebook page.

12. Track and analyze your results

The final step in your strategy is to keep an eye on the metrics you identified earlier when setting goals and analyzing results. This also includes determining the return on investment.

Facebook is a giant planet in its own right. If you don't monitor and measure your Facebook marketing efforts, you are missing out on a great opportunity to increase the customer base on the platform.

Facebook's metrics can be overwhelming, which is the number one reason small business owners ignore it.

But to ignore it would be a big mistake. If you really want to drive highly targeted traffic to Facebook, you need to monitor, measure, and improve your efforts.

You do this by paying attention to Facebook metrics.

Here are the metrics to note:

Fan Reach: This is the total number of your fans who saw a specific post. These views took place straight away without any action from a friend or fan. The metric helps you measure how attractive your content is to your fans.

Organic Reach: This is the number of individuals who viewed a specific post organically (fans and non-fans).

Engagement: This is the total number of individuals who clicked anywhere on your post. This includes usability, comments, and sharing. This also includes people who viewed your video or clicked on links and photos.

People who talk about it (or narrators): Not many people understand this metric. This metric is made up of just three actions: shares, likes and comments. It is totally different from the "engagement" metric because it considers these three actions alone.

Click-through rate: As earlier stated, this statistic has been around the web for many years. The click-through rate is the same on Facebook as it is in AdWords advertising, email marketing and landing pages. It's good to know how many individuals have viewed your content. And how many people act on it.

These five parameters must always be checked. Make a continuous effort to improve them.

Chapter 7: Tracking and Measuring Result with Facebook Analytics

If your business uses Facebook, you should use Facebook Analytics. It's full of ideas and one that can help you get the most out of the social network which reaches 1.62 billion users per day.

Why Use Facebook Analytics?

Adopting a structured approach that links social media efforts with our real business objectives and goals when we make use of Facebook for business is recommended. You must always keep track of your results to be a successful marketer, this is where Analytics comes in handy. Analytics help you refine your strategy and measure your return on investment.

Having a clear understanding of how and when people respond or interact with your Facebook content is also an important way to ensure that the algorithm of Facebook works for you and not against you.

This Facebook Insights guide will help you understand how and why each metric matters to your overall social media strategy.

Facebook Audience Insights Vs. Facebook Page Insights

Facebook Audience Insights and Facebook Page Insights are Facebook analytics tools. The two tools have some overlap between them, but they have very different purposes. The key to using each is in the name of the tool:

- Facebook Audience Insights helps you understand your audience on Facebook, so you can better target your ads and create more relevant content.
- Facebook Page Insights offers an in-depth analysis of your Facebook Page, so you can track what's working, learn how people engage with your content, and improve results over time.

In this section, we'll explain how to use Facebook Page Insights.

How to access Facebook Insights

To locate Facebook Insights for your Facebook Page, go to your Facebook Page and click "Insights."

How To Use Facebook Analytics

1. Overview: How your Page is faring

The Overview tab of Facebook Insights does a lot more than it says. In addition to showing your Page's top metrics (Page Summary), it also shows top metrics for the five most recent posts and a brief comparison of the page to similar Facebook Pages.

Page Summary

The Page Summary section displays key metrics for your page over the past seven days, such as a Like, Post-Engagement, and Coverage. It also displays the percentage change from the previous period and displays the graphs for the period.

This area is great for acquiring a quick assessment of your Facebook Page performance.

For instance, if you are concentrating on growing your page, you can get to it quickly by checking your page's likes and cover. If you post multiple videos to encourage engagement, you can immediately see if your strategy is working by watching the video's views and posting engagement.

Your 5 most recent messages

This section shows the main information from your last five posts: date and time of publication, caption, type of post, segmentation, coverage and engagement.

This section is great for getting an idea of how effective your recent posts are and what type of post has been performing well recently. For instance, you may find that posts with selected links outperform other post types. Therefore, you can try to post multiple link articles.

Pages to watch

The pages are to consult one of our features favorite of the page Facebook. It provides a quick comparison of your page with other pages that you want to see. If you click on one of the pages, the first posts of that page of the current week will be displayed.

This section is great for viewing how your Facebook page works between colleagues and competitors. By looking at the main articles on these pages, you can also stay on top of trends in your industry or take care of great content for your Facebook fans.

Advice

Export your data (in the page summary): If you want to better analyze your page data, you can export the metrics of the page, post or video as a Excel spreadsheet or CSV. Facebook gives a lot of data in the spreadsheet.

Click to view more insights (on your 5 most recent articles): Click on the article title to see a detailed analysis of an article's performance.

Find out what works (on which pages to watch): If you click on any of the pages, you will receive a pop-up with the top articles on that page, ranked from most engaging to least engaging.

2. Likes: Where your Page Likes came from

The Like tab allows you to go beyond knowing the number of likes on your page. It shows growth, averages and tanned sources.

Total Page Likes as of Today

This graph shows the general trend in page likes. If the chart is showing a plateau or a downtrend, it would be good to investigate and understand the cause.

Net Likes

This graph shows the daily growth of Likes on the page and dividing the percentage they like and not I like (organic or paid) that your page receives. While it is good to have positive net likes, it is also useful to monitor the trend in the aversion.

Where Your Page Likes Happened

This graph indicates where the likes of your page come from, directly from your page, from your advertisements or suggested pages that Facebook offers to users. For example, if you post likes on the Facebook page, you should see the "Ads" section increase.

Advice

Define the period: at the top of the page, you can define the period that interests you. You can drag the indicators on the chart, select "1W" (for a week), "1M" (for a month) or "1Q" (for a quarter) or set the specified start and end dates.

Know the sources of your like and unlike: If you click or drag to select a period in any of the charts, they will show the similar and different sources for the selected period.

Compare your averages: If you click on one of the metrics to the right of the charts, you will receive two averages for that metric: your average for the last period and your average for the current period.

3. Coverage: what is your reach and what factors influence it

The Coverage tab lets you know about the reach of your Facebook page and posts and what factors are increasing or decreasing your reach.

Post Reach

This graph shows the number of people reached by your posts (organically or through promotions). This can be a quick way to measure your organic reach over time and find out if your ads are working.

Reactions, comments and shares

When a post receives an engagement, Facebook delivers it to multiple people, because the post engagement implies that people have interest in the post. More involvement, more reach.

Reactions

It looks like this graph only appears if you have a high number of reactions to your Facebook posts. It's a great way to judge the feelings of your posts.

Hide, report spam, and unlike

"Hide Posts," "Report As Spam," "Unlike Page" and "Hide All Posts" are considered negative comments. This is how users tell Facebook that they don't want to see a page's posts. Facebook will show these posts to fewer people. Since you want this negative feedbacks to stay low or zero, it's a good idea to watch this chart.

Total reached

Full coverage is the number of people who saw activity on your page, such as your posts, your posts on your page, ads, mentions, and check-ins. Much like post coverage, it's a great way to see how your organic and paid coverage has grown.

Advice

Set the time period and compare your averages: Just like on the Like tab, you can set the date range at the top of the page and compare the averages for each metric by clicking on the metric.

Understand your post activity: If you see increased coverage, engagement, or negative feedback, click or drag to select the section of the chart and learn more. Facebook will display active posts during this time, in descending order of impression.

Show reaches Breakdown: If you prefer numbers over visuals, click or drag to select a time period on the Total Coverage chart to view full, organic, and paid coverage in tabular form.

4. Pages viewed: who viewed which section of your page

The Pages views tab is much like the traffic report in Google Analytics. Here you will discover your page views and the main sources of traffic.

Total views

The total number of views is the number of times people have visited your page. If the same individual has visited your page twice, it will be treated as two views.

Total number of people who viewed

The total number of individuals who viewed it is the number of people who viewed your page. If the same individual has visited your page twice, it will only be considered once. This value must be equal to or less than the total number of views.

Top sources

This graph shows the top five sources of traffic that brought people to your page. Knowledge allows you to increase your efforts on these sources if you want to increase your page views.

5. Actions on page: what individuals did on your page

The Actions on Page tab lets you understand what people are doing when they're on your page. The few actions that Facebook takes into account, click on "Directions," phone number, website and action button.

Total actions on the page

This graph shows the number of actions individuals have taken on your page. If you are a local company, you might be more concerned with the number of times people want to come to your house or get your phone number. If you are an online business, you may be more concerned with the number of clicks on the site. (The action button is the huge blue button on your page.)

People who clicked the action button/Get Directions/Phone number/Website

This graph and the following graphs show the number of people who have taken the respective actions on your page.

Advice

Set the period: like the previous few tabs, you can set the period at the top of the page.

Data Details: Just like page display charts, you can divide the actions performed by charts based on certain characteristics.

6. Posts: the performance of your posts

The Posts tab shows all the information about your posts, such as coverage and engagement. You can also improve your posts directly from this tab.

When your fans are online

We believe there isn't a universal best time to post on Facebook, but there's a better time to post for your brand on Facebook. This section will assist you. It shows how active your Facebook fans are, every day or week and every hour of the day, on average.

You can hover your mouse daily to see an overlap in activities that day, compared to the averages.

Post Types

This section explains how each type of post (for example, links, photos or videos) is rated in terms of media coverage and average engagement.

From there, you can figure out which post type is most effective on your Page and tailor your posting strategy accordingly. For example, if you think videos have higher average reach and engagement, try posting more videos.

Top posts on the pages you see

This section is very similar to the Pages to Watch section of the Overview tab. Although the Overview tab item shows the overall performance of these pages, this section displays the first post of the week for each of these pages and the engagement received.

All published posts

This section lists all the posts that you have published on your Page and the relevant information - date and time of publication, the caption of the post, type of publication, targeting, coverage and engagement.

Advice

Sort your posts: You may sort your posts by date, cover or published appointment (clicks or reactions on the posts) by clicking on the column title.

View different metrics: You can view different coverage and engagement metrics. To achieve this, you can select:

- Reach
- Reach: Organic / Paid
- Impressions: Organic / Paid
- Reach: Fans / Non-Fans

For engagement, you can select:

- Reactions/Post Clicks, Comments & Shares
- Comments/Reactions/Shares
- Post Hides, Reports of Spam, Hides of All Posts, Unlikes
- Engagement Rates

7. Events: the success of your event pages

If you regularly organize events on Facebook, the Events tab allows you to have more data, providing the main data of your events. You can discover what doesn't work and what works with the promotion of the event. Get data like the number of people who viewed your event, the demographics of your audience, and the total number of individual who responded to your event.

Event statistics (awareness / engagement / tickets)

In this section, you have several graphics on the notoriety and engagement of all your events. Here is the available data:

Awareness:

- People Reached
- Event Page Views

Engagement:

- People Who Responded
- Event Actions

Tickets:

- Clicks on Buy Tickets

(For specific event data, see suggestion below.)

Event statistics (audience)

In addition to awareness and involvement, you can also get a detailed analysis of your target audience by age and gender. This can tell you what kind of person is most interested in your events.

Upcoming/Past

The second half of the page displays information about your past and future event. You can switch between the past and the upcoming by using the drop-down menu in the top left.

Advice

Click for more insights: If you click on the title of an event, a pop-up window will appear with the data for that specific event. Since it only displays data for the last 28 days, you might want to save it after the event.

8. Videos: performance of your videos

The Videos tab shows how well the videos are performing on your page. It mainly reports the number of video views, divided into:

- Organic vs. Paid
- Unique vs. Repeat
- Auto-Played vs. Clicked-to-Play

Video views

This graph illustrates the number of times your videos have been viewed. Facebook considers 3 seconds or more to be a video display.

10 seconds views

This graph illustrates the number of times your videos have been viewed for at least 10 seconds. If your video is not more than 10 seconds, Facebook counts a 10-second view when people are watching 97%.

While this number is always lower than video views (i.e., 3 seconds), I think it is more representative of the number of views involved.

The top videos

This section presents the top five videos that were watched for at least three seconds or more. This can provide you with a quick idea of what kind of video is performing well among your fans.

Advice

Show different subdivisions: in the upper right corner of each graph there is a drop-down menu where you can choose between different subdivisions.

Compare your averages: If you click on one of the metrics to the right of the charts, you will receive two averages for that metric: your average for the last period and your average for the current period.

Click for more insights: Click on a video title to display a pop-up window with more information about that video. You can click on any of the statistics and see more information.

9. People: people who liked, seen or involved in your page

The People tab is an overview of the individuals who liked your page, viewed your posts, or were involved with your page or posts.

Your fans

Your fans are individuals who liked your page. This section divides fans by age group, gender, location and language. From there you can tell which demographics are most interested in your p will gina.

People reached / people engaged

Reached people are people who have seen your posts in the last 28 days, while people engaged are those who liked, commented on, or shared your posts or who interacted with your page (for example, posts) during the last 28 days.

What's interesting is that the people who saw or interacted with your posts aren't necessarily just your fans. This creates a percentage of differences. For example, while 41% of our fans are women, 55% of those involved are women. This may imply that our posts tend to be more interesting to women than to men.

Advice

Know more with Audience Insights: Audience Insights, a tool of Facebook Ads Manager, is much more powerful than the People tab at understanding your fans. Even if you don't display information about who has viewed or interacted with your posts, they do display a lot more information about your fans.

In addition to demographic info, you can discover data like other pages that your fans like. (You can use this information to define your pages!)

To access Audience Insights, go to Facebook Ads Manager and select "Audience Insights" from the drop-down menu in the upper left corner. You can also navigate through this direct link: https://www.facebook.com/ads/audience-insights/

Once you are there, select "People connected to your page" and the page that interests you.

The US is selected as the default location. You can deselect it if you want to watch your audience worldwide. However, family and shopping information is currently only publicly available in the United States.

10. Messages: Response times and Messenger analytics

The Messages tab displays performance metrics for your conversations with people on Messenger.

Here's what each of the metrics means:

The total conversations is the number of conversations between your page and people on Messenger.

Your responsiveness is the percentage of messages you replied to and the average response time.

Excluded conversations are the number of conversations with your page that people have excluded.

Marked as spam is the number and percentage of conversations on your page that are marked as spam.

Blocked conversations is the number and percentage of conversations on your page that were blocked.

Advice

View up to 180 days: For messages, you can view statistics for the last 180 days. You can select a period by clicking on "Last 7 days".

11. Others: promotions, branding and local content

The remaining tabs may not be relevant to most people, like the ones above, or they may not even appear to you. Let's look at them all, in case you're curious about them.

Promotions

The Promotions tab provides a quick overview of your recent promotions. It's a great place to check out your recent promotions on Facebook Insights. You can also use Facebook Ads Manager, which can be more comprehensive.

Branded content

When you receive mentions from a verified page (a Facebook page with a blue checkmark), the Branded content tab will appear in the list of tabs and posts will appear there.

You'll be able to see coverage and engagement stats, as well as your posts. These posts can even be shared and promoted.

Local

If you are managing a local business page, you will have a Local tab. On this tab, you'll find information about foot traffic in your area, demographic information about people close to you, and the percentage of people nearby who have seen your Facebook ads. (Unbelievable!)

Chapter 8: Getting Started with Facebook Advertising In 2021

When you start advertising on Facebook, you may think there are many checkboxes. Is your copy attractive enough? Am I targeting the right people? How much should I spend?

However, the overwhelming Facebook advertising nature prevents many people from experiencing it.

But with such a large and diverse collection of users, Facebook offers marketers a unique opportunity to promote their brands, an opportunity that can even bring more contacts to your business than any other paid channel. Below we will follow the steps to start advertising on Facebook, making sure to produce the right ad at the appropriate time.

Creating A Facebook Ad Campaign

The first thing to know in the Facebook advertising checklist is understanding the terminology. On Facebook, any paid advertising can be divided into three elements:

- **Campaigns**: A campaign hosts all of your resources

- **Ad Sets**: Ad sets are ad groups that target a specific audience. If you are targeting multiple audiences, you will need separate sets for each.
- **Ads:** the individual ads that you post on Facebook, each with its own colors, copies, images, etc.

When you create your first post, Facebook offers two options for publishers: the ad manager and the Potenza editor. Ad Manager is the best option for most businesses, while Power Editor is designed for large advertisers who need specific control over several campaigns. For these instructions, we will use the Ad Manager. To find the Facebook ad manager, go to your home page and look for "Ad Manager" in the left menu.

Before creating an ad, you need to choose a goal. Facebook offers 11 choices, divided into three categories: awareness, consideration and conversion.

How To Target And Optimize Ad Sets

After selecting a goal for your campaign, Facebook will walk you through a few steps to set the audience, budget, and schedule for your ad unit. If you have used Facebook's advertising tools, you can select a registered audience here. Otherwise, specify demographic information, such as gender, location, gender, and language.

You can make your targeting more specific in the detailed targeting area. Choose one of the predefined Facebook categories or enter the name of a specific business page that might appeal to your audience.

In the "Placements" section, select "Automatic channels (recommended)." So choose your budget and your calendar. Facebook offers the possibility of defining a daily or a lifetime budget:

- **Daily Budget:** If you'd like your ad to run endlessly, select Daily Budget. Choose the total amount you are willing to spend on this specific ad per day. Remember that this is an average; therefore, on some days you can go a little above or below.

- **Lifetime Budget:** If you'd like to run your ad for a specified period, choose Lifetime Budget. Facebook will try to evenly distribute the selected amount over the period.

Depending on your choice, you can choose the appropriate calendar for your ad unit. Decide if you'd like your ads to start immediately or later. With the ad set options selected, click "Continue."

Facebook Ad Formats

Now that you've designed your campaign and your ad unit, it's time to create your ads. In this section, you will select the format, medium, text and links to create one or more advertisements.

First, Facebook offers two ad format options.

Once you've decided how you want your ad to appear, upload your creative stuff and write a selectable headline. For each format, Facebook will offer some design tips, including image size, title length and more.

Before now, if 20% or more of an ad image was text, Facebook would refuse the ad. Since then, Facebook has adopted a new system, but always favors the images with minimal text. Ads containing more text will now receive less or no delivery.

Finally, edit the text and view the ad to view it on your computer or mobile. Then place your order.

Measuring Facebook Ad Results

Now that your ads have been launched worldwide, we recommend that you monitor their performance. To see the results, return to the Facebook Ads Manager. If you've run ads, you'll see an overview of all of your campaigns.

At the top of the overview, the dashboard will highlight an estimate of the amount you spend each day on ads. The panel is divided into columns to simplify filtering by results, coverage or amount spent.

There are many parameters to consider when determining the success of your ads, including the audience, impressions, clicks, click-through rate, etc. However, here are some examples of special attention:

- **Actions:** In the first stage of creating a Facebook ad, choose a goal for your campaign. Always take the initial logic into account when evaluating the success of your campaign.

- **Cost per action:** it is not enough to look at the number of actions that have taken place. See how much each action costs and compare it between your different ads in the ad unit.

- **Frequency:** Frequency is how often someone has seen your ad. An ideal frequency must vary depending on the type of ad being broadcast. For example, you probably want someone to see the promoted content only once. But it can take multiple views of a page-type ad before someone takes action. If one of your ads has a very high frequency but is underperforming, it may be time to remove it.

To export your data, look out for the drop-down menu on the right side above the results.

Facebook Advertising Strategy In 2021

If you have less than no idea on how to kickstart your Facebook advertising strategy today, you are not alone.

It's no doubt that Facebook's organic reach has been affected. Recent algorithm changes have forced companies to invest in paid campaigns or to abandon ship. But before you rule out Facebook as a lost cause, think again.

Facebook is still a favorite place for 97% of marketers to run paid ads for a reason. After all, Facebook has the largest user base of all social networks and one of the most compromised.

In other words, if your audience are of all kinds, there's a non-zero chance that they 're already active on Facebook. Combine that with the fact that Facebook ad targeting is incredibly deep and it's very clear why your business should always be on board.

Obviously, this doesn't mean that Facebook ads are infallible on their own. In this Facebook advertising guide, we'll go over some best practices for Facebook ads and what you must know to get started.

1. Define your target audience

The greatest benefit of Facebook ads is the ad targeting feature which allows you to find specific people most likely to buy.

And only these people.

Unlike previous PPCs, modern Facebook advertising allows you to become granular with ad targeting, only serving ads to relevant users. Below is a little explanation on how to target Facebook Ads so that businesses can analyze and define an audience ready to click and convert.

Create an audience

To get started, use Facebook to build an audience from scratch. Companies can define the audience based on specific parameters, such as:

Location: For instance, local businesses can target their cities or run ads in nearby neighborhoods, where new customers can wait

Age: If your audience is a large age group (think millennials or baby boomers), you can target your ads accordingly, rather than using a one-size-fits-all approach

Interests: Depending on user tastes and Facebook activity, the platform may highlight potential customers (think: a local bike shop that caters to users who follow the Schwinn brand page or who list "cycling" as an interest)

Demographics: Extra details, such as relationship status or education level, can help target specific social media characters who look like their real customers

Custom audiences

Also known as "remarketing ads," personalized audiences can change your Facebook advertising strategy.

In a nutshell, these types of ads are aimed at members of your target audience who have once interacted with your business.

Maybe they are past or current customers. It could be someone who has interacted with your Facebook page or visited your website.

With the availability of tools like Facebook Pixel, businesses have a sort of "second chance" to gain leads who already know who you are. Here's an overview of what you can use to build a custom audience, including a customer file, like the mailing list.

Lookalike audience

Another important feature of Facebook ads, Lookalike Audience allows businesses to target new potential customers based on their current customers. In short, you can target an audience on Facebook that is similar to your most loyal customers or to people who have interacted with your ad campaigns before. If your Facebook advertising strategy is focused on the exploration and reputation, a similar hearing is for you.

2. Choose the right types of ads

Just as businesses have many options for targeting ads, they are also hampered by choosing the types of ads they produce.

First, consider the three different types of goals related to your Facebook advertising strategy:

Awareness: Increase your reach and introduce your business to potential customers with Facebook ads

Consideration: encourage interactions between potential customers and marketing messages

Conversions: Take these 'budding' buyers and persuade them to become full customers

These goals will determine the direction you take for your ads, including the creatives and types of ads you choose. While some brands have recently gotten stronger on Facebook, there's no denying the new ad features launched recently.

As noted, remarketing ads are a verified way to bring back old customers, offering a sort of "Ah!" your Facebook feed.

And while Facebook Stories are still relatively young, many brands are killing it with full-screen ads to force people to click. With so many options, it's important to get familiar with Facebook's ad specs and new features.

And, in fact, that brings us to the next point!

3. Sort out your ad creatives

You probably already have creative ads and stylish product photos on the deck, right?

With that being said, what clicks with followers on Facebook is unpredictably specific. Based on what we've discovered through our research and some best practices, we have made these creative guidelines for your Facebook advertising strategy.

Don't overlook the value of entertainment

Being boring is a deadly kiss for any ad campaign and Facebook is no different. The more you like ads, the less they look like you. Whether it's humor or images that grab people's attention, try to avoid static and stuffy campaigns.

If possible, use video

You've heard it several times, but it's worth repeating: the content of the video is crushing it now. Videos are capable of showing your ads in action, which is perfect for raising awareness and grabbing the attention of users. Oh, and don't forget that Facebook has explicitly encouraged brands to embed videos with the algorithm change.

Think of a video ad as a kind of mini ad for your brand. When interrupting scrollers in their tracks, video is fair game for any business.

Create a compelling call to action

Any kind of engagement is a benefit in your Facebook ads, but in the end, you are looking for clicks. For these clicks to happen, a strong call to action is needed.

4. Test and monitor your campaigns

Before you dive into your Facebook advertising strategy, you first need to understand how to navigate the platform.

You have a learning curve. There are a lot of variables to analyze and metrics to track, so if any marketer is a little overwhelmed, no one can blame them.

With this, we always discourage beginners from increasing their budgets until they have run smaller test campaigns and understand more about how this works.

Speaking of budgets, Facebook can run your ads for you based on what they consider an "ideal" engagement, or they can run on a set schedule. There is no "right" answer to the budget; know that you can empty your money quickly if you do not impose restrictions.

Facebook allows you to limit your ad spending to keep a reasonable budget

Another key component of advertising on Facebook is the platform's reporting capabilities. Again, Facebook is getting incredibly granular in terms of what you can monitor. If you'd like to know if you're getting a positive ROI or a relevant click, look no further than your reports. By tracking specific events, scope, and amount spent, you have a wide range of data to understand what works and what doesn't.

5. Combine paid campaigns with organic activities

In most cases, it's in the best interests of businesses to adopt a hybrid social media strategy.

In other words, target organic customers by building content and communities, integrating your Facebook advertising strategy with paid campaigns.

It offers the best of both worlds. While the organic reach is really limited, that's no excuse to quit Facebook or ignore the advocacy potential of employees or customer service to connect with customers. While paid ads encourage conversions, an organic activity can help you build relationships and gain exposure to your brand.

Conclusion

Before I finish this guide, I felt compelled to include this section to really make your Facebook marketing campaigns work for you and your brand.

The advice I will be providing here is based on my Facebook marketing experimentations and experiences, as well as some expert social media marketing advice that I use with great success.

I hope these tips will help you reinforce the lessons you have learned throughout the guide. Everything I have included in this e-book has worked for me, and the things I am passing on to you are the product of my trial and error phase.

Although Facebook is an ever-evolving platform, the fundamentals of Facebook marketing are more or less constant and are expected to generate leads through outbound marketing techniques, promote relationships, and convert followers into paying customers.

Remember these basics and use the tips in this chapter to achieve your marketing goals more effectively.

Pin and highlight posts - In the Facebook group and on the business page, there is an option to pin posts at the top of the page to make it easier for you and your members to find content than they use as a reference, such as contact details or frequently asked questions.

Keep Up to Date - It's not enough to keep your timeline alive and active; you should also make sure that the appearance of the page and profile is up to date and fresh.

Show your appreciation - Showing your appreciation to your fans and followers is essential to strengthening the relationship you and your brand have with them.

Showoff Your Facebook Page - Just add social buttons, plugins, or widgets to all your website pages and blog posts to make it easy for visitors to share their content on their Facebook timeline.

Go mobile - The promotional techniques you use on your Facebook business page should be optimized for mobile devices.

Stay up to date - You've probably already discovered that Facebook is making a lot of changes to its layouts, offers, how-to, and rules. Keeping abreast of these changes is absolutely essential so that you can adjust and adapt accordingly.

And that is the end of the book. I hope you learned a lot? Facebook Marketing is an exciting field to enter and has produced measurable results for hundreds of brands around the world. The Facebook world is your oyster, so what are you waiting for? Go make your brand shine!

Instagram

Introduction

You may know a lot on Facebook marketing or be a specialist in e-commerce for Twitter, but when it comes to Instagram, that kind of social credibility means nothing.

Instagram, since its launch in 2010 has taken the world by storm. It looks like everyone - and their pets - are on the platform.

You may have also seen the increase in brands that have developed a presence on the platform. But is it worth spending time on Instagram and should your business be on the platform as well? The answer is yes.

Instagram is not like most other social networks. A huge 70% of its 300 million monthly users are located outside of the United States and most of these users are between 16 and 24 years old. If this is your target demographic, sit back and relax, because you're about to find out everything you must know to get started on this mobile-intensive social network.

Of course, Instagram is no longer just for personal use, whether for you or your pet. It is now a world-wide platform that allows brands to humanize their content, recruit new talent, present products and inspire their audiences.

Plus, Instagram users aren't just active; they're engaged. More than half of the active users of the platform visit the site everyday and 35% say they consult it several times a day.

Instagram can also help you get to know your brand better and introduce new products. 70% of Instagram users have spent time researching a brand on the platform. Instagram let you promote your product and brand in a friendly and authentic way, without hard-selling to your customers.

If you're targeting a mobile audience of international boys and girls in their late teens through the early 1930s, you've come to the right place. Instagram is popular with both men and women (although it used to be more female-focused) and users will probably access the network from a mobile app.

Things change quickly and the social audience can be a bit cruel, so your mission (if you choose to go along with it) is to learn all you can about smart marketing on Instagram before you create an account and post your first image.

Fortunately, you have come to the right place.

Even with all of these Instagram stats, you still might not know where to start. We know the platform can be a somewhat intimidating at first, which is why we created this guide.

Chapter 1: Getting Started with Instagram Business Account

With mora than 1 billion monthly active users, Instagram has come to be classified as a niche social network. It is among the most dynamic and popular social media platforms that your business should be using. If you haven't already, it's time to create your Instagram business account.

Sharing photos and videos is Instagram's goal. You can tell graphically rich and engaging stories about your business and brand through visuals. While other social networks place more emphasis on video and photo posts, Instagram is the perfect complementary network to add to your marketing mix to facilitate cross-posting of content.

Before we start with how to open an Instagram business account, let's provide answers to some of the questions we might be curious about as regards to Instagram Marketing.

Instagram And How It Works?

Instagram is a free social networking service based on sharing photos and videos. It launched in October 2010 on iOS and became accessible on Android in April 2012. Facebook bought the service in April 2012 and has owned it ever since.

Like most social media apps, Instagram lets you follow the users you care about. This creates a feed on the home page that shows recent posts from all the individuals you follow. You may like posts and comment on them.

Besides posting regular photos and videos, which stay on your page all the time, Instagram also supports stories. If you've used Snapchat, you'll know this. Stories let you post one or more video clips and photos in a series. Anyone can view them for 24 hours, after which they expire.

Apart from that, Instagram also supports direct messaging so that you can chat with friends privately. You can also browse profiles to see what interests you the most. We'll show you how it all works below.

Why Instagram Is Important To Your Business

In all fairness, Instagram can be the best marketing medium for your business or it can be a waste of your time. I wouldn't say it's important to every online retailer, but when it works, it really work well. If your demographic includes young women and men and your product or service lends itself to a visual strategy (and most do), Instagram can't be ignored.

Let's check some of the reasons why this network is so important to many businesses.

Instagram for business

The world is growing, and so are businesses! The ever-increasing competition in the business world has made it necessary for every business to connect with its audience more effectively. This is important not only to survive in the market, but also to successfully run your business. But the question we should ask ourselves here is "How do we do this?" Instagram is among the best social media platforms that can help you do this. Today, over 60% of the world's best brands use Instagram for marketing.

More audience

In just a few years, Instagram has managed to attract more people than any other social media site. It has attained more than 150 million active users. So if you are not using Instagram for business it means that you could lose millions of potential customers.

More shareable

The main goal of any marketing program is to get the word out. The more people who know about a business, the more likely it is to be successful. Instagram helps you reach a wider audience. It let you share videos and photos with other social media sites. This way, with just a single post, you can attract multiple users from different platforms, like Facebook, Twitter, etc.

Get to know the trends

Using Instagram for business can help any business get a better view of trends and customer demands. With likes and public comments on any image or video posted, the organization can say what consumers want.

Building friendly relations

People are more and more attracted to new things and innovations. Instagram allows a business to sell more than just products. It can help create better word of mouth. Reaching the audience through a platform like Instagram makes relationships with the target audience more user-friendly.

Show your personality

A picture is better than loads of sentences. It is better to tell your story to people through pictures rather than words. With a variety of filters offered by Instagram, you can edit images and share them with people. This helps them better understand your business and may be interested in becoming your customer.

Changing people's perspective

What could be better than using Instagram for marketing when it may be the only way to change people's perspectives? Effective marketing relies on invoking the desire of customers to obtain the product or service offered. Connecting with customers on a platform where they already spend a lot of time is the best way to achieve this.

Success indicator

Instagram can also help you get a feel for where you stand in the market. The higher the number of followers, the greater the success of this brand. And if you start to lose your followers, it's a warning sign for a business that existing customers aren't happy, or the marketing strategy isn't strong enough to grab attention.

What Does Instagram Business Account Mean and Who Should Use It?

Instagram business account is one of two free business profile options available to Instagram users. A business profile offers more marketing tools and services than a personal account, such as:

- Instagram analytics for impressions, reach, and follower demographics
- The capability to promote posts and run Instagram advertisements
- Various contact options for your business including phone number, email address and physical address

- Integration of appointment scheduling

You will benefit from an Instagram business account if you own a brand and intend to use the platform to sell products, market your business, or simply increase brand awareness through engagement!

Creating an Instagram Business Account

Now that we know what Instagram is and why it is important to our business, how do we create an Instagram business account?

Before you begin, it's important to note that Instagram is for the content of the moment. To stay relevant to your followers, you'll need to invest the resources you need to post regularly.

The best way you can engage your followers is to keep your Instagram profile up to date. Below we will see how to create and maintain a successful Instagram profile.

If you don't already have it, download the Instagram app from the App Store or Google Play Store. You can view content on the Instagram website, but you cannot upload it through the desktop. You will need the app for this.

Configuring your Instagram account

When opening the Instagram app, you will have two options to create your account - Login with Facebook or register by phone or email. Make sure you sign up with a professional email address so that your Instagram profile is not linked to your personal Facebook account.

Then enter your account details. Under Full Name, enter the name of the real business so that your profile is recognizable to visitors. This name is what is displayed on your profile; this is not the username of your account (or handle, for those Twitter people).

Username is a unique name for your profile and allows other accounts to interact with your brand.

Choose a recognizable and easy-to-find username. If your business name is used, try to include the first part of your business name in your username. Note: You may update your username later in your account settings. So don't be disturbed if you want to change it in the future.

Optimizing your Instagram account

Now is the time to choose the appropriate profile picture. Your profile picture is definitely your first impression on new visitors. For this reason, keep the image consistent with your brand and visual indicators.

Consider using your logo or other familiar images. Instagram profile photos are automatically cropped in a circle, so leave space for the corners of the image.

Next: your Instagram bio. The Instagram bio has a maximum of 150 characters, so your goal here is a straightforward, concise summary of the person you are and why people should follow you. Inform your audience about your business using a touch of personality. Instagram bios can not be searched, so don't worry about hashtags or keywords (which we'll cover later in this book).

In your bio, you can persuade users to take specific actions, such as visiting your website or using a specific hashtag. Your bio is the only permitted area where you can submit a clickable URL and drive traffic to an external website.

Due to this fact, it is ideal for businesses to update the highlighted URL to align with the most recent post. If you decide to add a link, use a link shortener to keep your profile from looking disorganized. Tracked URLs also let you better understand the amount of traffic Instagram is driving to your site.

For future changes, click the Edit Profile button on your profile to edit your photo, name, username, bio, and URL.

Managing Instagram settings

Finally, let's review your account settings. Click on the three overlapping lines in the upper right corner of your profile and click on Settings below the window. (In your username, you'll see a few links that we'll talk about later in this book.)

In your settings, you can do things like changing your password, see the messages you like, turn on notifications, and more. Here are some major things you should check out immediately.

Story settings, where you can set who can see and respond to your Instagram stories. We recommend that you allow all of your followers to view and reply to your stories to increase brand engagement. In your settings, click **Privacy> Story** to access the story controls. (You can also have access to it by clicking the gear icon in the upper left corner when posting a story.)

Switch to a business account, which let you identify your profile as a business profile rather than a personal profile. Instagram's Business Tools feature makes it effortless for users to contact you, provide information, and allow you to promote your post. Your business must own a Facebook business page to upgrade to an Instagram business profile. In your settings, **click Accounts> Switch to a Professional account** to have access to these features.

To switch to a business profile, follow this setting, sign in to Facebook, and allow Instagram to have access to your pages. Choose a Facebook page to connect to your Instagram profile. (You must be the Facebook page admin before you can connect to the two platforms.)

Then Instagram will automatically import appropriate information from your Facebook page for editing. You now have a business profile on Instagram. Make sure to check your profile information and your account settings!

Private account, where you are permitted to change your profile from public to private. Instagram will automatically set your profile as public - we don't recommend changing it! As a business, you want people to see your posts and follow your business unhindered. In your settings, click on Privacy> Privacy account and check if it is disabled.

Comments, that allows you to hide comments with certain phrases or keywords. To do this, you need to enter specific words and phrases in Instagram settings and activate the function. Receiving feedback is exciting and encouraging, but some can run counter to the values of the brand or offend your audience. In your settings, click on **Privacy> Comments** to update them.

Added additional Instagram accounts, where you can add up to five accounts and switch between them without signing in and out. This feature also let you have multiple people logged into an account at the same time. To add additional account, click **Add account** at the bottom of the settings. Input the account username and password you want to add. To switch between the accounts, go to your profile and select your username at the top of the screen. Choose the account you wish to switch to.

Benefits of A Business Instagram Account

You can only schedule automatic posts with a business Instagram account

Or not, the main advantages of having a business profile on Instagram are the ability to enable automatic posting. This is a useful resource for business owners who want to manage Instagram content ahead of time.

At this time, the Instagram API only allows auto-posting for business accounts. This means that you cannot have a personal or creator account and use this feature.

If planning and creating consistent content for your Instagram account is mandatory for your business or brand, an Instagram business account should be your first choice.

The booking function for Instagram business accounts

After creating an Instagram business account, booking for your business will be easier than ever.

In addition to the additional contact options, such as email, call or visit your physical location, your customers and clients can also book an appointment with a quick touch!

Most appointment scheduling and tracking software integrate with Instagram to make it even easier. Some popular providers are:

- Appointments by Square
- Acuity Scheduling
- StyleSeat
- BeautyDate
- Schedulicity
- MyTime
- Shore
- And many more!

Having an Instagram business account makes it easy to book your business!

Creating and managing ads with an Instagram business account

Instagram business accounts have a simple function of creating ads and promotions on your profile.

With a business account, you are allowed to advertise on Instagram and even easily promote a post right from the Instagram app. Just tap the Promote on Instagram Profile button to create a promotion from an existing post and select the final destination (Instagram profile, website, or direct messages).

You will have the choice to select your audience or create a custom audience, select your budget and submit your ad for approval! Simple, isn't it?

Now you can also work directly with creators and influencers, promoting the branded content they create (when they identify you as a business partner).

Do you want to guarantee a return on your advertising expenses and work with the chosen influencer? You can track the performance of branded content through Facebook!

Exclusive Instagram Business Account Analytics

Every good marketer needs usable analytics, and a business profile on Instagram delivers!

By using Instagram analytics, you can see precisely who your followers are, when they're online, and more! And when using this information, you never have to worry about posting in a bad time.

You might be really astonished to find out who your followers are. These are the types of things we all need to know to market more effectively.

In addition to overall account performance, with an Instagram business account, you can view information about your individual stories and posts to see how people are interacting with them. To learn more about what works, look for common topics in articles that generate more engagement.

Possibility to add a contact button

A useful addition allowed for accounts with a company profile is the ability to add a contact button to your profile. When someone clicks the button, you can configure them to send an email, make a phone call, or provide a map showing their location.

Your sector will be displayed on your profile

When you have created your Facebook page, you are asked to select the sector in which your business operates. So when you connect Instagram from your business profile to your Facebook page, pass that information to Instagram on your profile. You can edit this information directly on Instagram, if needed in the future.

Ability to add links to Instagram stories

Among other things that are frustrating about Instagram from a marketing standpoint, is that you usually can't use clickable links. If you maintain a personal profile, the only link you can use is your own.

However, Instagram Stories offers another option. A useful option for some Instagram accounts is the ability to add a URL to your Instagram story.

This is especially important when, as reported, 75% of Instagram users act, like visiting a website, after viewing a post.

However, the ability to add links to Instagram stories is not available to all businesses. You must have a business profile with 10,000 followers before Instagram allows access to this feature.

Changing to A Business Profile From A Personal Profile

In your personal Instagram account, go to your profile page and click on the Settings icon (a gear symbol). Scroll through the provided list of options and tap the Switch to Business Profile link. Make sure you haven't set up your account as private.

It will ask for your Facebook profile and a Facebook page to connect to. Enter the relevant details. You must be the Facebook page admin.

Instagram will ask for your business contact details. Remember to write them down the way you would like your customers to see them. This includes your work email address, phone number, and address.

After completing the steps above, you will officially have a business profile on Instagram.

Lastly, business profiles provide a better marketing experience on Instagram, whether you're a business that wants to pass your message across on your own or you're an influencer who builds your followers and engagement.

How to Succeed In Instagram Marketing For E-Commerce?

While Instagram differs from other social media in a number of ways, the basics of getting started successfully still apply. Before you begin posting, pay attention to what your users (especially those in your demographic) react to. Pay attention to what other brands post. See what happened and what failed. This will give you different ideas of what might work for your brand.

Employees - Social networking, when done well, takes a long time. If you're like most entrepreneurs, you don't book time. So, instead of working hard, decide what part of the process can be outsourced and get it done. You might want to get involved in the strategy and review phases, but you can leave the social tracking, posting, and reporting to someone else. It all rest on on your comfort level, but be aware that most businesspersons cannot successfully concentrate on all elements of an Instagram marketing campaign when running a business. Be ready to trust someone else with part of the responsibilities.

Money: Depending on your strategy and level of involvement, you may not need to invest a lot to start using Instagram marketing for eCommerce. To create a budget, consider who you will need to hire and if photos need to be taken by a professional photographer. In most cases, a quick snapshot for iPhone or Android will work just fine. It's more about authenticity and personality than about being a business.

Time: Social media marketing takes time. If you are short on time, employ someone to manage it (based on your advice). But understand that this is much more than laborious, it can take months to build an audience and gain trust in any social network, so be patient.

Software: As you get to know Instagram better, you'll be happy to know that some parts of the posts can be automated. An app like **Instatag** can help you find the right label to increase followers and likes. **Instafollow** is great for discovering relevant users to follow and **Pic Effect Studio** adds a more creative touch to your images than standard Instagram filters.

Creativity - Brands need to be more creative on Instagram for a variety of reasons, and that creativity isn't just about finding the right images to post. Your whole strategy should be approached with a creative mind. Maybe you are creating a contest to let users upload and tag images, or maybe you create a little game that involves images of your brand (find something in the photo or something similar). Regardless of what you may decide, you should know that posting images of your products or staff will not be enough. You must let your head out of the box and create posts that are worth sharing.

Chapter 2: Top Influencer Strategies In 2021

Now that we have discussed about how to create an Instagram business account, it's time to propel it to a higher level with some of the most recent influencer strategies in 2021.

Becoming an effective Instagram influencer is not easy, and it's no secret that Instagram is a very different platform in 2021 than it was a few years ago.

The days when you are guaranteed hundreds of thousands of new followers when you getfeatured on a larger profile are long gone.

Posting a three-word caption and seeing steady growth? This doesn't fly anymore. Even the old follow-unfollow "hack"? That doesn't work anymore either.

It is vital to remember that while growth is more of an uphill battle today, it is still more than possible.

And what's even more inspiring is that you don't necessarily need hundreds of thousands of followers to be effective as an Instagram influencer in 2021, as brands are increasingly in tune with the power of micro-influencers.

Who Is an Influencer?

The best definition we can give to an influencer is someone who got involved in social media as a result of creating content based on an ambitious lifestyle. Influencers are also usually referred to as bloggers, content creators, vloggers, and thought leaders.

What Is an Instagram Influencer?

An Instagram influencer is someone who uses this social media sharing platform to build a personal brand and increase their followers. Instagram is the ideal platform for most influencers and brands. However, this is not the only social media platform that influencers can be successful.

What Is Influencer Marketing?

If you want to monetize your social media profiles as an influencer, you need to know what influencer marketing is. Influencer marketing is what brands and businesses do when they collaborate with influencers to raise awareness about a product launch, build brand recognition and credibility with social media users. Typically, this involves influencers creating content about a product, posting to their social feeds, and recommending an authentic tone of voice to their followers.

There are many ways to do influencer marketing and if you are an influencer partnering with a brand, you need to be aware of your brand's marketing goals in your influencer marketing campaigns.

What Are the Types of Influencers?

Influencers are generally defined in terminology based on their reach. It helps to be acquainted with the terms used by marketing experts when working with influencers.

The micro, power-middle (intermediate) and macro and celebrity influencers are some of the terms that marketers use when working with influencers.

A micro or power-middle influencer is commonly referred to when people describe influencers with fewer social media followers. Macro-influencers and celebrities have a larger number of followers.

There is no quick and concrete definition of the number of followers that make up a micro, macro, and celebrity influencer.

A Guide to Followers

- Micro/power middle influencers: between 3,000 and 100,000 followers

- Macro influencers: between 100,000 and 1 million subscribers
- Celebrity influencers: they have more than a million subscribers

So far, the general rule where reach has been prioritized is that higher following equates to higher payout for influencer brand collaborations. The dynamics are changing now, as brands see more value in collaborating with more influencers, with smaller, more engaged followers. Good news for those who have just started!

Followers Vs. Engagement Rate

The higher the number, the lower the engagement rate - this is the general rule. Influencers with fewer followers have a closer relationship with their followers than those with more followers.

Why Become an Influencer?

Merely thinking about what to do to become an influencer means you are taking the first step on what can be an incredibly powerful, rewarding, and creative journey. It's an interesting business to join brands that are increasing budgets year on year and social platforms, introducing more and more resources to help influencers and content creators. Without a doubt, you've seen other influencers on social media, like Instagram, collaborating with brands, eating delicious food, and traveling the world - just to name a few or opportunities.

Living the digital nomad lifestyle may appeal to you for several reasons. In other words, building a personal brand that is independent of your creative skills allows you to be your own boss. You can even quit your 9 a.m. to 5 p.m. There are many different reasons for wanting to become an influencer. Knowing your primary goals is essential to understanding your personal brand and style of photography.

It may surprise you that not everyone who does this in the industry initially intends to become a social media influencer. For many social media stars, the transition from Instagrammer to an influencer is completely organic. These unwitting influencers were first a hobby, and they were surprised by the dramatic growth in audiences.

Seven Steps to Becoming An Influencer

The lifestyle of an influencer is envied by many individuals. What we often don't recognize is the constant effort they have to make to live a life of luxury and glamor.

The truth about this is, there is no easy answer to the question of how to become an influencer. However, there are a several steps you can take to steer your efforts in the right direction.

1. Increase your subscribers

To start getting brand collaboration opportunities, you'll need to cultivate your following. Your social media channels should demonstrate something that you are passionate about with creative, engaging, and unique content. With a lot of work, time, and persistence, followers should come naturally. There are no shortcuts, but there are things you can do to speed up your subscriber growth.

Develop a number of loyal and engaged followers, actively engaging your existing audience and contributing to the wider Instagram community. This means responding with genuine comments and actively engaging with the wider Instagram community with meaningful comments. Be consistent with the time of posting, the type of content you post, and the tone of your voice. Provide your followers with the chance to get to know you through behind the scenes (BTS) content from their Instagram Stories.

Some influencers were quickly hit as they became Suggested Users on Instagram. This means Instagram follows you, and for two weeks you become a recommended account for new Instagram users.

Whatever you do, don't be tempted to cheat the system. If you're buying followers or using bots, you might think you're taking the easy route. Playing a prank until you get close might seem like a shortcut, but it's not smart. This is certainly not the key to success. Brands are now using technology to identify influencers with fake followers. Influencer marketing platforms like Vamp's pre-vet influencers to ensure the authenticity of your followers.

2. Develop follower engagement

Your engagement rate can be calculated with this simple equation:

(The number of likes and comments / Number of followers) x100

So if you have 300 likes, 40 comments, and 4,000 subscribers, this is how your engagement rate is calculated:

(340/4000) x100 = 8.5% engagement rate

Instagram's benchmark for engagement rate is 3%. This is a good minimum to be pursued consistently.

One way to indicate that someone has fake followers is if the engagement rate is low.

You can increase follower involvement by creating a community. Ask your followers questions in your caption copy, use Instagram stories to engage your followers individually, send DMs to old and new followers. You can track your engagement analytics if you have a business Instagram account. Analyze which content is most affected by your subscribers and use that knowledge to plan your content calendar.

3. Develop a personal brand

Before you can become a successful influencer, you need to develop your personal brand. Your personal brand is essential and will help you stand out from the crowd.

Most of the time, people like to know what to expect from you, and a strong personal brand will increase the likelihood that you will maintain your followers' loyalty.

Things to remember

- Find a niche and keep it. Instead of trying to be fashion, art, foodie and travel all in one package, create a cohesive message. The same goes for photographic styles. If you want to be the expert of flat-lay and that's why people follow you, stick with it at least 80% of the time. There are successful accounts that maintain a consistent and experimental element with different variables in their imagery to know how their audience will respond.
- Make sure your Instagram highlights feature the type of content you're posting and the stories people

can expect to see. Use the bio to better visualize your tone of voice and content.

- The first nine posts in your feed that appear on your profile should always display the best content. Don't be afraid to delete or archive posts if it hurts your feed's own aesthetic (as long as a brand hasn't paid to keep that content in your feed, of course).

- Have a consistent aesthetic across the feed and across all social channels.

- Highlight products relevant to your Instagram Story that you really like.

- What is your influential tone of voice? How do you communicate in an engaging way with your followers?

- How often do you post? Successful accounts regularly post to their target audience without sending spam. How often you post on Instagram depends entirely on your audience, but once or twice a day during peak times is usually the weak point.

4. Be authentic

You must be authentic to be an effective influencer, build trust, and respect your followers and the brands you work with. Be honest in your posts and encourage your followers to respond by asking questions in their posts.

There are many versions of our authentic self that we share with the world. Our work ego may, for example, be different from the version of ourselves we share with our friends or grandparents. Each is true in a different way to you and how you interact with the world. Likewise, your social media profiles should be authentic to you.

The way you talk about a product shouldn't be seen as a tough sell. It is not influencer marketing. Positioning products according to lifestyle will always pass product approval.

People love influencers because they are seen as more trustworthy than brands trying to sell things or big-name celebrities. So it is simple. Only recommend products to your followers if you really like that product or brand. It can be tempting to say yes to all of the opportunities that initially present themselves to get you started. A more sustainable and authentic long-term approach is to say no more than to say yes to opportunities.

Don't let your Instagram feed be completely filled with branded promotions. Find the time to create organic content in between. This way, your followers shouldn't worry if you get paid to promote a brand because they think you like it too.

Authenticity builds trust and it's one of your most valuable assets as an influencer.

5. Win work with brands

Brands will like to work with you if you check the boxed of what they do expect in your collaborations with influencers. Depending on your goals, this may vary from business to business. The main points sought by most brands are:

High-quality content: Invest in a good camera and learn how to use it by taking a class, reading blogs, and watching YouTube tutorials.

Followers: Create a real follower of like-minded people who will love your content. Get a business account and get ready to share your business analysis, if brands want to see it. If your posts are working well, it will help them justify spending more money to work with you - a win for both parties. The brand's commerce generally requires that you are working with influencers with a business account.

Engagement: Brands want to see their followers engaged in their content. Ask questions in the captions and respond to all comments. Thank people when they follow you and try to get to know them better so they know what content they prefer. Post at times of the day when your profile will generate the most traffic. Eliminate bot-type accounts when they follow you to maintain high engagement.

Similar Aesthetics: Brands with a similar aesthetic to yours are more likely to choose to work with you, as it will help send the message they want to your subscribers and potential customers.

Professionalism - This is the icing on the cake. Brands want to know that you will follow their brief, respond quickly and professionally to emails, and behave well when posting their content. Discover how to build a great reputation as an influencer and get reps.

6. Network, network, network

If you want 202 1 to be the year you finally start collaborating with brands, you need to get out there.

Creating cohesive content and building a community on Instagram without coming into contact with brands is like winking at a guy in total darkness ... they won't notice you.

Here are few tips for making your next collaboration:

Get on Instagram influential marketing platforms

Discover platforms like Fohr, Popular Paga and Collectively. After your profile is fully set up, you will be contacted if one of the brands on the platform considers you suitable for one of your campaigns.

Find PR companies and make presentations

PR firms are firms that represent several brands and organize marketing campaigns for influencers. Use Google to find PR companies that represent brands in your niche.

Introduce yourself via email without asking or intending to work with any of your brands and ask to stay up to date on future opportunities. If you stay in the same city as one of these agencies, set up a date for a coffee and, if not, a phone conversation.

Create and send your media kit

Every time you launch a brand or make a presentation, send your media kit! When creating the media kit, make sure it contains the following:

- Your social logins and website
- Audience size on all platforms
- Audience demographics (age, gender, location)
- Examples of imagery that you have produced in the past to give you an idea of the kind of content you would create to publish them. Depending on the brand you launch, you can change these images!
- A list of brands you've worked with before (if applicable)

7. Diversify your platforms

No influencer should completely trust Instagram. Not only is it risky because you don't 'own' your target audience on a third-party platform and you can't control the vagaries of the algorithm, but it's also a missed profit opportunity.

By increasing your target audience on another platform, you increase the value you can receive for collaborations with brands.

For instance, if a brand asks you to hire Instagram posts, you can add a promotion and blog post to your email list and boost the rate significantly.

What other platforms should you use? It's all down to your strengths and interests and which platform is best suited for your niche.

If you are good on camera and are in a niche where visual communication is vital, YouTube may be the place for you. Do you have something of value to communicate and speak well? Think of a podcast! Have you always liked to write? Try to start a WordPress blog!

Building your mailing list is also extremely important, as this is the only audience that you actually "own" that is not based on the existence of a platform.

Here are some initial steps to take to build the list:

- **Deliberate on the knowledge you have about your audience:** what are they struggling with? What do they want to learn or receive from you? Maybe it's a video tutorial that walks you through the best yoga flows to help you relax, a PDF packing list, or a guide with ten ways to pair a blazer for fall.

- **Create that gift:** it can be in video, PDF, or template format.

- **Build an opt-in page:** similar to this one, which will allow people to input their email address to receive the gift. There are some technical works to be done here to make sure that once they have input their email address, they will receive the guide, but it's not something you can't learn through the Google university. I prefer building opt-in pages with LeadPages and MailChimp or ActiveCampaign for email marketing.

- **Begin to promote your freebie on all your social media:** Explain the transformation or results people will get from consuming your freebie and connecting them to your opt-in page.

- **Watch your list grow!**

How To Win Repeat Work With Brands

In science and art, great marketing campaigns start with great ideas and great content. But that's only part of the equation. Equally important is understanding what drives a consumer to choose your grocery store over their competitors. You may do this by going through the painful process of learning the many principles of psychology or by applying a fundamental marketing strategy.

1. First Impressions Count

Your profile photo is always the first impression of your brand. In the midst of increasing competition, a profile picture can make or break your campaign app. Make sure your profile picture reflects your aesthetic. This helps brands instinctively know if you'll align with their brand.

A candid self-portrait usually works best. Pick an image with the changes/filters you naturally use. For instance, don't use a black and white photo if there are some colorful tones in your feed. Avoid logos, graphics, or cartoon images, as they likely won't accurately reflect the aesthetic you carefully create in your feed.

2. Me, Myself And I

Your Instagram bio should reflect your personality and the main themes of your account. Brands and followers will connect with you on a more personal level if you include your name in your bio.

Avoid cliché phrases (e.g., I love life!) And find something that is unique to you. Remember to include in your Instagram bio the best way for brands to contact you to avoid missing out on opportunities. Using Instagram Stories Highlights now is also a great way to show off your personality behind the scenes of your profile. Avoid long connections. If part of a brief requires you to include a link in your bio, you can refine it with sites like bitly. Include relevant hashtags in your bio to help the right people find you.

3. Communication is the key

Find out your way around your email. If you don't use a third-party app for brand briefs, this may be the only point of contact with your client. It's a powerful and easy way to promote yourself in the brands you work with.

Everyone has that personal email account you created in high school. Consider switching to a more professional nickname. For example, myinstagramhandle@gmail.com instead of anything with confusing letters/numbers and avoid anything that is misleading at all costs. (babe2000@hotmail.com anyone ?!).

Setting up an electronic signature creates a professional impression. Being a graphic designer to make your electronic signature look stylish and to have a solid reputation is not a must - Canva is a great place to create professional branding features, if you're not a Photoshop professional.

If you are leaving or if you feel overwhelmed by personal or other commitments, use the field office to let brands know that you will respond as quickly as possible. They will know that they are not waiting for an immediate response. Remember that the best way to get in touch with the brands is via chat application for all campaigns on which you are currently working. Honesty is always the best policy. Brands can smell a white lie from a mile away. If you fail to produce quality content on time, be honest and try to explain.

4. Think like a brand

When taking your photos, it's important to think like a brand. This will miximize the likelihood that you will be selected by brands for additional usage rights. This means more money and more exposure to your content on a wide variety of media, including email, print, social media ads, and more.

Be sure to create the brand's logo/product on your images. Refer to the summary during your photoshoot to make sure the photos you create meet campaign requirements. Always treat your professional reputation as a brand would. This way, you will find yourself repeatedly working with your favorite brands.

5. Search for and ask questions

After accepting a brief from a client, do more research on the brand. Browsing social media accounts is a good place to assess your aesthetic style and content. Always endeavor to contact them for more details on what the brand is looking for. It will make a professional impression and help build a stellar reputation.

6. Professional development and networking

As an influencer, you need to keep growing and following trends. There are plenty of resources online to help you with your Instagram game. You can have a blog dedicated to keeping influencers up to date with the most relevant articles. You also have regularly invited a few items - some of them our most talented content creators.

Sign up for a photography class or test yourself to participate in a videography class to develop your skills. Stay on top of the latest Instagram and industry developments   to make sure you don't   get   left behind. Connect with other influencers to share tips, tools and advice

7. Be Consistent

One of the major areas of your reputation is your ability to be consistent. The brand chose you because they love your content. Make sure to reproduce this quality in your campaign images.

The power is with you simply to say yes to summaries that you can fully commit to. By making sure that you are reliable, you won't be disappointed, even with your fellow designers.

Be professional and treat your Instagram like a brand name, that doesn't mean having the creative fun that you can have with it. The fun will really begin after you secure more opportunities.

In conclusion

It requires more efforts to become a successful influencer, but hopefully after reading this you feel like it's a passion that you are inspired to follow.

In the end, what you put in will be what you get. After all, if you are passionate about creating content, you will thrive.

Being an influencer involves the maximum combination of creativity and strategy; community and individuality.

You may have the chance to work with some of the best brands in the world who are looking to spread the word and inspire action. And in return, you will continue to become a very intelligent marketer.

Influencer marketing will continue to develop and evolve. Follow industry changes, new Instagram features, and collaborate with associated brands and influencers to thrive.

Chapter 3: How to Reach Million Real Followers In 2021

Giveaways, sweepstakes, and other contests have always been great ways to go viral and quickly grow your audience.

If you want to quickly miximize your number of followers, organize a giveaway. Or team up with an influencer to cut costs and give that extra boost and level of credibility. With that said, let's explore a quick strategy on how you can do this.

Hosting A Giveaway

Everyone loves free stuff. There is something in our psychology that triggers an emotional response when we receive something for free - in fact, it makes us appreciate the product more.

Economists call this the zero-price effect. And that's what makes Instagram pay homage to such a powerful tool.

An effective Instagram giveaway can have a direct impact on your brand perception, increasing awareness of your business and its commitment to your content.

So how do you make sure you get it right?

We've put together a six-step tips to assist you in making your first Instagram giveaway the best it can be.

6 Simple Steps to Creating Your Instagram Giveaway

Creating a successful Instagram giveaway takes planning and a clear understanding of what you want to achieve as a result.

As you go through the procedure of creating your first offer, be sure to tie all decisions to your business goals.

1. Determine what to expect from your giveaway

If you don't set a predefined goal for your Instagram giveaway, you're essentially giving away something for free. Even though it's good for your followers, it doesn't serve your business.

The first step in the offer should be to get exactly what you want to achieve when the offer is full.

The goal you choose will impact all other decisions you make, including your reward, the content you create, and how you promote your tribute to fans.

By creating a gift with a defined and achievable goal, you can maximize your potential to achieve your goal.

It also let users easily understand what they need to do to participate and ensures that they won't have any issues with regulating Instagram content.

2. Familiarize yourself with Instagram rules

Once you understand what you want out of your offer, it's time to take a look at what Instagram requires of you to actually get it done.

There are several specific rules for creating a tribute on your platform and you should follow to make sure your bonus is working properly and avoiding the risk of being closed.

To ensure you have no issues with Instagram's free terms of service, be sure to include the following information:

- The rules for your giveaway.
- The eligibility conditions of participants.
- Any relevant regulations related to your giveaway (age limits, etc.).
- Acknowledgment that Instagram is not responsible for the giveaway.

All of this should be included in the comments section of your giveaway post. If you are unclear in any way, Instagram reserves the right to remove your content.

Do not worry; including that information does not detract from the impact of your giveaway. It's a standard way to keep everyone involved on the same page.

Now that you are fully aware of these rules, it's time to get down to the fun part.

3. Pick a prize that your audience likes

If your giveaway isn't appealing to your target audience, you won't see any implication.

When planning your giveaway, take a look at what your followers are interested in and think about how you are to offer something valuable and brand.

It's easy for consumer products and e-commerce vendors who sell specific products. A SaaS or software company will need to do more research if they want to offer more than one discount or trial.

A way of doing this is to segment by interest: Searching for Instagram Insights will provide insight into what is relevant to your audience.

Your gift on Instagram can also be an opportunity to collaborate with other brands.

It's a great way to attract an already engaged audience and increase brand awareness for everyone involved.

This makes the whole tribute more valuable and tempting for Instagram users and therefore more powerful for the brand.

4. Write the appropriate giveaway caption

Now that you have selected your prize, it's time to write your Instagram post for the giveaway.

This is where you will target users so they can find out more about what they will earn. Think about how you want subscribers to engage with the content (via shares or comments?) And customize the content based on those needs.

An effective caption will not only promote the items you are offering; it will provide all the necessary information that people need to find, know and participate in the competition.

This is where hashtags can come in handy.

In addition to a specific hashtag for your giveaway, include relevant hashtags, such as #contest and #giveaway. It's also a great idea to add more information and hashtags about your industry.

When writing your caption, think about how you can give your brand some personality as well.

Your tribute can be the first impression you make on new subscribers or it can strengthen the relationship you have with your present audience. Either way, it's time to increase your chances of participating, so be attractive.

5. Promote your giveaway on Instagram with ads

When your giveaway is up and running, use Facebook and Instagram ads to promote it. This can increase awareness of the giveaway to a wider audience and potentially also increase overall engagement with the publication.

When posting your ads, use the same type of interest targeting described above in the "Pick a prize ..." section.

It's important to ensure that you are attracting an audience that is not only interested in your product or service, but has the potential to subscribe and report the increase in your post.

These ads are also an opportunity to double the value of your giveaway.

Experience the fact that you are giving something away for free; all the user has to do is follow their account or tag one of their friends on the post. It is important to clarify how low the effort is for potential participants.

6. Keep Track of the Results

After choosing the giveaway winner, see how the process affected your original goal. It helps you see a return on investment and create better performing gifts in the future.

In Instagram Insights, search for interaction and discovery reports. Both will provide valuable information on the success of your campaign.

If you originally created your offer to increase engagement, the Interactions report will tell you what you need to know who clicked on your post. Among these, you can track who returned to your site or who became a follower as a result.

The Discovery Report is more valuable if your goal was to maximize brand awareness. Provides information on the number of potential new subscribers who saw your post in your feeds.

Use this information to determine how your donation really impacted your goal. Once you figure this out, it's easy to refine the process and look for opportunities to improve it for your next tribute.

Partnering with An Influencer

Brands are now investing more in influencer marketing and growing relationships with influencers. The global influencer market is expected to reach $ 22.3 billion by 2024. Indeed, consumers seek authenticity and marketing from influencers.

However, to be successful with influencer marketing, you need to find the right influencers for your brand. You can do this by finding the ones that have similar values to your brand. Plus, they need to be active on channels where your target audience is present.

Once you've seen your influencers, you need to figure out how to collaborate with them. This section explains how to collaborate with Instagram influencers. It also offer advice on how to manage these potentially powerful partnerships.

How to collaborate with Instagram influencers

Partnering with Instagram influencers can increase your reach, engagement, and sales. CivicScience found that 81% of consumers buy products because influencers promote them.

Influencers will have built loyalty and trust among those who follow them. And 88% of consumers believe in recommendations from people they know.

By collaborating with Instagram influencers, you expose your brand to a wide audience. Influencers can also increase their search rankings with qsuality backlinks to their blogs. Also, they can help you drive traffic to your website through your posts.

Now that you know the benefits of partnering with influencers, let's take a look at how to collaborate with Instagram influencers.

1. Establish partnership goals

You must first define your goals and key performance indicators (KPIs) before you can collaborate with Instagram influencers. Having them will help you measure the performance of your influencer strategy.

It also helps to channel your efforts towards this goal. You need to also have knowledge of what to expect from the influencer before you actually approach them.

Some of the influencer marketing goals include:

- Increase brand awareness
- Attract a new audience
- Generate sales
- Promote a product launch
- Increase your Instagram following
- Retain current customers
- Extend reach
- Generate engagement

Your Instagram influencer marketing goals must also be SMART, which means they should be specific, measurable, achievable, realistic and timely.

After you define your goals, you can determine the KPIs to measure. For example, brand awareness metrics can include impressions, engagement, and coverage.

Having goals will also help you clearly define your target audience.

2. Look for Instagram influencers

Once you've recognized your goals, it's time to find the right influencers for your business. The influencers you select should be from your niche and should have values similar to your brand.

Another important thing to consider when finding an influencer is the quality of the content. Mediakix has found that marketers consider the quality of content to be important when meeting an influencer. They also control the target audience and engagement rates.

Some of the other things to check include:

- **Engagement:** A high rate of engagement means the influencer knows what their audience wants and can convince them to take action. Check the comments on your posts. Note the number of comments and also their quality. Also check if they respond to fan comments.
- **Follower Quality:** Are the influencer's followers similar to your target audience? Can they connect with your brand?
- **Number of followers:** The number of followers also determines your coverage rate and your potential engagement. Influencers with fewer followers often have higher engagement rates.
- **Quality of content:** the analysis of the content will help you understand if they write relevant content

for your niche. It will also help you understand the quality of the content. You should also check if they can naturally infuse your brand into your content without being overly promotional.

- **Budget:** can you afford it? Some influencers agree to buy free products in exchange for a feedback, but some may want monetary compensation.

  You can calculate the cost of an influencer based on different factors. This includes the number of followers, engagement rate, industry, and audience size. However, it's vital to note that the more followers an influencer has, the more it will cost.

- **Voice:** Finding the appropriate voice will depend on your business. Do you want your influencer to be professional with serious, relaxed and friendly messages? You want an influencer with a good sense of humor? Their voice should be aligned with that of your brand.

Once you've found an influencer who matches your account, find a way to connect with them.

3. Build a relationship with influencers

To collaborate effectively with Instagram influencers, first build a relationship with them. Do a deep research, follow the Instagram account and find out what it is.

This will give you a compelling reason to approach them. You will also find out how they can make a difference in your campaigns.

The relationship should also favor the influencer, so you need to demonstrate the value of the partnership. If you can understand their interests and passions, you are in the best position to deal with them.

You must start building the relationship by starting a conversation with them through comments and messages. Share informative content with them to further strengthen the relationship.

Once you have a solid relationship with them, come up with your idea of collaboration. Explain why a partnership would be beneficial to your business and what they would gain from this partnership.

4. Decide on a partnership structure

Once they've accepted your offer, it's time to strike a deal with Instagram influencers. Discuss how collaboration works so you can run a smooth campaign.

Factors to consider when choosing a partnership structure:

- Timeframe: what will be the duration of the campaign? What are the deadlines?

- Campaign type: Will the influencer share a sponsored post or write a review? Do you want them to buy your account on social media or promote giveaways and contests?

- Content Quality: Accept what you expect from them in terms of content. Do you want photos, videos or branding mentions? Or maybe the features of Instagram Stories?

- Clearly communicate your expectations to avoid problems later. However, give influencers complete creative freedom to produce content that resonates with their followers.

- Rights to use content: the influencer retains ownership of the content, but it is necessary to request the right to use all of the content. You can reuse this content later after collaboration.

- FTC Regulations: Make sure the influencer understands and acts in accordance with FTC regulations and guidelines.

- Payment: agree on how and when payments will be processed. Will it happen by mail or by other means? Agree on the method of payment and amount before the start of the collaboration.

5. Measure campaign progress

When you collaborate with the Instagram influencer, you need to know if your efforts are paying off. Most marketers measure success using engagement rates, impressions, and brand awareness.

The metrics tracked will depend on the campaign goals. The information you get will help you improve your Instagram influencer marketing strategy and achieve better results in future campaigns.

Other Common Ways to Grow Your Followers

1. Optimize your Instagram profile

Your Instagram profile is the first property a potential follower sees. It is extremely important to optimize the profile space for maximum potential. There are four main components in an Instagram profile:

- Profile Photo
- Username
- Website Url
- Instagram Bio

2. Develop the aesthetics of your Instagram feed

Instagram is a visual platform, which implies that your photos must be top-notch. No exception. With iPhone pretty much being the standard, it honestly surprises us when a bad photo shows up in our feed. How is it possible?! This to us, and almost everyone, communicates laziness.

If you'd like to get hold of the attention of your audience and turn them into illusory fans, you have to impress them and make them stop scrolling.

Think of your Instagram feed as a grid of 9 images. You have 9 changes to make someone like you and follow you! If you think of your favorite feeds to follow, emulate a certain sentiment or vibe to them with the images they share.

The major important thing in an Instagram feed is the balance of space and color.

Color: Enedeavor to keep the color as uniform as you can. The trick to doing this is to maintain a filter. Editing photos in the same way always improves the flow.

Space: For continuous flow, space is needed. Whether it's empty space or whether the main lens of the photo is closer or further away. Think of space like zooming in on a camera - you need a balance between narrow and wide shots to make it more appealing.

3. Use hashtags

If you've heard of the changes to the new algorithm, it will likely become much more difficult to dominate

Instagram. Now, it's absolutely vital to keep engagement in the flow.

This is where hashtags come in. The hashtags are like your best friend. You need it to help you.

Currently, up to 30 hashtags are assigned to a photo. USE ALL. These are your keywords. People will use these words to type in the search box and find relevant photos or accounts to follow.

4. Tell a visual story

No one except you knows what happened before you took this photo. Share the story behind it with people. Where was he taken? How is it? What is happening in the photo? Let's connect to the picture and pull the strings of our hearts.

You have to be sociable. Put yourself in your audience's shoes and study how they communicate. Find your ideal customer and find out what interests them. It's okay to have a liner every now and then, but try to take it further.

5. Plan ahead

To post daily, you need to plan ahead. We recommend that you create a social media calendar to help you become more consistent with Instagram. When planning your content, allow room for change. Sometimes you can go to a really cool bar mid-week and want to post a pic of your cappuccino. If all of your messages are already scheduled, you won't be able to do it.

6. Tag Brands

Tagging brands and suppliers in your photos is essential for quickly building your Instagram follower. It will not only notify the people you have tagged, but also expand the scope of your photo. Chances are, the person you've tagged will want to re-share the photo in their feed and tag you! This will result in increased visibility and credibility for your business.

7. Use geotags

A geotag is like a Facebook record. If you have a physical setting for your business, you should set it as a custom location and tag it with each post. If your business has a worldwide presence, use the location where you took the photo or the city from which you want to attract customers. According to the simple metric, Instagram posts that have a position have a 50% higher engagement rate.

8. Use call to action

Ask for something and they will get back to you. Create conversations and a very engaged audience. People want to participate and feel included in the discussion.

Think about what your audience might respond to. When asking questions, show that you care about your audience and that you're not just numbers.

If you are concerned that your question might be received with crickets, do not stay. If you want to create a sequel, you have to overcome this fear. More people will fold your photo than they will comment on. Change their behavior by sending a question at the end of each caption. Whether they respond or not, they will always have the opportunity to do so. The easier it is to answer the question, the bigger the answer.

9. Respond to comments

We admit that as you gain more subscribers, it becomes more difficult to respond to every comment. Often times people leave comments blank like "great" or "nice," and it doesn't seem useful to respond. Worse yet, it could be an automatic bot leaving these comments.

However, it is worth taking the time, just because they took the time to write them down, and therefore you should return the favor. If it's a bot that left the comment, you'll always let the person who left the comment know, forcing them to take a look at your Instagram feed.

Unless you have thousands of comments on every photo, there's really no excuse for not spending a few minutes writing acknowledgments. Be social! Respond to all comments to keep the conversation going. Visit your subscribers' accounts and also interact with their posts.

10. Publish every day

Not a must to post on Instagram every hour, but certainly every day, if you want to stay relevant. Consistency is what will keep you going. If you post too much, it will saturate your subscribers' feeds and bore them. Track your commitment to see your optimism after the days and hours.

People will like to know that you are trustworthy and that you can count on your content. Keeps you relevant. Most of us gave up before we see results, but we promise that if you keep going, you will gain traction.

If you don't have a solid Instagram strategy to follow, it can get confusing and overwhelming trying to grow your account.

If you want to increase your Instagram in 2021, it's time to start planning NOW.

Chapter 4: Types of Instagram Posts

After creating and optimizing your Instagram account, it's time to start posting some great content. Instagram let you post different kinds of content, including photos, videos, and stories.

It's time to talk about the different kind of Instagram posts and some best practices for inspiring engagement.

Images

An image post is the most common post on Instagram. When you post images, you are sharing multiple photos. The variety will show that your brand is diverse and engages your followers in a number of ways.

It's also vital to remember that Instagram users look for genuine branded posts, not blatant ads. Try to capture the culture of your business with lifestyle photos and behind the scenes looks. Avoid posting too much photos of your product.

To get started, we've compiled a list of some types of successful Instagram images.

Behind-the-Scenes Posts

These posts provide insight into the part of your business that people don't normally see. It is important that they do not appear staged: authenticity is the key!

Reposts from Your Employees

Great content may sometimes be right in front of you … on your employees' Instagram. (Be sure to credit or tag the original poster.) Reposting employee photos is an easy way to take care of authentic content and humanize your business. Your target audience will not only engage with your brand, but will also begin to "bond" with your employees.

Educational posts

How-to posts provide advice on how to make or do something. Photos or videos usually have instructions quickly and easily.

Influencer Posts

Influencer posts use the fame of a well-known public figure or celebrity to promote their brand. These posts typically include a view of the influencer who uses or interacts with your product. One of the main advantages of influencer posts is getting the attention of another audience.

Motivational posts

A motivational post combines a simple image with a quote overlay or uplifting text. These posts inspire your audience and amplify your brand values. While they are effective, try to post them sparingly to avoid sounding confused. Apps like Typic and Quipio can help you add text to your photos in a way that meets your brand's guidelines.

User-generated content

Similar to employee repositories, User Generated Content (UGC) is curated by fans and subscribers. Your posts tagged and your posts with your brand's hashtag are a great source for UGC.

Sharing photos of your followers and fans not only make the original poster feel good, but it also means you really care about your customers. Make sure to credit the original post with a tag or caption. To repost user-generated content, take screenshots and crop the original post or use an editing app like **Repost for Instagram.**

Newsjacking (Trending Holiday Posts)

There seems to be a "vacation" for everything these days. Events like National Brothers Day and National Ice Cream Day generate a lot of engagement on social media. Join the fun by participating in a local, national or global trend. A newsjacking post is a better way to post humorous content related to carefree events.

How to Capture and Edit Instagram Photos

After exploring what you can post on Instagram, let's take a look at a few ways to make sure your content is successful. Unlike other social media platforms, the simple layout of the Instagram profile forces you to focus on the content quality and not the quantity.

While this is essential for engagement, it also means you can't hide poor content. Do your best to use high-resolution images in your Instagram feed.

Square images must be 1080 x 1080px. Landscape images must be 1080 x 566px and profile images must be 1350 x 1080px. Regardless of the size uploaded, each image will be displayed as a square in your profile feed.

How to take a good photo with your smartphone

You might be wondering how to capture a perfect high-quality photo without a high-quality camera ...? Relax! The phone's camera technology has become so advanced that it now rivals $1000 cameras.

Extraordinary photography is no longer limited to those with professional cameras. You (yes, you!) can take some compelling photos that your audience will love using a tool you already have on your hands. Here are some tips for encouraging Instagram follower growth and engagement.

1. Follow the rule of thirds

To instantly improve photo composition, turn on camera grid lines. Try placing the subject at the intersection of a series of horizontal and vertical lines. This technique, referred to as the rule of thirds, is popular with painters, illustrators and photographers.

Positioning the object off-center creates a slight imbalance that catches the viewer's eye. To activate the grid lines (on an iPhone), go to **Settings> Photos & Camera and activate the grid.**

2. Focus on a single subject

A background filled with multiple subjects in a single frame only distracts the focus of the photo. It can even get your audience confused.

Instead, focus on a single subject in every photo. Remove distractions by cutting them out or finding a clean background for the shot.

3. Take advantage of negative space

The empty space around the subject is known as negative space. Leaving negative space around the object will draw attention to the desired focus of the image and prevent it from appearing full.

4. Look for interesting prospects

People are used to seeing the world at eye level. To create interesting and new photos, use photos from different angles. Change your shooting perspective to capture an aerial view or a worm. Try different angles to find new perspectives in common places.

5. Take advantage of patterns and symmetry

The human eye is obviously drawn to symmetrical objects and shapes. Sometimes it's best to center the scene in the frame and break the rule of thirds. Guidelines are another more specific form of symmetry that stands out in the photo. People are also drawn to standards. A pattern can be man-made, like a tile floor, or natural, like flower petals or vines on a wall. To make things interesting, your should break the pattern with the topic.

6. Use natural light

Standard ambient lighting creates strong shadows and highlights that create an unwanted dark and bright areas in your photos. To avoid this, make use of soft natural light as much as possible. Try taking pictures next to a window and, for pictures outside, a half-hour before sunset and after sunrise lighting typically offers the most surprising, because the sun is low in 'horizon.

Add filters and edit photos

Have you ever questioned why some photos are so beautiful? It probably has to do with your modification. Editing photos will only take some minutes and can dramatically affect the quality. Thanks to Instagram's built-in filters and tools, editing photos is very easy. Follow these tips to make your homemade lunch photo a culinary masterpiece.

First of all, start with a great photo (using our tips above). No editing can correct photos if they have little composition or lighting.

Consider editing your photo with other apps. Snapseed is a free editing app that lets you apply effects like tonal contrast and HDR, as well as adjust saturation, brightness, and contrast. VSCO is also another common editing app with several free filters that look like popular movies.

When your edited photo is uploaded to Instagram, the photo is automatically cropped to a square. To return to the original width, tap the icon with the two arrows pointing outward. At this point, you can add more Instagram filters, but don't go crazy. Each Instagram filter has its own unique personality, which can dramatically change a photo.

So try to adjust your lux photo. According to Instagram, "Lux balances exposure and provides the necessary brightness" for photos. Lux make can make your photo more vibrant and highlight details. To do this, tap the wand icon at the top of the screen and adjust the level.

Make the final edits using Instagram's editing tools. Tap Edit to adjust photo alignment, brightness, contrast, texture, and more. Tap Next when you're done adding the latest details and posting.

Video

Instagram also allows you to upload videos, as long as they are a minute or less long.

You can download finely edited videos from your computer or edited videos in a mobile application. Splice is another free editing tool (from the same guys who made GoPro) that lets you trim multiple clips and add transitions, titles, and music.

Instagram videos are preset for playback without audio. For this reason, make sure that at least the first few seconds of your videos don't need audio to be understood. You can use the caption or ask viewers to turn the sound back on.

Boomerangs

Open Instagram and tap the camera icon in the top left corner of the main screen. Here is the app camera. You can also have access to it by sliding your finger to the right of the screen.

Observe the settings below. The **Normal setting**, where the camera is **set** by default, takes pictures. You'll see the first setting on the right is Boomerang, which records three-second looping videos that play back and forth.

Boomerangs let you put a quirky spin on a traditional video. Boomerangs created using a series of photos and stitching them together for a small, repetitive video. These types of posts are fun for circumstances like jumping, grilling with glasses, or five more.

You can also download the Instagram Boomerang app to have a separate location to capture boomerang videos.

Hyperlapse

Do you have a really long Instagram video? Check out the Instagram Hyperlapse which allows long videos condensing into shorter content and greater content capacity.

Create smooth, fast-paced videos with built-in stabilization. To create your Hyperlapse videos, download the app and assign it to access the camera. Click on the circle once to stop and start your recordings. Once the recording is done, you may choose a playback speed between 1x and 12x. Save the final Hyperlapse video to the reel for later upload.

Instagram stories

Stories allow Instagram users to post at a higher frequency without clogging up and over-posting on their main feed. Stories often feature less-polished, more organic videos and images. Like Snapchat stories, your Instagram story vanishes after 24 hours.

The stories speak of authenticity. While your Instagram feed should contain polished photos, the stories can be a little crueler. Use this feature to take a glance behind the scenes of your brand or introduce the culture of your company. Do you have an office that accepts dogs? Share photos and videos of dogs on your story. Stories are also a useful tool for showing live events that your business is hosting or attending, as this feature is much more time-sensitive.

Instagram Live

As stated above, Instagram has a live video option that allows you to share content in real-time. To start a live video stream, launch the Instagram camera, scroll to the Live setting and click the button to start the live video.

As soon as the live video starts, all followers currently on the app will receive a notification that you are live. Viewers can also add comment to the live video using the built-in chat feature. The live video should be used in moderation to showcase exciting, real-time content or captivating moments like questions and answers or reveals.

IGTV

Instagram TV, or IGTV, is Instagram's latest video offering. Available for viewing through the Instagram app or IGTV, users can view long-running vertical videos from Instagram's creators. Think cooking videos, celebrity interviews, product reviews and tutorials ... this is the content you normally find on IGTV.

What is the difference between Instagram Live and IGTV? IGTV is a downloaded movie that offers users the ability to edit and adjust the video. Instagram Live is filmed and sent live.

To start posting, download the IGTV app, create a channel, and upload a video between 15 seconds and 10 minutes. Verified accounts can play videos up to one hour long. Currently, IGTV videos can only be viewed on mobile devices through the Instagram app or IGTV: the platform does not support desktop viewing.

How to Write Instagram Captions?

A picture may be worth more a thousand words, but there is something to be said about the context those words provide.

Writing amazing captions can be tricky, which is why we've found some tips to take some of that pressure off.

Don't rush the process

Write several drafts and ask your friends or colleagues for advice. Yes, your content should be timely, but also engaging. Instagram just changed its algorithm to organize each user's feed to show what they are likely to find interesting. The visibility of each post will be dependant on the number of likes and comments received. Take your time to create content that will engage and delight your customers.

Consider the length of your caption

Captions may be up to 2,200 characters long. (For comparison, Twitter allows 140.) Regardless of the size, users can only see the first 3-4 lines of each caption. They have to click on More ... to see the rest. For this reason, insert the most important content at the beginning of the caption so that it is always visible.

That said, don't be afraid of long captions. In fact, Instagram is a great way to tell stories.

Engage, Engage, Engage

Ensure to always put a call to action in the caption. Inspire your audience to comment, share, and like your photo.

You can also use the caption to direct users to your bio link, where they will have the opportunity check out a new product or blog post. Don't forget to edit the link to match your most recent post. Tip: Use collapsed follow links in your URL so you can see traffic coming from your Instagram account or a specific post.

Include geolocation. Did you know that the publications associated with a position are more than 79% engaged? Adding geolocation gives users another way to find your content, which can lead to more engagement.

Find your Instagram voice

Each social platform has a distinct voice. What works on Twitter may not work on Instagram. Posts with a light-heart authentic tone tends to work better on Instagram. Try out emojis and other fun tools to give your brand a distinctive look. Don't expect to be successful the first time - it may take some time to develop your brand's voice.

If you have any question about what to write, be quick. There is little correlation between caption engagement and length, but short captions allow your visuals to speak.

How to Use Hashtags On Instagram?

Hashtags have taken over the internet. Hashtags refer to keywords or key phrases written without spaces and preceded by a pound sign (#). They are typically used to refer to events, conferences, pop culture, entertainment, or recurring themes and are an effective way to make your content more visible.

Initially distributed on Twitter, hashtags are now present on various social networks.

Use of hashtags on Instagram

Instagram feeds are continuously changing, which makes sense given that 80 million photos are shared every day. With so much content, it may be hard to get noticed on your own. This is where hashtags come in handy.

Hashtags aggregate posts from a large number of users into one feed on Instagram ... although only public accounts can be viewed when searching for hashtags.

Instagram makes it easy and simple for users to find tagged content. When you search for a word or phrase, the search results page has four parts:

- **Top**, which shows the main Instagram accounts and hashtags positions that include your keyword

(typically accounts that you're following or that are popular)

- **Accounts,** which displays the best Instagram accounts that include your keyword
- **Tags,** which suggest popular hashtags that include your keyword and the number of other Instagram posts have been shared with that hashtag
- **Places,** which shows nearby locations that include your keyword

For example, if you plan to tag your post with #coffee, you can add related hashtags like # coffeebar, #coffeeholic, or #coffeehouse to expand the coverage of your post.

Making use of hashtags is easy! Simply create hashtags using emojis, characters, or numbers; you can add up to thirty to the legend. Remember that your account must be public for your posts to appear in hashtag feeds.

Choosing an Instagram hashtag

How do you choose the best hashtags for each post? Our best answer is to think about related keywords and find relevant trends, which is actually easier on Instagram itself.

Start on the Explore tab (the magnifying glass icon in the bottom menu). There you will find popular articles and see which hashtags have been used.

If you already have a special hashtag in mind, you may also use this page to find popular and related hashtags. In the search bar. enter the hashtag and filter the results by tags to see how many posts have used that hashtag and other related hashtags.

Try to mix generic and trending hashtags and specific hashtags to increase the coverage and relevance of your posts. Also consider creating your own personalized hashtag.

Many businesses use their hashtags to implement a new product, run an Instagram campaign, promote an event, and collect user-generated content. If you are doing this for your brand, make sure yours isn't used for any other purpose ... and therefore encourage your audience to use it!

Formatting an Instagram Hashtag

Now let's see how to incorporate hashtags into your content. First of all, don't be spammy. Hashtags must be natural in your caption. Most businesses make use of 2.5 hashtags per post. Try to use one to four hashtags to avoid overwhelming your audience and making the captions hard to read.

If your hashtags don't blend naturally with the caption, paste them at the end or even in the first comment. They will work the same regardless of where they are.

Chapter 5: Instagram Marketing Strategy In 2021

Many companies feel pressured to be present on all social media platforms ... and forget about strategy. Don't make that mistake.

Since Instagram is so different from other popular social sites, it requires a different marketing strategy.

Begin by creating your Instagram strategy using this overview. By following these action steps, it is possible to set a clear visual story that can be achieved when working internally or with other organizations. The strategy will help shape your brand vision by creating great branded content and keeping the brand promise.

Here are the main steps to create a winning Instagram strategy:

- Choose a simple promise and send a sophisticated message
- Create a unique visual story
- Create your story on the four pillars of visual storytelling
- Choose your narrative path
- Match your message to the right occasions

Choose a simple promise and send a sophisticated message

The most effective Instagram brands promise to deliver more than photos and videos to their followers - they create emotional connectivity with their brand experience. Like all great marketers, this strategy is based on a unique understanding of consumer and brand insight. A brand's promise must be clearly visible from its presence on Instagram.

In essence, this promise should provide unique insight via Instagram to support the brand. Intuition needs to deliver content to capture audiences and bring them closer to the brand. The form of intuition can come from a heritage, inspiration, lifestyle, utility, or a variety of other aspects. Above all, the message must be natural, unique and clearly linked. Intuition should involve an intrigue of how your brand connects to your mission.

The best promises are simple and carry a sophisticated message.

Successful brands on Instagram are fully embracing the story through images. Storytelling is a fundamental skill in building a brand and Instagram provides an engaging framework for implementation. A story differs from a traditional marketing message or conversation in the way it is conveyed to consumers. A story brings consumers closer to execution. A story shares an ongoing journey with the consumer. A story connects the consumer to the brand promise in an engaging, engaging and interactive way.

Create a unique visual story

Instagram brands are recognized for expressing unique stories. Consumers expect consistent, high-quality content.

Users follow great content quickly, but they also stop following if the content is unattractive or produced slowly. Every brand must look for a way to create personalized content that delivers on the brand's promise, maintains consistency, and balances different themes.

Create your story on the four pillars of visual storytelling

Pillars of effective visual storytelling:

- Sensory
- Authenticity
- Relevance
- Archetype

Sensory: Images are common because they make use of a sensory medium to engage the minds, memories and sensations of consumers. Viewers pay more attention and retain more information when the images subtly involve various senses. Images can prompt minds to associate them with an experience, involving the senses even more. Smell, touch, sound and taste can be stimulated by information gaps in an image, asking the viewer to provide details missing in their mind.

Authenticity: The abundance of content and the wide reach of the Internet have made it very easy to find almost anything imaginable. As such, the viewer's gaze has become much more sophisticated in identifying "fakes."

People want real images and appreciate messages that are personal, unpredictable and familiar. Genuine photos don't use excessive retouching or obvious post-production. People refer to apparent flaws because it makes the content more tangible and real. Perfection is an abstract concept that can be different for each individual and therefore should not be the goal of Instagram content.

Relevance: Globalization and the expansion of internet use are constantly changing cultural relevance and social ideals. Take, for example, the growing cultural contempt for Photoshop and the resulting impact on general perceptions of beauty. Brands that defy standards and provide localized content have the opportunity to build lasting relationships with their consumers.

Archetype: Archetypes provide a powerful framework, making a story relatable with ideas that are widely applicable and timeless. Therefore, archetypes can be used to develop the strategy of brand communication and visual story.

Choose your storytelling path

A powerful Instagram account starts by identifying the main pillars of content that fit the brand's storyline. Is the brand storyline linear, circular or disturbing? What brand archetype are you trying to say? These are important factors in mapping a brand's content roadmap, planning for post-frequency, providing photos and videos for each pillar, and highlighting relevant content.

Instagram users want to be sold in a story. Brands need stories that can be told over a long period of time. A brand story requires sufficient depth to continue the narrative, introduce, develop, and distort new content. The story needs to be something that consumers see as unique, deep, and socially relevant. Identifying which archetype (s) best represents a brand helps deliver personalized results to consumers. Archetypes provide a powerful framework that can be understood and correlated with viewers.

The best brands are storytellers. Our stories are always the most memorable ones. Personal stories and desires evolve based on the human need to strengthen their worldview and self-esteem. Consumers want to be able to clearly understand the purpose of the brand in order to measure its compatibility with their choices. The authentic brand's story visually highlights the context and characteristics of the product, giving consumers a cohesive view.

To compose a nice visual story, a brand team needs to ensure a clear understanding of the following:

- The desire for love
- The desire for justice
- The desire for order
- The desire for validation
- The desire for pleasure
- The fear of the unknown/ unknowable
- The challenge of morality in choices
- The fear of death

Storytelling paths, a classic narrative concept, are powerful narratives that resonate with buyers. They are not the same as the story, plot, or genre. A narrative path is deeply rooted in essential human desires, fears, and challenges. They evoke emotional elements that guide us, move us and hold our attention.

Match your message to the right occasions

Opportunities are the physical manifestation of a brand's character. It is an experience or moment that represents the history of the brand. Opportunities are tangible building blocks that support narrative themes. A group of friends camping, a panoramic image of a sunset, or a person climbing a mountain are all occasions that can represent an aspect of the brand. Your brand's visual storytelling will be guided by these opportunities to create a cohesive storyline for your audience to follow.

Viewers can refer to the individual moments that create the sum of what a brand stands for. Opportunities are specific guidelines on what your content should be. There must be specific topics included in your strategy that can be implemented to stimulate the desires, fears, and morals of viewers. Opportunities are things your brand advocates do, can relate to, or are inspired by. Having a clear vision about the way your brand can express your opportunity is important to show the larger image of your brand.

Improving Your Instagram Marketing Strategy In 2021

It is essential that businesses have an active social media presence in order to survive. A social media marketing strategy is incomplete without Instagram. It has become the best platform for brands, advertisers and consumers.

This platform has over 800 million monthly active users. And more than 500 million Instagram profiles are active daily. Here's another thing that might surprise you: 70% of Instagram hashtags are branded.

What does this tell you? If you're not active on Instagram, your competition certainly is.

Those individuals who have already created an account is on the way. But having an Instagram profile doesn't necessarily translate into sales. If you want to increase sales and make money with Instagram, you need to come up with a viable strategy.

Now, we're going to guide you in the right direction with 18 tips and strategies you can apply to your Instagram marketing strategy today. Let's start.

1. Increase your audience

One of the first steps in a successful Instagram marketing strategy is to increase your subscriber base.

Without a lot of subscribers, you will have a hard time seeing your posts. Generating sales without followers won't be easy.

For those who are new to their Instagram page, it can be intimidating to start with the number zero. But if you are not a completely new business, you already have customers.

This is the best place to start looking for subscribers. Your existing customers are interested in your business. Tell them about your profile and implore them to follow you.

Start by sending messages to your email subscribers. Just make sure you get them to follow you.

For example, emails can only be sent a few times a month. Tell your followers that if they want more frequent discounts and promotions, they'll find them on Instagram.

If you use this strategy, keep that promise.

Besides contacting your email subscribers, you can have an Instagram badge on your website. Also promote your Instagram profile through other social media channels.

After following these steps, another effective way to get more followers is to follow other people. That said, don't follow random users.

Find the right followers for your target audience. It will be the best solution to generate new leads and increase sales.

How do you find people who fit your target market? It's a bit complicated and you will have to work hard. First, you must find accounts similar to yours.

I'm not saying you should steal followers from your competition, although that works too.

Instead, you may search for Instagram profiles that post content related to your business. It takes time, but it will work. Once you've found an account like yours, check out your followers and start following people.

Users will be notified and will verify your page. If they appreciate what they see on your profile, which we'll talk about soon, they'll likely follow you.

Once thousands of new followers are added, your Instagram strategy will make it much easier to increase sales.

2. Focus on your page first impression

First impressions count. This statement is true in the real world and in the virtual world.

As a marketer, you have to recognize this. It's the same reason why writing a compelling blog post presentation is vital to your content strategy.

When a user of Instagram clicks on your profile, what's the first thing they see? They see your profile picture, bio, and most recent posts. Coming back to the last point on following users to increase their subscriber base, when a user clicks on their profile, they shouldn't have any questions.

What I mean by that is this. Your profile should tell you who you are and what you do.

Having your logo as a profile picture makes more sense. It's much more recognizable than a random image of a person or one of their products.

3. Post content regularly

If you only add one photo or video to your profile once a month, that's not a great strategy. I wouldn't even refer to it as an active profile.

You want your business to always be fresh on the minds of your followers. Also, you don't want to inundate user timelines and be seen as irritating. You have to find a better medium here.

I wouldn't recommend posting more than once a day. If you have a lot of content that you want to share every day, it is best to add it to your Instagram story.

How often should you post on Instagram? Research shows that the best brands on Instagram post an average of 1.5 times per day. That works out to about 10 or 11 posts per week.

The timing of these posts is also crucial. The best brands typically post content during office hours during a standard workweek.

You need to recognize this and plan your posts accordingly. Regular posting increases your exposure and the likelihood that as many people as possible will see your content.

4. Don't be too "salsey."

We just established that you have to post every day. But we have not talked about the content of the posts.

Obviously, you want to boost your sales. However, that doesn't mean everything you post has to be a product promotion.

This will irritate your followers and end up having the opposite effect of what you are looking for. Mix up your content.

Be fun. Post photos of your employees. Don't stray too far from your business image.

While it's good to post content that doesn't promote a product, you want to avoid controversial topics. I am referring to topics like religion, politics and race. Offending your followers won't help you increase your sales.

Again, avoid too many promotional messages. Posting lots of promotions is the first irritating social media move for businesses, according to users:

Whenever you post a promotion, do it at random. You don't have to type words in all the capital letters and include tons of stars and quotes around it all.

It's boring. Be brief and to the point.

5. Go live

Instagram has a live streaming feature. Users love it and brands use this information to their advantage.

Live video provides the ability to connect with your audience in real-time. During the broadcast, they can comment.

Be sure to respond to these comments and do your best to recognize these users. This will help you increase engagement metrics.

There are endless possibilities with your live broadcasts. You can present new products, visit its facilities or even introduce some of your employees. I like the idea of hosting a question and answer segment to provide a more authentic connection with your audience.

Another way to use Instagram Live Story is to work with other brands. Instagram is the best social platform for brand collaborations in the world.

You can try to stand out in the live broadcast of another profile, with the aim of promoting your brand.

As a result of this, this strategy can assist you in exposing your brand to a new audience, maximize your followers, and ultimately generate more sales.

6. Add photos and videos to your story

As I briefly discussed earlier, your story is the best place to add daily content. You can post your story content multiple times per day, as this does not affect the schedules of users who follow you.

But that doesn't mean you overdo it and post 20 different photos and videos in your story every day.

People won't be looking at each one, so it's a waste of time and resources. Engagement and opinions will decrease with each additional post of your story.

You should also make sure that the post time of your story is relevant, as it will disappear 24 hours after uploading.

I recommend that you use your story to offer discounts, run contests, or tell people what you've been doing so far in the office.

The idea here is to always keep your brand in mind. If they're thinking about your brand, they're more likely to make a purchase.

Just like your live video strategy, you can even use your Instagram story to collaborate with another brand for a survey. You can rent their account and they can post content to yours as well.

Again, this will make it easier to expose your brand to a wider audience.

7. Collaborate with social influencers

Making use of social influencers to promote your brand, products, and services is an extremely effective tactic.

In fact, 94% of marketers has said their social influencer strategy has been effective for their business.

This is because the followers of social influencers trust them. We know that 82% of individuals are likely to follow the recommendations of micro-influencers. And 94% of buyers believe these influencers are very informed.

Basically, if you get an influencer to promote your brand, you will get sales. Instagram is the main social platform for influencers around the world.

It is an economical marketing strategy. Most influencers only charge a few hundred dollars for a post. However, if you prefer to work with famous influencers, be prepared to spend a lot more.

However, it is not always necessary. I recommend looking for influencers with followers between 10,000 and 50,000. These people have higher engagement rates and more authentic interactions with their followers.

In addition, the cost per post will be lower.

8. Add hashtags to your captions

Captions are just as vital, if not more important, than the videos and images you post.

Hashtags are absolutely necessary. There are many different approaches to this. To begin, you can use an existing one so that other people can see it. For example, you can choose a hashtag that promotes a national event.

Another concept is to create your own hashtag. It would be much more specific for the brand.

You can use a hashtag with just your brand and the name of your campaign. If you like to run contests on Instagram, you can have an exclusive hashtag for everyone.

9. Encourage the UGC

UGC is the abbreviation for User Generated Content. This is my last point on using hashtags to promote contests.

Promotions like this encourage people to post photos and videos related to your brand on their personal profiles.

As a result, your brand is exposed to all followers who are friends with that particular user. This type of content serves as a recommendation, which we just talked about as an effective promotional method.

Apart from running contests, the best way to encourage user-generated content is to feature user photos on your profile.

10. Post targeted ads

How can people who don't follow your account be reached on Instagram? Certain strategies, such as position coding, managing contests, and collaborating with social influencers, can do this.

However, these strategies don't always expose your brand to people in your target market. Targeted ads will be shown.

Instagram was acquired by Facebook. Ads are being set up the same on both networks.

You can use parameters like age, gender, and position to select your target audience. You may decide to go a step further and target users based on their interests.

11. Organize contests and giveaways

Giveaways and contests are two of my favorite strategies for brands to engage with their audience on social media.

If you learn how to make a profitable giveaway, your hard work will result in more sales.

I am aware of what some of you are thinking. How can you earn just by donating your products?

12. Take advantage of the "swipe up" function

The swipe up function is a turning point for businesses. For years, you've probably struggled to get Instagram users to browse your site from a specific link. You would post content and get people to click on a link in your bio.

But this strategy has many flaws. First of all, this is another step for the user. They should go to your profile page and click again.

People prefer not to go through this stress. What if you want to promote two separate landing pages? Or maybe three? Or four?

You will no longer have links in your bio. It is very confusing. The scroll up feature eliminates this issue. Now you can make use of your Instagram Story to drive traffic directly to specific landing pages.

Simply promote a product or service in your story and add the scroll feature with a link to a landing page in your promotion.

If you are promoting a specific product, a logical landing page would be the product description on your website. There the user can see other photos and add the product to the cart.

These lead magnets are a great way to drive more traffic to your website and ultimately increase conversions.

13. Use shoppable posts

If you have an e-commerce brand, you need to take most advantage of shoppable posts.

This strategy let you sell products directly via the Instagram platform. The reason I love this feature so much is that it increases your chances of convincing your current and potential customers to buy something. Here's why.

Right now, you depend on consumers browsing your website to buy your products. This can come from organic traffic, paid advertising, or direct browsing.

The problem is, people probably don't do it every day. But they are active on Instagram every day.

In fact, 500 million people use Instagram daily. So, there is a chance that your target market falls into this category.

14. Publish the same product multiple times

If you post a product once and no longer promote it, people might forget about it.

Think about user behavior on Instagram. They quickly scroll through the streams. When they see your product for the first time, they might not have a reason to buy it. But you are seen more than once, it may start to interest them.

According to a social study from Sprout, more than 60% of people need to see something on social media two to four times before buying it.

I'm not saying you can post the exact same photo four different times to your Instagram page. It's annoying and may even prevent you from following it. Be creative.

Start with just a post about the product. After some days later, you can share another product image in your Instagram story. The following week, he organized a competition to promote the same product. A few weeks later, you can share a video of the same object used in a demonstration.

Posting the same product different times increases the chances that people will buy it.

15. Respond to comments and messages

I know this might appear like a long and tedious task, but you need to respond to your followers on Instagram.

Responding directly to comments on your post will add a human element and a personal atmosphere to your brand, which people appreciate a lot.

This strategy is particularly important if people are asking questions or complaining about your business. Respond to these pi ù observations as quickly as possible to find a solution.

Show other users who are aware of your responses on social media that your brand values customer service.

Buyers will pay more for good service. You can expect increased sales by communicating effectively with your customers on social media.

16. Use your story to showcase products

Previously, I talked about examples of posting content to your Instagram story. But now you can make use of your Instagram Story to sell your products the same way you did with the posts that can be purchased in-store.

As the material purchase feature is new, the post contains additional text to inform users that the post is clickable.

If you tap the button as shown, you will be taken to the brand's website. From there you will be shown the option to purchase the product displayed in the story.

Use this strategy if you are running an online store. As I said before, users need to see a product different times on social media before deciding to buy it. Add purchasable stories to the list of ways to showcase their products.

17. Connect your followers to your Facebook page

If your business has an Instagram profile, it probably has a Facebook page as well.

Since the acquisition of Instagram by Facebook, these two platforms have many features that work together. I've talked about this before when I talked about targeted ad serving.

You can now sync your Instagram followers with your Facebook business page. Once this process is complete, you can nurture those users with messenger bots.

There are over 300,000 bots per month active on Facebook Messenger. Obviously, other companies are already taking advantage of this strategy.

Get on board now before your competitors' bots steal your customers.

18. Offer discounts to your followers

Everyone likes him very much. Share discounts with your followers on Instagram to inspire them to buy.

Instagram is a great flash selling platform. Since your story vanishes after 24 hours, you can use this type of post to share a promo code.

This will let your followers feel like they're getting an offer that others don't know about. This feeling of exclusivity will also encourage them to go shopping.

Don't think that your promo codes should be limited to posts and stories in your profile.

Combining this deal with a targeted ad can be extremely effective. This is because your ads will feature CTA buttons that redirect users directly to your site.

Chapter 6: Instagram Hacks and Tips

Let's explore some little-known Instagram hacks to get the most out of the platform. We implore you to download the latest version of the app to follow along.

Post to Instagram At The Best Times

On average, the most effective time to post on Instagram is between 2 p.m. and 3 p.m. CDT. Though, the level of engagement you get can change drastically, depending on the day of the week you decide to post. The recommended day to post on Instagram is not only at 3:00 p.m. but also at 5:00 p.m. on Thursday, 11:00 a.m. and 4:00 p.m.

As mentioned above, while 2:00 p.m. is considered the recommended time of day to publish on Instagram, the day of the week you post can affect the engagement you actually receive at 2:00 p.m.

Why? Think about the small differences in your mood and your daily routine - the ones you might not understand - and how they affect your behavior. The same goes for everyone who follows your Instagram account. Here is some more information on when to publish Sprout Social data is optimal to show you what I mean:

- Posting 5:00 a.m. CDT Tuesday through Friday generates some of the biggest engagements: People typically don't check their phones until they wake up.

- Posting between 11 a.m. to 3 p.m. on weekdays also takes a lot of effort: people typically check their phones during lunch or when they start to run out of mental power at the end of the day.

- If you want to post on weekends, post on Saturdays around 11:00 am CDT, when people are having brunch or going out with friends.

So, when using Instagram, don't go alone during this time. Consider the day of the week and the industry you're in (we'll talk about that in a minute).

On average, here are the best times for Instagram during the week in each time zone around the world:

- Sunday: Between 11.00 a.m. and 2.30 p.m.

- Monday: 10 in the morning - 5 p.m. in the evening (maximum engagement is 11 a.m. and 2 p.m.)

- Tuesday: Between 8 a.m. and 6:00 p.m., * 7:00 p.m.

- Wednesday: 5 a.m., * 11 a.m. - 3 p.m.

- Thursday: 5 a.m., * 11 p.m. - 4 p.m.

- Friday: * 5:00 a.m., 9:00 a.m. - 10:00 a.m., * Between 11.00 a.m. and 2p.m., and 2:00 p.m. - 4:00 p.m.

- Saturday: 9-11: 00

= particularly high levels of involvement

Do you want easy work orders based on this data? Post on Instagram between 9:00 a.m. to 6:00 p.m. Tuesday through Friday. This way you will get the most consistent engagement.

The Recommended Times to Post on Instagram for Tech Companies

- Recommended time: Wednesday at 10:00 a.m. CDT
- More consistent engagement: Wednesday to Friday, 10 a.m. to 5 p.m., CDT
- Recommended day: Thursday
- Not recommended day: Sunday

The Recommended Times to Post on Instagram for B2C Businesses

- Recommended time: Friday at 11:00 a.m. and 1:00 p.m. CDT
- More consistent engagement: every day from 10 a.m. to 3 p.m. CDT
- Recommended day: Wednesday
- Not recommended day: Sunday

The Recommended Times to Post on Instagram for Educational Organizations

- Recommended time: Monday at 8 p.m. CDT
- More consistent engagement: working days from 11:00 a.m. to 4:00 p.m. CDT
- Recommended day: Monday
- Not recommended day: Sunday

Recommended times to post on Instagram for healthcare companies

- Recommended time: Tuesday at 1 p.m. CDT
- More consistent engagement: Tuesday to Friday, 9:00 a.m. to 4:00 p.m. CDT
- Recommended day: Tuesday
- Not recommended day: Saturday and Sunday

The Recommended times to post on Instagram for non-profit associations

- Recommended times: Tuesday at 3 p.m. and 9 p.m., Wednesday at 3 p.m. and 4 p.m., Thursday at 2 p.m. and 3 p.m. and Friday at 10 p.m. and 2 p.m.
- More consistent engagement: working days from 12:00 p.m. to 5:00 p.m.
- Recommended day: Tuesday
- Not recommended day: Saturday

The audience for each brand is different. To build a big and engaged audience on Instagram, you must know who your followers are. And another way to get to know your audience and grab their attention is to know exactly when they like to browse the app.

Link Your Instagram To Your Facebook Page

One of the major things that makes Instagram special is that you can perfectly share your content on other social networks.

Automatic login to other social platforms, such as Twitter and Facebook, is not recommended; what works on Instagram doesn't always produce the same results on other channels, especially when you get up and run. For this reason, modify your content to fit each platform.

However, linking your Instagram to other social accounts like Facebook increases the number of eyes on your posts. Remember that your Facebook page will already be connected to your Instagram if you create a business profile on Instagram.

How you can connect Instagram to your Facebook page

1. Start with your Instagram profile.

The first step is opening your Instagram account on the phone and select the profile icon in the lower right corner. Next, select the gear icon. (It may look like 3 vertical dots if you're using an Android device.)

This will take you to your options, where you can adjust many of your preferences, including social settings.

2. Configure (or update) your linked accounts.

When accessing your options, we recommend that you scroll down to where it says **"Settings"> "Linked Accounts."** This is where you detemine where you want your Instagram photos to appear on social media.

Tap on **"Linked Accounts"** and you will see all the options for which you can connect to social networks with Instagram.

3. Log into Facebook.

You must be currently logged in to this network before you can grant permission to share content there. You will need to sign in to Facebook on your phone for this step to work: when done, tap "Facebook" on the sharing settings screen.

You will be asked to continue as you do: press this button.

You will then be required to give your privacy preferences. Since you are sharing your photos on a company page, you can select "Friends": the people who will actually see your photos are the ones who like the most on the page you are posting to, in the following steps.

After selecting "OK," then you will be taken to the sharing settings, where Facebook should now be selected. Otherwise, select it: the logo should appear in blue to indicate that you are sharing your posts on Facebook.

4. Choose where you share on Facebook.

After connecting Facebook to Instagram, we recommend that you use the sharing settings to determine where you will share Instagram posts on Facebook. If you have now only allowed Facebook to connect to Instagram, the images will be shared on your personal Facebook profile by default.

Tap **"Share To"**: every place on Facebook where you can post your Instagram photos will be displayed. Includes personal history or any company page where you have an admin role.

After choosing the Facebook page where you want to post the photos, go back to the sharing settings.

Now you need to specify that your Instagram photos are posted to your favorite Facebook business page.

5. Make sure to share responsibly.

If you use Instagram for personal and business accounts, remember - you'll need to change these settings anytime you want to change where your photos are posted.

If you are really concerned about the possible downsides of using the same Instagram account for both, you may decide to create a specific Instagram ID for the business that is completely separate from your staff.

In this case, you must follow the same steps to connect your Instagram account to Facebook. The good news? Instagram has a sleek feature that lets you switch between accounts, take a look here.

6. Start sharing!

You are all connected! You can now navigate to the home screen and choose the photo you want to post.

When you're ready to share your photo, make sure you've selected Facebook as one of the places you want to post your photo.

How to use Instagram in connection with Facebook

Now that you're signed in, what kind of content should you share?

At the basic level, you need to post content that is relevant to your brand and target audience. This includes things like behind-the-scenes footage of what your brand does to delight customers, inspirational quotes, and humor.

See Posts You Have Liked

Most of the major social networks make it easy for users to find their favorite posts. Instagram doesn't.

On Instagram, when you press the heart button on a photo or video post, it seems to be lost forever, unless you copy the post's URL and send it to yourself. However, your favorite posts are not lost before and there is a hidden place in the app where you can find them.

The following instructions apply only to the mobile version of Instagram.

Where to look for your most popular Instagram posts

To find the posts you recently liked on Instagram, follow these steps:

1. Log into your Instagram account and tap on the profile icon on the menu.
2. Make use of the hamburger menu button to choose Settings.
3. Select Account from the list.
4. Tap Posts You've Liked.

Being able to access the posts that you have liked previously is useful for many things. Come back and see what you've already liked, so you can:

- Find new accounts to follow in the posts you liked in the Explore tab.
- Read the long caption of a post you didn't have time to read when you liked it.
- Read the other comments added below and a discussion on a specific post, as others see in your feed.
- Leave a comment on a post that you liked, but haven't had time to write something yet.
- Go over useful information that you want to review in detail later, such as a product, service, competition, workout routine, recipe, makeup tutorial, or something else.

What you like on Instagram isn't just a friendly gesture to let the poster know that you approve of their posting. It's an incredibly useful way to mark things interesting and valuable for review.

Limitations on reviewing liked posts

According to Instagram, you will only be able to see the 300 most recent posts (photos and videos) that you liked. It's still a lot, but if you are an experienced user who likes Instagram hundreds of messages a day, or if you feel the need to look at something that looks like it has several weeks, you might be unlucky.

Liked posts are only shown if you liked them using the Instagram mobile app or on the web. However, you can only see your favorite posts in the app. It is not known if all the posts you liked from a third-party Instagram app like Iconosquare are displayed, but if that doesn't work on your Instagram web platform, chances are it won't work for third-party apps either.

Finally, if you commented on a photo or video but didn't like it, there is no way to find it if you lose it. You will be able to see the posts you like just by tapping the heart button (or double-tapping the post) in the "Like" section of your profile settings, not just posts you commented on. So if you want to review a post later, hit the heart button, even if your main intention is to leave a comment.

That's all!

Sharing your Instagram photos on a Facebook business page allows you to bring strong images to multiple platforms with just a few clicks and offers the possibility to show the personal side of your business. It can helpful in engaging with your target audience: Visual content is over 40 times more possible to be shared on social media than other kinds of content.

Reorder Instagram Filters

Instagram is one of the most comprehensive platforms in the world. In fact, the photo-sharing app has hundreds of features, which millions of users enjoy every day. But do we all use them? Of course, Instagram's number of features is too large to be fully utilized.

So it's fair to say that there are some things we don't use very often. For example, the topic channel bar contains a lot of items that we might be interested in. However, we don't rely on all of them.

In other words, there are topics that interest us more than others. The same is true with Instagram filters. There are a lot of them, but we definitely have a group of favorites.

So what do we do with these filters that we don't actually use? Now, we can just rearrange them. And today we're going to teach you exactly how to do it.

How to rearrange Instagram filters

First, you need to add a new message and wait for the filter list to appear. Then navigate to the right of the screen and tap where it says "manage."

This will direct you to a fresh window with all the filters Instagram has to offer. Once there, you can choose which filters you want to display at the beginning and which filters you want to place at the end.

So, to rearrange them to your preference, keep your finger on the three gray lines on the left side of the filter you want to move and drag it up or down.

Additional tip

Besides being able to rearrange the filters, you can also choose to hide them. To do this, simply go back to the manage menu and deselect the filter you don't want to see on the screen.

Then just tap the checkmark (✓) and edit your message again. Finally, note that some filters are not selected in the management menu. So if you want to try new ones, you already know where to find them. It's that simple!

Insert Line Breaks In Your Captions And Bios

Adding spaces on Instagram isn't rocket science. However, many people find it difficult to do this well.

Many people are on Instagram, so they can consume funny and / or aesthetic content. They are not there to read a story. Therefore, finding a long, unformatted caption may be inconvenient for them. The same goes for unformatted BIOS which is just plain confusing.

But for some influencers and brands, there are times when you need to write a long post for your caption. In this case, adding spaces between the lines is not something you can just ignore. You must add a pause to improve readability.

For example, you might need to create an article to promote a contest or tribute. And you must include all the details of how to enter and some important disclaimers in the caption.

So obviously you need a long caption for this.

As for your Instagram bio, be sure to list all the important results when describing yourself.

You can share a lot of information through captions, hashtags, and bio. This means that you might make reading difficult without proper formatting. In this case, you end up losing interest in the people you are trying to impress or engage in.

So, I decided to write this section to guide you on how to add spaces in Instagram captions and bios.

In this section, you'll gain a better understanding of all the steps required to properly format bios and captions to attract and engage your followers.

How to add spaces on Instagram

Before we discuss the steps to add spaces to Instagram captions and bios, there are some best practices you should remember.

Following these recommended practices for adding spaces on Instagram will help minimize the frustration when trying to format captions and bios correctly:

1. Avoid writing directly on the Instagram app

You can read this book now because you tried to format IG captions and bios directly in the Instagram app and it didn't work.

If you try to add a paragraph and line spaces in the app, the app will automatically post your post with zero-spaced formatting. And this is part of the main causes of frustration for those who know that good formatting works, but haven't been able to successfully format Instagram captions and bios.

So how can you add spaces to Instagram captions?

So instead of writing the caption directly in the app, try writing it in the Notes app on your phone first. You can copy and paste this completed copy into the app when you post a new post. You can even use the messaging app to create a draft of the caption.

So what is the result here? What should you keep in mind when adding spaces between paragraphs on Instagram?

The main rule to follow is that you should avoid writing directly to the Instagram app because you cannot format it properly this way.

2. Remove extra spaces

Another solution to solve your spacing issues: remove any extra space in Instagram captions.

If invisible line breaking works, you need to eliminate the extra space between the last word or punctuation and invisible space.

For example, if you end a sentence with a period, avoid pressing the space key as you normally would. Instead, immediately press the "Enter" or "Return" button and add the invisible space.

Two ways to add spaces in Instagram captions and bios

There are several ways to add spaces to Instagram captions and bios. You can select from these options, depending on what is preferable and convenient for you.

1. Make line breaks with symbols

The easiest way to add spaces to Instagram captions and bios is to use symbols. It's also the quickest option and you can even type directly into the Instagram app. You can make use of characters like a dash or a dot, as well as emoticons whenever you need a line break. And that extra character will act as a space between paragraphs.

The main problem with this option to add spaces to Instagram captions is that the symbol will be visible, which may not make it viable for some people.

Here's how to add spaces using this option:

- Type the caption in the caption box on Instagram.
- When you need a line break, press the "Enter" or "Return" button on the keyboard.
- Add the symbol on the next line. You can add a point to make it as visible as possible.
- Press "Enter" or "Return" again and start typing the next paragraph.
- If you want more space between two paragraphs, you can continue to repeat steps 1 and 2, if necessary.

2. Make invisible line breaks with the Notes app on your phone

What if you don't want symbols or lines in Instagram captions? There is another tweak by which you can include spaces.

If you want to include invisible line breaks, there is a way to do that using the Notes app on your phone. If you are using a scheduler app, you can also use it to create the draft instead of the Notes app.

Here are the steps to add invisible line breaks using this option:

Type the caption into the app.

- When you want to add a line break, paste these invisible spaces on the next line. The spaces are inside the brackets.
- [   ]
- Paste multiple times if you want to add more than one pause line.
- Remove the brackets.
- Copy the entire draft and paste it in the Instagram caption space, if you are using a Notes app.

If you're making use of a scheduling app to type in your draft, just upload it to Instagram as usual. You will see the line breaks copied automatically along with the rest of the copy. Post as is and Instagram will post your caption with the necessary spaced formatting.

Other Instagram Tricks And Tips

Hide posts you have been tagged in.

If you are tagged by an individual in a post, it will appear when you click on the person icon in the menu under your Instagram bio. Even your followers can see it.

A tagged post can be hidden in two ways. One way is through each image. Open a post you want to hide and click on the three dots in the upper right corner. **Click on Photo options** and from there you can select **Remove me from post** (remove the tag and hide it completely) or **Hide from my profile** (leave the tag, but hide it in the profile).

If you don't want to permanently check and delete the checked messages, you can choose to manually include only the ones you like. To do this, go to **the privacy tag settings** and turn off the **Add automatically** option. Henceforth, you will receive a notification when someone tags you in a photo. When this happens, tap on the photo you've been tagged with and choose **Show on Profile.**

On this screen, you can also manually hide multiple photos and videos from your profile.

Save photos and build collections.

There are several amazing content on Instagram. You may have seen content from competitors that you want to emulate or found user-generated content that you want to repost. Can this content be saved and accessed later? Well, Instagram makes it easy - thanks to saved content.

In your Instagram feed, you can like, comment, and post. You can also save them by making use of the ribbon icon in the right corner. When you tap it, you'll see the Save to Collection pop-up window at the bottom of the article. If the image or video you saved is part of a collection, as inspiration or UGC content, you can create a collection for that content.

Access saved content via your profile. At the top right corner, tap the three lines and click on **Save** on the list. In **All**, you'll see all of your saved content in chronological order. In **Collections,** you will find content organized into Collections.

Chapter 7: Instagram Analytics

Have you recently looked at your Instagram numbers? Maybe you are following your likes or have an idea of how your number of followers is growing month by month. But have you really explored the analysis and analyzed this data? If the answer is no, it's time to do it!

Watching your Instagram analysis will help you understand how the platform works as part of your general marketing strategy, and it will also let you improve and grow your business with this highly populated, powerful social platform.

In this chapter, I'll explain why your Instagram analytics is important and walk you through all of the analytics options available. I'll point out which data is most important to your business goals, so you know exactly what to focus your attention on, and finally, I'll share a shortlist of our favorite Instagram analytics tools. Ready? Let's start.

Why Should You Care About Instagram Analytics?

With more than 25 million brand profiles on Instagram globally and over 200 million Instagrammers visiting minimum of one every day, it is clear that businesses are finding value in this advertising platform. However, if you do not know who is viewing your profile or seeing your ads, how your posts and stories are performing, and what your account is worth, spending time posting on the platform can be a waste.

If you don't regularly review your Instagram review, the following are probably the mistakes you could be making:

- Too frequent (or infrequent) posting.
- You are targeting the wrong audience.
- You are driving irrelevant visitors to your site.
- You are ignoring any mentions that may lead to future partnerships.
- Driving calls of an ad type that you only used once!
- You missed opportunities for brand engagement in your comments or stories.
- You are posting during sub-optimal hours of the day or during the week.

This is just a shortlist of things you could do better if you dig into Instagram data more often. The insights collected from the data will help improve the way you use the platform to drive more value for your business, which can make Instagram an even more critical part of your online marketing strategy.

Without further ado, let's dive into the data!

Instagram Profile Analytics

Your profile analyzes are those which you access directly on the "My profile" page, where your publications are located.

This page displays information for one week. You might have seen your profile information before, but you might not have delved into the metrics. Let's see what you can access here:

- **Impressions:** How many times peoples viewed your posts during the period.

- **Interactions:** the number of actions performed on your account.

- **Reach:** how many unique accounts have seen one of your posts.

- **Profile Visits:** The number of profile views during the week.

- **Site Clicks:** The number of times visitors clicked on the site link on your profile page.

- **Call/email clicks:** the total number of times visitors clicked the **Call /Email** button on the profile page.

- **Mentions:** The number of times your account manager has been mentioned by other users.

Instagram Audience Analytics

Who is your target audience? I bet you have the ideal demographics of the followers you are looking for. But does that match the people who view and interact with your Instagram posts? Fortunately, there is an entire section of your Instagram review dedicated to educating you about your audience.

Here are the main factors to note:

- **Top Locations:** This information lets you see the top five cities and countries where your followers are located.

- **Age group:** how old are your followers? It's an easy way to find out. Instagram shares it with the multiple ranges.

- **Gender:** your followers' distribution separated by women and men.

- **Follower Hours:** A very useful statistic to see the average time of day your followers are on Instagram.

- **Follower days:** Also useful, this section displays the days of the week when your subscribers are most active.

Individual Post Analytics

Once you've determined that your profile is receiving actions from the right audience, we recommend that you review individual posts to see how a specific post resonates with your audience. It's a useful way to check that your content is performing well with your audience.

Here are the individual posts statistics available:

- **Interactions:** actions taken directly from your message. Whether you visit your profile, a hyperlink, or use the call/email button on your post, these items are tracked and logged here.

- **Discovery:** Anyone who is addicted to Instagram like me has probably used the discovery feature. This allows you to find new account content that you may not be currently following and, yes, your business account may appear on this page. Instagram will report the number of accounts reached through discovery that are not currently following you.

- **Follows: the** number of new subscribers you have received from a message.

- **Reach:** how many unique accounts have been reached since publication.

- **Impressions:** The total number of times your message has been viewed. Instagram also divides by category to see where on the platform the post has been seen at home, in hashtags, on profile, and on other people.

- **Saves:** The number of unique accounts that have saved your post to the saved personal folder.
- **Comments:** the number of comments on your message.

Instagram Stories Analytics

Finally, we have Instagram stories. If you don't post stories on Instagram, you are missing out on a substantial opportunity. This feature of Snapchat, similar to Instagram, continues to gain popularity and provides another opportunity to expose your brand to more users or increase the exposure of your current audience.

Once your story picks up steam, here are the stats you can follow:

- **Impressions:** how many views your story has seen.
- **Reach:** how many unique accounts has viewed your story.
- **Exit:** the number of times someone left their story halfway.
- **Responses (Replies):** The total number of responses to a video or image in your story.

- **People Info:** Accounts that have seen a specific item in your story will be listed.

What Data Should You Track?

OK, there are several information on your Instagram analytics! To help you feel less stressed with the sheer volume of stats available, here are some tips on what to focus on.

Before beginning to analyze the data, it is essential to know the overall purpose of the platform. Is your strategy aimed at targeting multiple site visitors? Maybe your Instagram was launched as a community for customers to share ideas. Or maybe you have launched an Instagram presence to maximize your brand awareness among your target audience. It is also possible that you have different goals for your account. Some messages can be created to raise awareness, while others can try to increase sales. You must know what you're looking for to make the most of Instagram analytics.

Here are three basic goals with the three main steps to follow in each.

1. Increase brand awareness

If you are a new business looking to build an established business or name, trying to present a new product or enter a new market, Instagram can be the best place to increase brand awareness. It's a great target for this platform because your target audience is more likely to be on Instagram somewhere.

Here are the stats you'll need to focus on:

- **The followers count:** an increase in followers corresponds to an increase in brand awareness (and pleasure of the brand!). If there is a rise in the total number of new accounts after your own, it's a sign that your business is resonating on Instagram. Some useful ways to increase your followers are by posting ads for this purpose, collaborating with relevant brands in joint campaigns, and running contests where you encourage people to follow your account and publish your post.
- **Impressions:** The more people who view your articles and stories, the better! If you want to increase your brand awareness, make sure your impressions, history, and accounts increase as well.
- **Reach:** Reach also tracks views by post, story, and account. The difference between your reach and impressions is that the coverage refers to unique accounts (not the same account that shows your Instagram post multiple times). When it comes

to brand awareness, increasing Instagram reach is crucial.

2. Generate sales/leads

This is a very mutual goal among marketers. Who wouldn't want more sales? You have several tactics that can be used to increase sales through Instagram, including showing targeted ads and posting special offers to followers. But how can you assess their success?

There are three main indicators to monitor:

- **Site Clicks:** In your ads, posts, and stories, you're probably encouraging people to make a purchase or complete a form on your site. The track of the number of people who actually will help you understand if your efforts are paying off.
- **Call clicks/Email clicks:** Calls and emails are great indicators of the arrival of conversions. An increase in these contact points is a signal in the right direction of conductor conversion.
- **Follower Days/Hours:** Paying attention to when your audience is most engaged will help improve your Instagram strategy. You can plan to show your ads when your target audience members are most active, which increases engagement.

3. Building a community

With so much fun and visually engaging content on Instagram, there couldn't be a better place to build an interactive community. If this is your major goal, you should continually monitor, respond to, and evaluate the following metrics:

- **Comments:** a community speaks. Having a conversation over your posts is best way to do this. With this, you will also be chanced to respond and interact with members of the community. As a general rule, never ignore comments, even if you like them.

- **Story Replies:** This is another way to assess the level of activity in your community. Stories are a nice tool to use if you want to interact with followers to build a community. If viewers are taking too long to respond, that's a good sign.

- **Engagement:** Finally, engagement is essential when it comes to building a community. Tracking the engagement of Ads, Posts, Profiles, and Stories will ensure you are working towards your goal.

The Top 5 Best Instagram Analytics Tools

We are all busy and searching for Instagram Insights in various places on the platform can be time-consuming and frustrating at times. Good news! There are tools to make tracking and ranking your Instagram analytics easier and faster for you. Here are the best five that I recommend checking out.

1. HootSuite

I've been a huge fan of Hootsuite ever since I used it for social planning, long before Instagram was a thing. Today, their software has become even more robust, and they have great analytical tracking tools built into their plans. For Instagram, Hootsuite is the perfect place to focus on goal metrics to track your progress and even create visual reports.

2. Squarelovin

Squarelovin focuses specifically on Instagram Insights, so it provides some really useful reporting features to improve your strategy. For example, they display engagement graphs to see when your content is driving the most interactions, as well as graphs illustrating the best days and times to post.

3. Socialbakers

Socialbakers gives free and visually appealing Instagram analytics tools to help you share hashtags, filters, more interesting posts, and more. This tool also provides a graph detailing the distribution of your posts over the past one year, which can help you to continue being consistent. Socialbakers will also check your profile and classify you as a leader, sleeper, spammer, or shy to determine the effectiveness of your strategy.

4. Social Sprout

If you want to build customer reports and spy on your competitors on Instagram, Sprout Social may be the platform for you. Track your subscribers' growth, likes, and comments with a visual graph and track similar data from your competitor's accounts to see how you are doing against the competition.

5. SocialRank

SocialRank is a tool focused on understanding the Instagram audience. Think of follower patterns, the popular word used in bios and posts to his followers and popular emojis that are used among your target audience. Apart from helping you to better understand your audience, it will also set you up to tailor your content more effectively. Not too shabby!

Whether you decide to use a tool to help you with your analytics tracking or follow the native ideas of Instagram, I hope this chapter has inspired you to better use the data at your fingertips to grow your business through this powerful platform.

Chapter 8: Getting Started with Instagram Advertising In 2021

So you do paid searches and show ads on Google, advertise on Facebook, LinkedIn, Twitter, and even some industry-related niche social sites. You may be running guerrilla advertising campaigns or advertising through NPR. But for some weird reason you ignored Instagram, you don't know if it can generate a return on your investment.

Well I'm here to tell you that today is not the day to skip Instagram! Even though Instagram is younger, with fewer users, than its parent company, Facebook, Instagram is the successful family star everyone wants to sit next to at the Thanksgiving table. Instagram provides a platform for visual storytelling across various ad formats, and many advertisers have seen this channel generate a higher ROI than their other ad campaigns.

Today, Instagram, according to Statista, has over 800 million active users, and the rapid growth rate seen since 2013 is quite surprising. Take a look at the table below.

But with so many active people browsing the feeds all the time, how does a small business like yours stand out?

This is where Instagram advertising comes in. Similar to Facebook, clutter comes with popularity, and organically breaking down that mess to have a real impact can seem nearly impossible. To focus on the appropriate people, at the right time, with the right message and the right images, Instagram ads are your powerful vehicle to get there.

Here, we will talk about all you need to know to launch an advertising campaign on Instagram.

What Is Instagram Advertising?

Instagram advertising is a means of payment for posting sponsored content on the Instagram platform in order to reach a more targeted audience. While there are many reasons why a business or individual may decide to advertise, Instagram advertising is often used to increase brand exposure, website traffic, generate new leads, and move current prospects down the funnel (and hopefully towards converting).

Since Instagram is more or less a visual platform, text ads are not a thing there. Instead, you need an image, a set of images, or videos (which can be accompanied by text) to reach your audience with ads on Instagram.

Similar to Facebook ads, investing money behind a post will lead to more exposure for your business, as well as more control over who can see your post.

Should You Use Instagram Advertising For Your Business?

This lead us to the obvious question: who are the people on Instagram? Is it just teens taking selfies? Or 20 years plus looking for recipes? What about older populations? Are they "gramming" their grandchildren?

Unfortunately, for all marketers looking for demographic grandparents, Instagram tends to reach a younger audience, with the highest percentage of users in the 18-29 age range (55%), therefore between 30 and 49 years of age (28%). Only 11% of Instagram users are between 50 and 64 years old and only 4% are adults over 65.

According to Hootsuite, 18% of users in the country, 28% of users live in the suburbs, and the majority of Instagram users live in urban areas (32%). Although there are more women on Instagram than men, the gender gap is not as big as it used to be.

If that doesn't sound like the target audience, you still shouldn't dismiss the social network as a wasteful opportunity. Similar to Facebook, more and more adults over 34 are likely to join the Instagram movement as the platform continues to grow. Plus, if you're working with 4% of adults over 65, you can still target those demographics directly.

Similar to many other platforms of social advertising, Instagram provides granular control over the objectives specific to gender, age groups, locations, interests, behaviors, etc. You can even target custom or similar audiences to only show ads to your direct list of prospects or those with a similar tip.

What advertisers should really stick to is that Instagram uses Facebook demographics to serve ads to the right parties. This makes it an very valuable tool for advertisers who want to reach a niche audience, as Facebook already has a full history and in-depth demographic targeting options.

Advertising on Instagram can be particularly powerful if you are in a creative or visual industry, such as the craft marketing or restaurant business.

How Much Is Instagram Ads?

The answer to this is complicated, as the costs are based on multiple factors and, as you may have thought, these factors are not always revealed by the platform. The model is based on CPC (cost per click) and CPM (cost per impression), and prices are determined based on the Instagram ad auction.

Some advertisers think Instagram ads are usually more involved, but it can come at a cost to them. The costs of Instagram ads are slightly higher than those of Facebook.

On the positive side, advertisers control how their budgets are allocated. For example, you can choose between a daily budget to limit how much you spend per day, or a lifetime budget to set your ads to show for a period while the budget is exhausted.

Other ways to control ad spend on Instagram include setting up your ad schedule (for example, you can decide certain times of the day that you want your ads to show), setting your ad delivery technique (there are three options: link links, impressions and one day cover), as well as the definition of the amount of the auction (manual or automatic).

6 Easy Steps to Start Advertising On Instagram

Learning the details of a new advertising platform can at first seem overwhelming. The good news here is that if you are advertising on Facebook, there isn't much to learn. In fact, Instagram ads can be configured directly through Facebook Ad Manager.

If you're not advertising on Facebook, don't worry. We'll take you through the process below and it's also possible to create simple ads right on the Instagram app.

Advertisers who are more advanced or who serve a relatively large set of ads can also choose to configure their ads through Power Editor or Facebook's Marketing API. Instagram Partners are also available for businesses that need to buy and manage multiple ads, manage a large community, and deliver content on a large scale.

In this book, we will focus on creating ads through Facebook Ad Manager, which is the most common method, thanks to its ease of use and the ability to personalize those ads to a greater level than is likely in the app itself. While setting up Instagram ads isn't very complex, there are a few steps to keep in mind. Start with ..

1. Go to Facebook Ad Manager

To access the Facebook Ad Manager, simply click on https://www.facebook.com/ads/manager/ assuming you are logged in to Facebook.

Note: there is no separate Ad Manager for Instagram; Instagram Ads are handled through the Facebook Ads UI.

2. Define your marketing objective

Now the fun part, choose your campaign goal. Fortunately, the goals are self-explanatory. Do you need more traffic? Select the traffic destination. Do you want to maximize your brand awareness? Choose the brand recognition goal. You understood.

It's important to remember that Instagram ads only work for the following purposes:

- Reach
- Brand recognition
- Traffic (for clicks to your app store or website)
- Engagement (after engagement only)
- App installs
- Conversions (for conversions on your site or app)
- Video views
- Lead generation

While these goals are intuitive, some have additional setup steps, which I'll do for you.

Reach: If reach is your concern (how to maximize the number of people viewing your ads), just select your Instagram account when creating your own ad. It's also vital to take note that if you want to post an ad on Instagram Story, "reach" is currently the only goal you can choose. You can take advantage of Facebook's split test feature, which allows you to split two ad tests to see which one produces the most installs. NOTE: Split testing is also accessible for traffic goals, app installs, video views, lead generation, and conversion.

Brand recognition: prepare a very long lunch. There are no additional steps here! This is the most typical goal that will attempt to serve your ads to more potential people who are likely to be interested. How does Instagram determine this? It's a secret, but this goal likely exposes new and relevant people to your brand.

Traffic: If you want to send multiple people to your website or app store to download the app, this is the right destination for you. The only extra step you need to do is choose between these two options, enter any URL you want and get into the traffic jam!

Engagement: who doesn't want more shares, likes, and general involvement? If engagement is your goal, one thing to note is that at this time you can only pay to play "post-engagement" on Instagram. Facebook will allow you to pay for the "page participation" and the "responds event," but this is not currently available for Instagram.

App installs: If your primary goal is to install apps, you've come to the right place. To configure this, you will need to choose your app from the App Store during installation.

Conversions: We have Conversions. This goal allows you to guide your leads to take action and convert on your website or app. Additional configuration here requires you to configure a Facebook pixel or app event based on the website or app you're trying to promote; this will allow you to track conversions.

Video Views: The videos are often an investment in time and money; Therefore, not promoting your video on Instagram would be like purchasing a plane ticket to Hawaii and leaving it on your desktop. Fortunately, this goal is very simple and does not require any further configuration steps.

Lead generation: Last but not least, we have lead generation. Who doesn't want more leads? If this is your main goal, this goal is for you. Keep in mind that not all lead generation ads provide the same pre-populated Facebook fields. Instagram currently only supports email, gender, full name, and phone number. These ads also present a bigger barrier than Facebook's lead generation ads because when prospects click to open the ad, they have to click to fill in their information. On Facebook, prospects can fill in their information without any additional clicks. The other part of the setup is that you will need to create a lead form when creating your ad.

3. Configure your target audience

Now that you've selected your goal, you need to target the right audience to get your ads to the right people. That's the real beauty of Instagram ads, because you'll use Facebook's depth of demographic knowledge to reach the right people.

If you've done this for Facebook Ads, you've probably already created multiple audiences and are familiar with the process. If you're a novice to this process, here's a list of targeting options, which you can stratify to precisely target your audience. (For example, if you want to target New York women between the ages of 19 and 65 who are interested in yoga and healthy food, you can!)

Location: Whether you want to target a city, state, country, region, zip code, exclude or include certain locations, your geo-targeting will allow you to do all of this and more.

Age: allows to target groups between 13 and 65 years old

Gender: choose between everyone, male or female

Languages: Facebook recommends leaving this space blank, unless the target language is common to the target location.

Demographics: Under "Detailed Targeting" you will find demographics, which has several sub-categories with even more sub-categories. For example, you can target **"Demographics">   "House">   "House Ownership"> "Renters".**

Interests: Interests are also found in "Detailed Targeting" with several sub-categories to explore further. For example, if you are looking for people interested in spirits, sci-fi movies, and aviation, these options are available to you!

Behaviors: and another "Detailed targeting" option with several subcategories to explore. Whether it's shopping behaviors, work roles, birthdays, or other behaviors, the options seem endless.

Connections: Here you can target people who are connected to your page, app or event.

Custom Audience: Custom audiences allow you to upload your contact list, allowing you to target the existing prospects in your pipeline or customers you're trying to sell.

Lookalike audience: If your personalized audience is leveraged to their potential, create a similar audience. This will allow Instagram to find people with similar characteristics to other audiences.

After setting up your audience, Facebook will also provide a guide to your audience specificity or breadth (like the one below).

This is an important tool to watch, because you want to find a balance between your target audience, by not being too large (since it is probably not oriented enough), but also by not being very precise (in the red zone) because there may not be a lot of people (if any) to achieve with so many layered goals.

4. Choose your placement

Now that you are targeting your ideal demographic, it's time to pick your placement! This is crucial if the goal of your campaign is to show ads only on Instagram. If you decide to skip this step, Facebook will allow your ads to appear on both platforms.

This doesn't seem bad, but if you have content created specifically for Instagram, select "Edit Placements" here.

From there, you can specify Instagram as the location, as well as whether you want these ads displayed in the feeds and/or stories section of the platform.

5. Define your advertising budget and schedule

If you know how budgets work on Facebook, AdWords, and other digital advertising platforms, this step shouldn't be too demanding for you. Otherwise, take a deep breath; Even if you're not sure exactly where to set your daily or lifetime budget when running your first Instagram ad campaign, it's trial and error as well as experience. And the good thing is, you can control whether your campaign is put to sleep or stopped at any time, if you think your budget hasn't been allocated properly.

So should you go there every day or your whole life? While I usually turn to daily budgets because it ensures that the budget is not spent too quickly, lifetime budgets allow you to schedule ad serving. Both options therefore have advantages and disadvantages. I also recommend that you explore the advanced options below. For example, if you bid manually, you control the value of each prospect to you.

As mentioned earlier, you can also run an ad calendar to target specific times of the day and days of the week when you know your audience is most active on the platform. It is an extremely valuable way to improve your budget. As a reminder, this is only accessible for those using a lifetime budget.

6. Create your Instagram ad

The next thing now is creating your Instagram ad!

We hope that after following the steps above, you already have some content in mind for the ad you are trying to promote. This part of the setup may vary depending on the purpose of the campaign, but you will still have a few option format ads to choose from. So, in the next step, let's discuss the different ad formats available.

Different Formats Of Instagram Ads

If you are not a good decision-maker, you may want to prepare yourself. Instagram offers six ad formats. (It's a lot less than Facebook!) Two of these are for Instagram Stories, which appear at the top of the feed in the same way as

Snapchats. The other four are formats created to power Instagram, which are most commonly used by advertisers.

1. Image Feed Ads

This is the most typical ad format and probably the one you see the most in your feed. These ads are individual images that will appear as a native experience as the primary target scrolls through your feed. The great thing about Image Feed ads is that they don't hear any ads, especially if they're done right.

Here are some more details to consider:

The technical requirements

- Maximum file size: 30 MB
- File type: jpg or png
- Minimum image width: 600 pixels
- Text size: maximum 2200 (* although Instagram recommends staying below 90 for optimal delivery)
- Aspect ratio: minimum 4: 5, maximum 16: 9
- Hashtag number: maximum 30 (* you can add some in the comments)

Supported objectives

- Traffic
- Reach
- Conversions

- Lead Generation
- App Installs
- Brand Awareness
- Product Catalog Sales
- Post Engagement
- Store Visits

Supported call-to-action buttons

- Book Now
- Apply Now
- Call Now
- Get Directions
- Contact Us
- Learn More
- Download
- Get Showtimes

2. Image Story Ads

The same concept as above, but these are for Instagram Stories! Instagram Story ad details below:

The technical requirements

- Minimum image width: 600 pixels
- Aspect ratio: 9:16 recommended

Supported objectives

- Traffic
- Reach
- Conversions
- Lead Generation
- App Installs

Supported call-to-action buttons

- Book Now
- Apply Now
- Download
- Contact Us

3. Video Feed Ads

Propel your ad to life with a video! If you've taken the time to create a great video, you should definitely promote it through your Instagram feed.

While most video files are Instagram compatible, they recommend using H.264 compression, square pixels, fixed frame rate, progressive scan, and 128 kbps + AAC audio compression (PRO TIP: If your video does not meet these criteria, you can still run the video transcoder, handbrake, to make these settings).

The technical requirements

- Maximum file size: 4 GB
- Video resolution: 1080 x 1080 px (at least)

- Video aspect ratio: minimum 4: 5, maximum 16: 9
- Video captions: optional
- Video length: 60 seconds maximum
- Aspect ratio: minimum 4: 5, maximum 16: 9
- Hashtag number: maximum 30 (* you can add some in the comments)
- Text size: maximum of 125 characters recommended

Supported objectives

- Traffic
- Reach
- Conversions
- Brand Awareness
- Lead Generation
- Store Visits
- Post Engagement

Supported call-to-action buttons

- Book Now
- Apply Now
- Call Now
- Download
- Contact Us

4. Video Story Ads

This is another great place to post video ads, as users generally expect to see videos in stories; therefore, the "selling" portion of the ad does not appear to be forced. The recommended video specs for downloading are the same as listed above, and here are a few more details to keep in mind!

The technical requirements

- Maximum file size: 4 GB
- Video resolution: 1080 x 1920 px (at least)
- Video aspect ratio: maximum 9:16
- Video captions: not available
- Video length: maximum of 15 seconds

Supported objectives

- Reach
- Traffic
- Conversions
- Lead Generation
- App Installs

Supported call-to-action buttons

- Book Now
- Apply Now
- Call Now
- Download

- Contact Us

5. Carousel Feed Ads

Next, we have carousel feed ads. How fun these are! This format allows you to display a series of scrolling images instead of a single image.

This type of ad is ideal for highly visual brands, such as food industry brands, furniture vendors, clothing options, vacation destinations, car dealers, and more. But they're not just for sexy companies; they can also work to humanize your brand or showcase your culture by showing the people behind your software or finance company.

The carousel format allows you to choose between a maximum of 10 images in a single ad, each with its own link. A video is also an option for these advertisements.

The technical requirements

- Maximum file size: 30 MB
- File type: jpg or png
- Minimum image width: 600 pixels
- Text size: maximum 2200 (* although Instagram recommends staying below 90 for optimal delivery)
- Aspect ratio: minimum 4: 5, maximum 16: 9
- Hashtag number: maximum 30 (* you can add some in the comments)

- Video length: 60 seconds maximum

Supported objectives

- Traffic
- Reach
- Conversions
- Lead Generation
- Product Catalog Sales
- Brand Awareness

Supported call-to-action buttons

- Book Now
- Apply Now
- Contact Us
- Download
- Call Now

6. Canvas Story Ads

Lastly, we have the state-of-the-art addition to the ad format family, Canvas Ads. The ads are actually eye-catching, which allows the ad to create a 360 ° VR experience within their story. They are only supported through mobile devices, and highly customizable for the advertiser, but you need some technical tips. These ads work with video, image, and carousel.

The technical requirements

- Minimum image height: 150 pixels
- Minimum image width: 400 pixels

Supported objectives

- Brand Awareness
- Reach
- Traffic
- Lead Generation
- Conversions
- Post Engagement
- Store Visits
- Video Views

Supported call-to-action buttons

- Book Now
- Apply Now
- Contact Us

Instagram Advertising Best Practices

Now that you've cut down the basics of Instagram advertising, it's time to get the highest ROI possible by following these Instagram best practices for creating great Instagram advertising.

1. Install each ad with personality

Whether it's a funny joke, an emotional video, or just an intriguing image that shows your culture, if your Instagram post doesn't look humanized, you won't reach your potential as a 'commitment.

People use Instagram for fun, to have fun, or to be surprised. Whether you're on the train to go to work or to relax after a long day at work, no one tries to jump on Instagram to see a boring corporate ad. That's why appealing to emotions is always the way to go.

2. Endeavor to make your ad relevant to the context

What works with one social media platform doesn't necessarily work with another. For example, your business is unlikely to promote the same content through LinkedIn as it would on Twitter, as audiences are usually in a different mood.

The same goes for Instagram. Put yourself in the target buyer's shoes and know where they are. On Instagram, do you think your prospect can download and read your 40-page eBook? Probably not. Make sure your ads aren't overly sales-targeted, as they're not normally used for Instagram.

3. Use hashtags

But not just hashtags #food or #love. Be more creative and research users to see which hashtags are most likely to be searched by your audience. Don't overdo the hashtags, either. It can make your post a bit sloppy and hopeless.

The ideal number? TrackMaven studied 65,000 posts and found that nine hashtags are the ideal number for maximum engagement. They also found that longer hashtags generally work better.

4. Organize a competition

Promoting a contest or tribute is by far one of the most effective ways to reach your goals faster with Instagram advertising. Why? Because people love competition and free stuff! What's the best way to boost your target audience for your brand?

5. Post at Optimal Hours

As discussed in the previous chapter, if you know your audience well, it shouldn't be too difficult to determine, but trial and error can work here as well. Keep your vertical in mind. If you are a retailer online, when do people usually buy clothes online? Or if you are a car dealership, what days of the week do you see the highest traffic on the site? Begin by asking these questions.

Without further ado, exhibit and advertise on Instagram! It is a platform that should not be ignored, and this single chapter should provide enough resources to become the insta-famous.

Conclusion

With over 700 million monthly active users, there's no denying the power and reach of Instagram. What was once a photo-sharing app has evolved into an immersive social experience that allows users to explore a company's visual identity.

The user of Instagram appreciates high-quality content. Create visuals that give your audience interesting information or display your brand in a new and unique way. Optimize your content by writing fun captions.

Creating and upholding a platform that captures your brand's visual identity can seem daunting, but Instagram makes it fun and easy. Follow our guide and get inspired to get the most out of your Instagram marketing strategy.

Youtube Marketing 2021

For Beginners. New Advanced Strategies to get views, subscribers and how to become a real influencer with a step by step process

Introduction

It's not every day we wake up to a miracle of an invention or innovation that promises to make life better. Back in the days, the next big thing since rising dough was the television, and people went about this invention with feverish excitement. But now, a TV is about as interesting to a newborn as a door knob at an orchestra. We are fortunate to exist in such a time as this—the internet age—where we have online systems in place to do things from the convenience of out whereabouts. We can bank, shop, message, and reach just about every part of the world without needing to move. How great is that! With the advent of Web 2.0 technologies, social media and social networking came into and changed the internet landscape forever. Enter: YouTube.

As a platform, YouTube has something for every kind of audience. You can catch web shows, tutorials, reviews, and basically anything you can think of. But beyond being a hub for entertainment, YouTube also serves as a means of generating revenue for the willing user. With a channel and the right tools in place, you too could earn on YouTube. In this book, I'll lead you through the steps of going from a noob to an established channel owner on YouTube.

Enjoy!

Chapter 1: Introduction to YouTube

What is YouTube?

YouTube is one of many different social media networks that has innovated digital media consumption, redefining blogging, social media, music, entertainment, and film industries. The innovation is in the name "You-Tube;" making media consumption more personal, "you-centric" or customizable, and interactive. The platform was founded in 2005, and 15 years later, it has immensely revolutionized online media consumption across the globe. But what's even more mind-blowing is that as great as YouTube is, it doesn't own any of its content. That's right. Just as Uber doesn't own cars, YouTube doesn't own any content. Instead, it depends on the contents created by its users, which it avails to everyone. This availability allows for a different means of content creation and self-expression known as vlogging; a word coined from blogging. Think of vlogging as an online diary entry. Even though vlogging has been practiced since the beginning of the internet age in the '90s, vlogging has only recently been adopted into the Oxford English dictionary. It refers to recording opinions and news about a specific subject through video(s) and publishing the recording online.

Vlogging can be done easily and can range from talking into a camera about your day-to-day life, interests, among others to recording parodies, short films, music videos, advanced sketches, tutorials, and so on. Since its creation, vlogging has grown into a complete entertainment for many and has an entire ecosystem of enthusiastic bloggers and fans on YouTube. The platform is mainly used by two sets of people, namely:

- Creators: As the name implies, this set of individuals' own channels publish their content for viewing. I'll be focusing on being a creator throughout this book.
- Viewers: This set mainly consumes content, interact on videos, and subscribe to channels of their choice.

YouTube is quite versatile; it can be accessed anywhere from a smartphone to a computer. Put simply, almost every internet-enabled phone in this day and age is capable of streaming and sharing YouTube content. YouTube is open to everyone and has something for every audience. Whether you are the CEO of a business with a big budget for a video ad campaign, or an individual who needs a creative outlet to get or publish content, there's something for you. Also, while its user base spans from young to old, it is especially popular among the younger demographic. The reason is that younger audiences are more attracted to a variety of content, instant gratification of content over traditional TV, and the interactive components of the platform. For many, YouTube is a means of relaxation and entertainment, keeping up with content creators like artists and filmmakers, and learning to do things (tutorials and guides). Due to how widely accepted it is, YouTube can be accessed from almost every country across the world. Even more: it's available in more than fifty different ethnic languages. Additionally, since the platform is owned by Google, it is relatively easy to set up a YouTube account. You only need a Google account to get started.

How it Started

Three former employees of the online remittance giant, PayPal, named Jawed Karim, Chad Hurley, and Steve Chen, created YouTube in 2005. The platform was one of the first social media that allowed its users to upload video clips on the internet. At the time, internet speeds were on the rise across the world, changing into the high-speed broadband we now want. With the increasing speed of network connections, it wasn't long before the world was ready for streamable videos. Enter: YouTube, which stood as the forerunner in this movement. The platform was so successful that only one year later (2006), it was acquired by another tech giant, Google. Under its new owner, with stronger backing and better guidance, the platform has grown at an impressive and enormous speed. The video platform was a perfect fit for many of Google's ongoing projects, especially their AdSense program, which links videos to target ads.

With such additions, video creators found a large audience to not only target, but also a means of earning money depending on the popularity of their content. Popularized by its early periods of being a haven for bizarre home videos and bootleg TV clips, YouTube has since become a key figure in the global media industry. Since its creation, YouTube has revolved around the notion of being social on the internet. It encourages users to subscribe, share, and interact with their preferred content.

Basic Parts of the Platform

To make optimum use of your content, ensure a great experience for your audience, and monetize your brand, there are three building blocks you should know: channel, playlist, and video.

1. Channel:

The moment you sign in to YouTube with a Google account, you will be given a personal channel to publish your content. The channel is made up of several divisions meant to show a list of information such as the following:

- Thumbnails of your video uploads

- A comment section to see the interaction of viewers with your content.
- A short section containing your personal description.
- Other members, you have subscribed to.
- Video contents from others that you have marked as favorites.
- A list of members with whom you're friends.
- A subscriber section.

You can visit the channel of others by clicking the username of the user. On the channel, you can find all the video or music content a user has uploaded and the one marked as favorites. Additionally, you can see other members to whom a user is subscribed to. Personal channels allow you to explore the platform in the same way as any other social media instead of as a simple database for video content. You can find other users with similar tastes as you and find out other content they also consume. Before publishing content on your channel, especially when you just create an account, your channel is more or less a digital desert. It's space and emptiness all around. Fortunately, it is much easier to covert that garden wasteland into an attractive and luscious virtual ecosystem. After imputing your profile details, got can tweak the color scheme of your channel. YouTube has an array of suggested color schemes, but you can also create a personalized one using hexadecimal color codes.

With the help of a menu, you can renovate your channel's entire layout to your tastes. You can even decide what to hide or display on your channel and choose what side of the screen they appear on: left or right. These options are great, and help to make your channel distinct in and of itself.

2. Video:

After setting up your channel, the next step is to fill the empty fields with content. You can go through the platform and source for content that you enjoy. Watching videos, streaming music, and clicking on the favorite button to add videos to your channel's "favorites" area can help. As I mentioned earlier, you can keep in touch with a user's uploads by subscribing to their channel. Whenever a new upload is made, you will find a screenshot of the content in the section marked "subscriptions." After uploading your own content, you will find it in the top right area of your channel unless you alter the layout options otherwise. Over time, as you upload more content (videos), the section marked "videos" on your channel will start to fill up. The upper right area of your profile will typically contain the latest upload on the channel.

3. Playlist:

Lastly, we have the playlist, a type of list comprising of several videos that play in a specific order, usually one after the other. When one video is completed, the next video is automatically played, saving the user the stress of searching for or playing the next video. Typically, playlists are made up of videos grouped according to a common subject. For instance, a playlist could be about a TV series or the music videos of a music album. However, this quality doesn't mean YouTube playlists are restricted. Quite the contrary. Even if a set of videos is related or not, you can create a playlist with them and share it with your viewers. You can also create a playlist to keep up with your favorite content. A YouTube playlist is typically found in a separate section of a channel. It can be as many as one desires. The videos that make up a playlist are queued up in the order you wish the viewers to watch them. Although one is also free to pick the content they wish to see in a playlist, the idea of queues is merely for convenience.

Chapter 2: Creating a Channel

Elements That Make up a Channel

Every channel is made up of several elements that make it stand out from others. These elements could be the details ingrained in the look, or add-ons that catch the eye and convey a message. Let's consider some of these elements below:

1. Art

Otherwise known as a YouTube banner or channel header image, channel art refers to the big banner placed across the top area of a channel page. It is usually used as a means of visual communication about the personality and brand of the channel. Due to its strategic positioning and underlying purpose, channel art is important to the success of a channel. It occupies the landing page that welcomes viewers. As such, to make a strong first impression on your viewers, your channel art must be good. Additionally, channel art is used to communicate important details about the channel, such as the tagline, upload schedule, and social media handles. A great channel art is one that represents the channel correctly. To do this, the image used should convey two main details to the viewers:

- The name of the channel; and

- What makes the channel different.

When creating a channel art image, there are three categories you can pick from:

i.   A creator image

As the name implies, this channel art is a picture of you or the creator of the channel. It is especially useful for personal vlogs and brands. Most personal brands tend to use a professional-looking image of the creator in a power pose. For example, the channel Charisma on Command uses a creator shot as its channel art.

ii.   A representative image

This type of channel art is a picture that depicts what the channel is about. Think of it as a picture speaking a thousand words. A representative image is the best alternative for reinforcing your channel's brand without the need for words. For instance, the popular Dude Perfect channel uses a representative image, which shows the guts that make up the group performing great stunts.

iii.   A picture collage

The beauty of channel art is that it isn't limited to a specific type. Why use one when you can use many different images? Many YouTube channels use a collage of pictures of their channel art. However, the images used in the collage are usually on subjects that concert the channel or brand. For instance, channel Think Media makes use of a collage of four images in their channel art, each representing the main issues they cover: photography, lighting, and cameras.

iv.   A logo:

This is another simple form of channel art, in which the logo takes center stage on the channel. For instance, popular chef, Jamie Oliver, uses his logo as his channel art. The infamous black and yellow logo serve as a representation of both his brand and channel.

2. The Tagline

A tagline is a form of description, typically brief and crisp, that portrays the channel's value proposition. It serves as a good way to convey the qualities that make the channel stand out in a series of words. Many different channels are going aboard the bandwagon of including a tagline in the channel art. Doing this allows new visitors to the channel to see and understand what the user is about right away. For instance, popular YouTube user, Jenn Johns, makes use of the tagline "Cookies, cupcakes, and cardio" on her channel art to convey to visitors what the channel is about. Also, it serves as an attraction point that sets the channel apart from other similar ones.

3. Descriptions

Descriptions are not a compulsory part of a YouTube channel. Matter of factly, the area is left blank by many YouTubers. However, that doesn't mean that descriptions don't play a role in the success of a channel. Quite the contrary. Descriptions have great power and can improve viewership, followership, and monetization for the channel when used correctly. As the name connotes, the description section of a YouTube channel is used to describe to viewers everything they have to know about the creator, channel, content, and schedule. You have to be careful with descriptions so as not to give off too much information. The description should be a method of getting viewers to subscribe to your channel and keep up with your content and get to know you better over time. It is also a good way to answer the questions visitors might have about the content and channel itself.

There are some factors of a description that cannot be done without. They include:

i. The description

Like it isn't already obvious enough, you will find that many tend to get stuck here for lack of knowing what to do. The aim of the description is to convey to visitors what to expect when they watch your content and subscribe to the channel. What kind of content would you publish? Are the contents geared at teaching them something? How frequently are you likely to publish new content? Ensure that they know and understand the benefits of subscribing to the channel, like easy and understandable tutorials, a good sense of humor, or tech knowledge.

ii.   Use CTAs (calls-to-action)

Endeavor to add a call-to-action in any content you publish to get your followers to do certain things. Do you want them to share your content? Subscribe to the channel? Turn on notifications? Sign up to receive newsletters? Support you on Patreon? Whatever the case, always ask them to do it. Convey it in such a way that they would not be able to resist doubt it. Also, add the call-to-action at the end of the channel description.

iii.   Personality

Anyone can create a generic description for the channel. Still, you alone can create something with a unique tone and style that appeals to your channel. Don't refrain from using a joke or slang, given that it is something you're used to doing. Stay true to yourself on your YouTube channel from start to finish, as it gives the visitors a chance to know you and what to expect.

iv.   Brevity

Nobody wants to read your application letter to Harvard, so do well to keep the description as concise as possible. Don't go over the edge with too much information, but don't leave too little information. Just leave enough to keep them on their toes, wanting to know more beyond the channel's basics. Doing this will pique their interest to consume your content or visit your social media pages. The preferred go-to is a short description that is straight to the point.

4. Links

Every YouTube channel tends to have more than one link that takes visitors to a channel's homepage. These links tend to look different from one another. Still, their functions are exactly the same: taking visitors to the channel. Let's consider some types of kinks below:

i.   ID-based links

These types of links are the generic or standard ones that every YouTube channel comes with. It is a combination of the channel's unique identity, explaining the use of letters and numbers at the end of the link. For instance, a link such as youtube.com/channel/UCEZHPZ9jIKrLtiW5LcyJBQJ is ID-based.

ii.   Legacy username links:

Depending on the time a YouTube channel was created, it may have a username of its own. In recent times, the use of usernames for channels is no longer in use; however, you can still use this link to drive traffic to the channel. Thus, even if the channel name has been altered since choosing a username, the link still works. However, keep in mind that already existing usernames cannot be changed once set. For instance, youtube.com/user/newphonewhothis is a legacy username link.

iii.   Custom links:

A custom link is a briefer type of link that is easier to remember, and thus, can be easily shared with an audience. Custom links are given to and operated by qualified channels. They can take the form of your present display name, a linked and verified internet domain, or a legacy username. To check if you can claim a custom link, visit the advanced account settings. An example of a custom link is youtube.com/c/WeCreateThings.

5. Section:

Channel sections are used for organizing and promoting the content that you want to highlight on the channel. In a channel section, you can group certain videos to help your visitors decide what to consume. There are no inhibitions in the number of sections one can have on a channel, so you can have as many as 10 sections. Creating a channel section is quite easy and can be done in a few steps:

  i.   Start by signing into YouTube.
  ii.   Just beneath your display picture located at the top right-hand area, click on your channel.
  iii. Click to turn on channel customization on the channel.
  iv.   At the bottom area, click on *Add a section.*

v.   Under the area marked "Content," click on the drop-down menu and click on the type of content you want to appear in a given section.

Videos: If you decided to group your popular videos.

Playlists: If you choose to create a specific section for your playlists.

Uploads: This will help you group published content and live streams.

Channels: This should help group your featured channels.

vi.   Click *Done* to complete the process.

Types of YouTube channels

So, you think you're ready to own a YouTube channel and publish content? That's cute. When you start setting up your channel, you'll be asked to enter a name for the channel, and then there's the section called *Channel Type*. When you click to pick a type, you will find several options to pick from. Which one is right for you? The likelihood of finding the right fit is higher when you plan on making a specific kind of content. However, the odds swing in another direction when your content has no specific category. That's where the real dilemma lies. Which option best addresses your content? Moreover, why does it matter which one you pick? The available options aren't quite as streamlined as you would expect. Still, it helps to know the type of channel you want to associate with your content, for obvious reasons.

When you start creating your channel, YouTube provides you with several options such as Reporter, Comedian, Director, Guru, YouTuber, and Musician. While these categories all seem self-explanatory in themselves, they have options peculiar to them. So, you better watch out. Perhaps your content is comedic, but you prefer the Director option, that's a crossroad. Alternatively, if you plan to make comedic content that isn't original, you can't use the Comedian Type for your channel. The reason isn't farfetched: the Comedian Type is for original content only.

1. The Musician YouTube channel

This channel type is used by aspiring musicians with original content. Again, you might be wondering what the fuss is about original content. This channel type isn't for uploading music videos from your favorite artists, or those old songs you managed to salvage and save on an SD card. It is specially created for upcoming and established artists trying to put out their content to several audiences. The musician channel type allows you to provide more details about yourself as a music creator, even allowing you as much as posting concert dates for shows. Among the musician type channels, the handle Dave Days is one of the most popular. It has many subscribers, although its views are surpassed by musicians with the VEVO branding, such as Justin Bieber, Lady Gaga, and Katy Perry. These three have some of the highest viewed videos on all of YouTube. Some of Justin's content is almost at the 2 billion mark in views.

2. The Comedian Channel Type

I briefly touched on this channel type in the introduction. Like the musician type, the comedy channel type only deals with original content, with the same perks as describing yourself in detail and publishing concert dates. You can't publish your favorite comedy specials on this channel type. Many comedians who go with this channel type are usually those who use portrait shots. You must have seen many of them, with only their heads visible in all their content. So far, one of the top comedians on this channel type is Ray William Johnson. He is known for his breakdown shows, which have since give viral. Additionally, his channel has one of the highest subscriber counts on YouTube, with more than 4.5 million subscribers. So, have you got a funny bone, and can pull off original content regularly? If yes, the comedy channel type is your go-to.

3. The YouTuber Channel Type

This type of channel is more suited for covering everyday life. Think of it as a kind of general account, where you can publish content without trying to cater to any specific audience. You just want to share your life with people, and get those you know to see what's going on with you. The aim of this channel type is neither fortune nor fame. However, many could be fortunate, depending on how entertaining audiences find them. The YouTuber channel type has default settings without the options peculiar to the other more specific channel types. So, don't expect to be revealed as a specific channel type. On the channels tab, the platform only shows the other more specific channel types. The YouTuber channel type is where you can publish content that isn't originally yours too. So, bring on all your favorite videos and whatnot.

4. The Director Channel Type

This channel type is specifically designed for more serious content creation, feature lengthier, and more sophisticated content. The director channel type is your go-to if you wish to create videos that exceed the 10-minute limit. You can also put a price on your content, just ensure that everything you publish is original to avoid copyright issues. A popular channel that falls in this category is Machinima, which has lots of subscribers and borders on a genre that lies on the fine line between borrowed or stolen and original content. For instance, the channel uses game footage to create new movies containing overdubbed dialogues. This sample should offer you an insight into the creative freedom available to the director channel type, with the only catch being that your content must be original. Here, genre doesn't matter and can be whatever you choose.

5. The Reporter Channel Type

This type of channel is for anything news-related, including hard-hitting news, latest gossips, etcetera. Basically, you're granted the freedom of a journalist when using this channel type. You will be granted access to events and stories as they unfold. You probably need to be a professional in journalism and mass media to use this channel type. However, the reporter channel type isn't limited to big news events alone. You can also cover entertainment, sports, and other relevant happenings. A channel in this category with the highest view counts is known as the Associated Press, with up to one billion views since its time on the platform. Another noteworthy channel is the Nucleus Medical Media, which reports medical news, and has high views.

6. The YouTube Guru Channel Type

It is quite unlikely that you haven't seen or looked up a how-to video on YouTube before. You might have when searched for one at some time. How-to videos are created by Guru channels. This channel type is used to offer help to the audience. Let's say you know how to cook, and wish to share your secrets or teach a specific recipe, this is the channel type for you. Interestingly, the guru channel type is that the channel FPSRussia has one of the highest subscriber counts on YouTube. The channel is a site for ammunitions and guns, so you can imagine how surprising that is. Asides that, there are several other channels dedicated to teaching pranks, hacking, programming, beauty, and fashion, among other subjects. For instance, the channel Michelle Phan is a run by a makeup and beauty expert and has one of the highest number of subscribers in this channel type.

7. The Special Request Channel Type

As the name connotes, this is an unusual type of channel mostly used by politicians, sponsors, partners, and non-profit ventures. This type of channel is only available on special demand. A non-profit channel is self-explanatory. The owners merely want to create awareness for a cause and educate the audience, without really needing some form of revenue generated by views. In this category, the Sesame Street channel is one of the highest-rated. Partners are usually a group of people uploading their different content on the same channel. The largest partner channel is VEVO, a music channel that carries almost every Kate's music video made by popular artists. The channel also contains lots of *behind the scenes* and *the making of.* It's a great channel for lovers of music. Sponsors channels are used by advertisers to show off their latest commercials. While there aren't many such channels on YouTube, there are still some thriving channels, like Old Spice. The channel takes in lots of views with its popular commercials on the Old Spice Man. Additionally, Sony and Universal publish the latest trailers and updates on new movie releases.

Niches

There are many different niches to pick from when creating a channel. Still, I'll focus on the main ones that have bigger audiences and can be easily monetized.

1. Storytelling

We all love a good story, so it's no wonder why this is a popular niche. Storytelling content comes in the form of a video where you sit before a camera and recant a true story to your viewers. The story could be from as far back as your younger years or a recent happening. Provided you are engaging and entertaining and can tell a good story, you should excel in this niche. Your story could be good or bad; there's an audience for every story out there. Content in this category makes for some good entertainment, and you can easily get a good view count. Also, storytelling can be a way of selling yourself to the audience.

2. Gaming

Like storytelling, we all like a good game. Sometimes, that game we love can quickly become a chore, especially when you find it difficult to finish a level. So, what do you when you can't get past a particular level? You go find the pros.

By watching gameplay videos, you can get a walkthrough on how to pass a level. There's a walkthrough for almost every game on YouTube, so it won't be hard selling a channel for it. To start your own YouTube gaming channel, you need the right equipment, which, although costly, can get you a stable audience and some revenue.

3. Tech reviews

There are many tech channels on YouTube that feature unboxing, testing, predictions, among others. These tech videos are interesting as they feature a range of gadgets, including phones, cameras, and accessories. With the rising influx of consumer tech, contents in this niche help you keep abreast of and understand how those techs work. This niche is one of the most popular ones on YouTube and tends to come across nearly everyone's feeds.

4. Vlogging

Vlogs are like online diaries in which people record their day-to-day lives and share it with others on YouTube. Think of it as an online electronic diary, except with visuals this time. Many people fall in love with YouTube because of vlogs, as it can be interesting to watch the goings-on in other people's lives. To make the most of this niche, you must have an interesting personality and some good friends, who can help spur your viewership and cement your vlogging channel. There are many different subdomains under this niche, which are peculiar to whoever is running the channel. There are kid vloggers, family vloggers, couple vloggers, single life vloggers, and military vloggers, among others.

5. Food Reviews:

Just how mind-blowing is it that you can create a channel and thrive on reviewing what you eat! To review food, you will have to get new menu additions from several restaurants and record yourself eating them. In the end, you have to grade the food on several factors you consider noteworthy to consumers. Additionally, to thrive in this niche, you have to have a great and entertaining personality, the willingness to eat many different types of foods, and a good sense of humor. Food reviewers thrive because people tend to be skeptical about trying new things and are hesitant to splash money on a new food item they may or may not like. So, food reviewers simply put themselves on the line to give others their impression of the food item. They also serve as watchmen over food outlets, helping to improve the quality and appeal of foods.

6. Tutorials:

We have all gone on YouTube to learn a thing or two at some point. Whether it's DIY projects, life hacks, cooking, recipes, how-tos, fixing things, etcetera. A lot can be learned by following tutorials on a specific subject from pros, who teach you the tips and tricks to ensure you reach a satisfactory result without errors.

7. Product Reviews:

Like tech and food reviews, product reviews revolve around exploring and describing a product to your audience. If you choose to create content in this niche, you will get products from companies who want to promote their products. You will have to try out the products and convince the audience whether the product is worth their money.

8. Pranks:

Who doesn't love a good prank? You'll be surprised just how much people love to see others get pranked. Just look up Jalal. There are many prank channels on YouTube, so to make it in this niche, you have to come with a different and captivating approach. Put simply, there has to be a sense of originality about your pranks. Your contents need attractive titles and thumbnails. Additionally, you need good equipment, so that your videos come out good. You'll be surprised how seriously people take pranks and are attentive to details.

9. Healthy Living or Weight Loss Videos:

With the pandemic still plaguing the world, people have been somewhat sedentary, causing them to eat more and expend fewer calories. Over time, people started to worry about their weight, and many have resorted to YouTube for weight loss and healthy living content. Videos in this niche could range from fasting to veganism to plausible diets to meal planning to workout routines and weight loss ideas. One big trend in recent times is intermittent fasting. If you're no stranger to that concept, you can create a channel to share your experience, and encourage and teach others to lose weight.

Chapter 3: Content Creation

How to Create YouTube videos

So, you've picked your niche and selected a channel type, now what? The next move is to begin producing your content. Creating videos for your channel can be a bit of a hassle, especially for a first-timer. You are entering a niche already dominated by many others. You don't want your content to get lost to potential audiences. Below, I'll cover some basic tips to help you prepare that killer video and announce yourself in style.

1. Watch other influencers in the same niche as you

There are many others in the game before you, and watching them could give you an insight into how they thrive. From appealing to their audiences to their mannerisms, style, dress sense, among others. Take note of how they structure their videos, from start to finish, as well as what they show to the audience and the points they discuss. You can use the knowledge gathered to create your own content. However, in learning from others, do not steal their content or copy them verbatim.

2. Figure out the target audience for your content

Sure, you've picked a niche, but that's not all that applies to audiences. For instance, followers of food channels may not always be interested in everything the channel offers for reasons like tastes, allergies, etcetera. The audience interested in shrimp salads might not like peanut butter sandwiches. So, it's important to pick the audience you're creating content for, as it helps you choose the kind of content to publish. When picking a target audience, go with the one you can relate to because you will identify what resonates with them. After selecting a target audience, endeavor to make the most of their attention by creating videos that they would like to see.

3. Create an outline or script for your content

Always make plans for what you will say on your videos ahead to time to avoid losing focus or forgetting when you start recording. You can write your points as bullets or create a full script, which you will memorize before going on. Ensure to go over the script as many times as possible, editing and proofreading it to take out errors and remove anything that sticks out oddly. You don't want to publish a video ridden with errors and unaligned sentences.

4. Make some research on the subject you cover in your content

Before publishing any informative content, ensure to make findings on the subject and find out what others know about it. The reason for research is to find engaging content and fact-check your content before going live with it. You don't want to publish content that is wrong or untrue. Sometimes, you might also have to learn more about a subject. You must source your content from reliable sources to avoid using the wrong data. To confirm the reliability of any information, fact-check it against many different sources. Doing this can also help you master a subject. If you're covering a news event, check local newspapers and news hour briefings for details before drawing your own conclusions.

5. Create a budget

Getting your content isn't enough to make it fly with the audience, you also have to think about the financial parts of things. You need several types of equipment to record and edit your content, so it's important to plan for them. Although it sounds daunting, since you're just starting out, you don't have to break the bank to get the necessary equipment. With a budget, you can plan to make the most of your money and get the best quality your money can afford. To succeed with budgeting, don't set your mind on expensive equipment. It's better to use a cheaper camera that you can easily operate than an expensive one you constantly have to use a manual for. Prioritize equipment to cover lighting, video, and audio, as they are the key focus of every YouTube video. Also, feel free to improvise. For instance, rather than get a tripod, you can use books arranged in a stack. But, of course, your improvisation should be in line with your environment and needs. Don't improvise to the detriment of your content.

Equipment for recording YouTube videos

Equipment plays a key role in YouTube content, and it's important to get them right when you hit the ground running. They help to improve the overall output of your video and attract audiences to your channel. Let's see some of the important equipment to have:

1. Video

What's a video without a camera? Many YouTubers start out using smartphone cameras or webcam. Although both are fairly good, they are limited. You can use either of them during the early periods of your channel, but as it grows over time, you might want to switch to a better camera. Again, be reminded that the most expensive products aren't necessarily the best. So, it's imperative to make do with what you have. Go for a camera that gives you great video quality, and can record 720p or 1080p videos. DSLRs are a common option for many channel owners because of their good video quality. These cameras are also easy to use, have high adaptability in low light conditions, and can record smooth and streamlined videos.

2. Audio

Once you have settled on a good camera for your budget, the next step is to get an equipment with good audio quality matching that of the video. If your content has good video quality but is poor sounding, audiences are less likely to want to watch your content. It's inadvisable to use built-in mics on laptops or cameras because they have a poor audio output. The reason is that these sorts of audio inputs are not suited for removing ambient sounds properly; thus, affecting the output. As such, you should invest in a good microphone when planning for YouTube equipment. There is a range of microphones to pick from when it comes to finding the right audio equipment for your videos. You can use a lapel, USB, shotgun, or condenser microphone. Your microphone choice should be in line with what you need and how you intend to use it.

The Shotgun Mic

The shotgun microphone is common among YouTube influencers. It provides high-quality audio when recording videos with smaller, high-end cameras. The shotgun mic comes with shock mounts that help lower noise from background disturbances or mechanical vibrations from the environment. Another quality of a shotgun mic is its ability to focus on the clear vocals and sounds right in from of them. This property prevents the microphone from picking up ambient noise from around and behind the microphone, even during outdoor recording.

3. Lighting

It's necessary to make plans for lighting equipment, especially when you are recording indoors or in poor illumination areas. Even when recording in environments with enough ambient light, having the right lighting gadgets can improve the mood and tone of the place. Additionally, lighting equipment help to even out the brightness of your recording environment. Softboxes are the recommended go-to for YouTube videos because they offer good value for your money.

4. Tripod

Tripods are important, especially to get that stable and well-defined video. So, it's imperative to get a sturdy and reliable one to round up your set-up gear and ensure good quality for your recordings.

Online tools to Master in 2021 and Beyond

1. Annotations

Annotations are those clickable buttons that pop up on a YouTube video towards the end or at the beginning. They come in the form of video suggestions, *Click to learn more* or even subscribe buttons. The use of annotations is on the decline in recent times, but their impact cannot be underestimated. A simple guide to annotating a YouTube video is explained below:

   i.   Log into your channel and click on the video manager.

   ii.   Identify the video you wish to annotate and click on the drop-down menu, and select annotation.

   iii.   Click on "Add Annotation" and choose any of the five types available: label, spotlight, title, note, or speech bubble.

Speech bubbles: As the name connotes, these annotations are text bubbles that pop-up within a video. The point of speech bubbles can be changed in any direction. Additionally, they are linkable.

Spotlights: These annotations highlight a given area of a video you have selected with a dark grey box. When a visitor drags the cursor over the box, it produces a clickable text box below.

Titles: These annotations appear as text overlays used to add titles to a video. They are useful when you publish a video without adding a title and aren't linkable.

Labels: These annotations look like spotlights. The only difference between both annotations is in their looks. For labels, the text appears inside the frame you created rather than below it, like in spotlights.

Notes: These annotations appear as clickable pop-up boxes that contain text, and can be used to add more information to your videos.

iv.   Next, add the text and customize it to your taste. Pick a don't, transparency, background color, and size.

v.   Pick a timeframe for the annotation: when it starts and ends. To include a link, click the checkbox marked "Link" and select the page type you wish to link.

vi.   Drag the annotation to any part of the video and resize it by dragging its corners.

vii.   Move the annotation to your preferred part of the video using the timeline.

Click in publish to finish the process.

2. Thumbnails:

YouTube thumbnails are the small clickable pictures that can be found next to videos. They are the first things that attract the notice of viewers when browsing through the platform.

i.   After logging into your channel, click on your avatar located in the top-right area of the screen. Click on YouTube Studio from the menu that appears.

ii.   On the dashboard of your channel, click on the button titled Upload Videos.

iii.   Select the file you wish to upload and publish.

iv. Input some details about the video and wait for the upload to finish processing.

v. Once the video has been successfully processed, an option of three automatically-generated thumbnails will appear at the bottom of your screen. You can pick any one of these thumbnails, especially one with the best appeal. Then, proceed to the next phase by clicking on the Next button to finalize the process.

vi. Alternatively, you can upload a thumbnail of your own. However, to do this, you need a verified account. Verification can be done via a registered phone number or email address.

3. Captioning:

Captioning allows people that consume your content to read what you say on their screens. Think of it as a subtitle. Captioning is especially useful for accessibility purposes for people with hearing impairments.

How to add captions to your videos:

i. Log into your channel and click on YouTube creator studio.

ii. Click a video and start editing.

iii. Click on subtitles or CC (closed captions)

iv. Click English (automatic)

v. Edit the captions to be in line with the audio.

vi. Click save to add changes before publishing.

Alternatively, if you have a custom subtitle file like an SRT file you will prefer to use, use the first three steps in the rundown above and continue with the steps listed below:

iv. Add a new subtitle or CC

v. Select a language

vi. Click on upload a file and select the chosen file.

vii. Upload and publish.

4. Call to Action:

Calls to action on YouTube are a mechanism for steering your audience in the direction you want them to follow. After deciding the audience, you want, the next step is to point them in the direction of more content you think would resonate with them.

How to add calls to action:

i. In the Description: On YouTube, every video has a description section below. This section contains only two visible lines containing text, while the rest are hidden in a link. You can add a link to any of those two lines. So, in your videos, you can include a brief description, a YouTube call to action, and a link for your viewers to click.

ii. Cards: YouTube allows you to add your websites to your videos on cards, provided your site has been verified. Ensure to add as many as five cards in your videos after publishing. You can do this by visiting the settings area.

iii. Using end screens: This is one of the best ways of using calls to action, as it gets more people than the others. Your end screen can be filled with many different elements, which can prompt viewers to take action. Just remember to add a link, as it is the most important part of a call to action.

5. Live stream:

A live stream is a process of engaging your audience in real-time using a chat, video feed, among others.

How to start a live stream:

i. Log into your channel.

ii. Click to create a video on the top right corner, and select *Go live.*

iii. You must have a verified channel to do a live stream. So, if you haven't already verified your channel, follow any ensuing prompts.

iv. The first time you live stream, enabling the option can take a whole day (24 hours). However, once in place, you can live stream at any time.

v. Choose your preferred method of streaming. There are three types of live streams, namely encoder, webcam, and mobile. Go for the option that best suits your streaming needs.

vi. Mobile streaming is good for making quick updates from your tablet or phone, and vlogging in general. But there's a catch. To implement this option, you must have a minimum of 1,000 subscribers, and a mobile device with a camera.

Chapter 4: How to Grow a Channel in 2021 and Beyond.

YouTube allows video creators a level playing field to grow their channel, using the many different data it provides for them. While you wouldn't be able to find out the names of your audiences, you can get useful information that you can use. To grow your channel, you must be conversant with the analytics section of your channel. The built-in segment provides aggregate data regarding your audience in a similar way to Google analytics. With this data, you can track and tweak the performance of your content and channel in general.

How People Find your Content

One key question to ponder as a YouTuber is how people locate your content. Identifying this means of traffic will allow you to optimize your content to capture more interests. To find vital data regarding how your content is discovered, visit the Reach Tab on your channel. There, you will find the unique views, impressions, and general views of your channel. You will also be able to trace the source of traffic for your channels. You will find if your audiences are discovering your content through external kinks, YouTube searches, or some other source. You will also find how often people used the thumbnail on your content, and whether or not the click resulted in watch time. Internal sources of traffic on YouTube include playlists, YouTube searches, YouTube ads, and suggested videos. External traffic can be generated from apps, mobile sources, and websites linked or embedded in your content.

To track these data, visit the Audience tab, which shows a breakdown of your viewers' demographic, including their geography, age, and gender. In the Device type section, you will find the type of device and operating system your audiences use to view your content. The devices could range from game consoles to smartphones to computers and televisions. You can also find the most common operating system used by the audience, whether there is more watching on-demand or live. Also, you can find the most viewed playlists.

Engagement and interactions

There is a tab tagged engagement that shows you important data in detail about how long viewers see your content. Here, you will find the most-watched of your content, the most efficient end screen content, and the top playlists based on watch time. The knowledge of this data can help track the interests of your audience and profile your content accordingly. As such, you will be better positioned to make the most of your videos by reaching more audiences, getting better watch times, more effective calls to action and end screens, and better interactions. With this in place, you will be able to grow your channel by carving out a unique brand and style that appeals to your chosen audience.

Maintaining the Channel

Maintaining a YouTube Channel involves growing the channel to the point of becoming your voice and face online. Asides consistently posting content and making your videos interesting, there are tactics that top-performing videos employ on YouTube that can make your channel a popular one. Beyond the tactics pointed out, it is important to stay up to date with top videos and analyze their new tactics to use them.

Using Metadata

Metadata is data that describes other data. Metadata are the labels of your content that inform your audience about your content. This metadata includes the title of your content, the thumbnail (the small picture on your content link used to represent the content), the description of your content, and the tags that you use to categorize your content.

This means that you must use accurate and quality metadata in representing your content. Quality keywords in your title can go a long way than excess words in your title, and precise tags can go a long way than 'tag-stuffing' with misleading tags that can be penalized on YouTube.

It is crucial to use keywords that can be enhanced by google search in your title. This means that you must understand what most YouTube users are searching for and use that for Search Engine Optimization (SEO). While some users search on YouTube, some search on Google directly and expect to get video content. Optimizing your keywords, therefore, is not for YouTube alone but also for Google search. There are tools to identify suitable keywords for your content like the Keyword Planner on Google Ads. You can then proceed to Google Search, whatever keywords you choose. This trial search gives you a list of results and the keywords where the top results are video contents are the most suitable for your title. For example, adding a word like 'Tutorial' or a phrase like 'How To' to the title that best describes your content is a good way to come up with an optimized title. Another method is to type your theme or topic into Google search and let autocomplete suggest keywords.

While at this, ensure to keep the title as short as possible, and let your keywords lead the way in introducing that concise title. The title must be captivating and must not be cut off during display because it is too long. Most professionals advise that the title should be kept at less than

50 characters. The keywords should be in the first half of the characters because that part catches the attention of readers and viewers the most. Additionally, it is imperative to ensure that every word used in the title is relevant to your content. Otherwise, your channel will no longer be trusted and might earn a reputation as a clickbait channel.

The effect of graphic, bright, and catchy thumbnails cannot also be underestimated in the number of clicks that your content will get on YouTube. It is important to create a unique and beautiful thumbnail for every content you post. The human brain tends to notice them first, according to research. Ensure the image used in your thumbnail is a close-up, high contrast image, add color and text to the image, use the right format and don't exceed the size limit, and finally, your resolution must be in multiples of 16:9, which is the aspect ratio that the thumbnail will be presented to your viewers.

The description of your content should connect your content with a suitable playlist and contain timestamps of each part of your video's content to get the viewer to the exact thing they want to see. This description should not pass the limit of 5000 characters. It should be introduced with plenty of keywords that are relevant to your content.

Finally, use a few tags relevant in the tag section that can help YouTube direct your content to the exact audience you want for your videos.

Identifying and Engaging Top Fans

It is important to know who your channel's biggest fans are and how best to engage them. The necessity to figure out who your audience is and what they want cannot be overstated. This is important because it guides the content of your production. You must give your audience what they want to see to be a successful content creator.

For a content creator who already has uploaded content, the best way to identify your audience is to go through your YouTube Analytics. The information given here will help analyze your audience and give you statistics on the level of engagement of each fan to help you understand who your top fans are. Other demographics are also available on YouTube Analytics as the location of the majority of your fans. This can help you finetune your content to best suit their interests.

After identifying who your top fans are, it is important to respond to all of their comments, even when you can not respond to your fans' comments. The response could be a like or a reply. What matters is that your top fans see that they matter to you. Your reply could be to appreciate their positive comment or give clarifying answers to important questions. Another thing to do might be pin a top comment to make it known that you appreciate the feedback. The strong attachment with which this gesture connects you with your subscribers cannot be bought.

Asides this, another cool trick is to do a giveaway for your fans or run a contest that repays your top fans. The contest you should host must involve getting people to subscribe to your channel and engage with your content. The procedure to enter the contest can be as simple as "like, comment, subscribe." The reward should be as relevant as something that is an important part of your brand.

Collaborations

A YouTube Collab involves different YouTubers working on different channels coming together to make a video that will engage all of their unique audience. It could be a challenge done together, or it could be a meet up where both content creators appear together in the video. The videos can also be done by both creators in different places and edited into one. Asides improving the variety of the content on your channel, a collaboration will ensure that there is more engagement on your channel or more subscribers generated from that traffic. A collaboration gets more productive when the channel you're collaborating with is much bigger than yours.

The important thing about collaborations is to find important meeting points for the ideas on your channel and that of the channels you wish to collaborate with. It could be joining another content creator to review a piece of trending music or movie, or it could be making a question and answer video on a subject that cuts across the main topic of the channels, the important thing is for the content to appeal to the audience of each channel participating in the collaboration. The interest of the audience and subscribers of your channel should not be sacrificed on the altar of collaborations.

Identifying the right people to collaborate with on these content ideas is another important part. A channel with a far bigger size of subscribers might not want to collaborate with your small channel because they have little to gain from the collaboration in terms of publicity. They would prefer to collaborate with channels that have many subscribers very close to theirs. Therefore it is more practical to go for channels with the size of the audience in the range of yours. It is also important to find a channel whose topic is not too different from your own. A channel that has a sharply different topic to yours will not be practical for collaborative content that can engage your audience, even if it gets you new subscribers. Other factors that can affect this include age, location, etc. An aged person and a teenager will rarely have meeting points to collaborate on except in rare cases. At times, collaborations can require meeting up, shooting the video, or appearing in front of the camera together, depending on the content. In this case, location is to be considered when choosing which channel to collaborate with.

Social Media Promotions

Promoting your YouTube content on social networks is another part of publicizing your channel. Sharing your uploads with other followers and asking for engagements like likes, comments, and subscriptions to your channel is necessary. It is very important to ask and not just assume that they will engage with the content you create.

This is a free content promotion and can be the most effective if mastered very well. You can share your videos on Facebook while including some interesting facts about the content. You can share a snippet of an interesting part of the video on your WhatsApp statuses and follow it up with your YouTube link on the next status. You can tweet your video, especially when it relates to an ongoing trending conversation on Twitter, by optimizing the few words you blog with the video on Twitter to include those trends. You can share the snippets of your video on Instagram and optimize it with trends on the platform. Most times, it is best to focus on the social media app where you already have a wide fan base.

Meanwhile, it is important to ensure that what you do on this social media app isn't similar to what you do on YouTube, so that you would not face the stress of following the same content of yours on different platforms. It could also be a behind-the-scenes or a teaser that you'll share. The concept must be different even when the creator is the same.

Creating a Social Media Ecosystem: YouTube + Facebook + Instagram + Twitter

Put simply, an ecosystem is created by the interaction of a community with the environment. Creating a social media ecosystem is a step ahead of social media promotions. On YouTube, it is possible to connect your Twitter and Facebook accounts to your channel. This means that automatic promotion is activated on your social media immediately. You publish a video. As long as you can authorize YouTube with your login information on other social media accounts, the sharing happens instantly. This goes beyond having a fan base but having a fan community to be related to. The aim of a social media ecosystem is to build a social architecture that is consistent.

The social media ecosystem involves users on their end on social media platforms, publishing, and sharing content with their different devices. This could also involve an SEO optimized blog post on a website for each of the videos published on the channel. The video content can be transcribed as a news post with the keywords of the title optimized, too, while the link to the YouTube video is in the content. Promotions can be done by email to ensure that fans and subscribers get emails of new content while going through the promotions section of their mail.

Building a social media ecosystem makes the channel a more viable business venture that brands have to associate with to get their product or services into the market of that community. Most companies would always want to reach young consumers. They would prefer to reach out to all social media as a community rather than build a separate account on many different social media platforms. For this, they'd prefer to relate with someone with a social media ecosystem to promote their brand. This is because most companies cannot face the challenge of being consistently active on social media, so they network and leverage different channels to build their social media presence. To achieve this, companies co-create marketing content with content creators for their channels and community.

Chapter 5: Monetizing your YouTube channel

You've seen them do it. The big YouTubers like MrBeast, Logan Paul, David Dobrik, who have an average speculated net worth of $20 million, spend hundreds of thousands of dollars on videos and seem to always be giving away something big. Where does all this money come from? How can a 10-minute video bring in one dollar, much less thousands?

Let's establish that earning money on YouTube or monetizing your channel and content is a choice. YouTube in no way makes it mandatory for creators to place a price on the content they release. If providing free content is your cup of coffee, cool. Suppose you want to find out how to make "big YouTuber money" or just earn a stream of income from your video content in this chapter. In that case, you will learn how to turn your passion into revenue.

YouTube is a truly amazing platform. It allows you, the creator, to share your ideas and creativity with a worldwide audience and earn a living doing it. Anybody can monetize their channel, and any kind of content can be monetized. You don't have to worry that your channel content won't bring income. YouTube has made its platform so that even the most random content (provided it's within guidelines) can generate income.

There are several methods of getting income by being a YouTuber. The major ways YouTubers earn income are through sponsorship deals, merchandise trade, advertising revenue, YouTube premium revenue, channel memberships, and the newly introduced super chats and stickers. The most popular way and what we will be discussing mainly in this chapter are earning through advertising revenue.

What is Advertising Revenue?

Advertising revenue or ad revenue is the money that internet-oriented companies get paid for in-app or in-site advertising. Production companies pay companies like YouTube a contracted sum of money to feature their products and services on their website or on their app. YouTube makes most of its profit from ad revenue, which amounts to nearly 15 billion dollars.

With YouTube, creators can earn an income from ad revenue by displaying the advertisements from production companies on the videos and channels of content creators. The advertisements show up in various formats on the creator's channel. We have bumper ads, display ads, overlay ads, skippable/non-skippable ads, midroll ads, and sponsor cards. YouTube allows you to choose all these formats when you want to display ads on your channel.

Great, right? You're all ready to get started, aren't you? Not quite. Slow down. We still have some ways to go before you can put ads on your channel and earn your slice of the ad revenue pie.

How to put Ads on your Channel

YouTube has guidelines for content creators seeking to monetize their channels by using ads. Surely, you didn't imagine it would be as simple as linking your account details to your channel, posting a video, and waiting for the alerts to roll in? Well, it can be, but we're getting there.

YouTube has established that there are three key players when it comes to YouTube monetization:

- The viewers
- The creators
- The advertisers

The relationship between these key players on the YouTube platform is very important. For the viewers, YouTube provides a place to satisfy entertainment, informational and educational needs; for the creator, YouTube provides a platform to reach a wider audience with their content; and for the advertiser, YouTube provides a platform to reach their target audience with precision. The creators build an audience of viewers, and advertisers buy ads to reach the said audience. The viewers watch the creator's videos with relevant ads, and then the creator gets paid.

YouTube works hard to protect the integrity of this relationship. That is why certain guidelines have been put in place for the creator that wants to become a part of and benefit from this relationship.

These guidelines work in a program called the YouTube Partner Program (YPP). Once you've joined the YPP as a creator, you can begin to earn through YouTube. Before that, however, you have to apply and be accepted for the program. To apply for YPP, you must first meet the minimum eligibility requirements stated below:

1. You must be in good standing with YouTube.

Follow every policy made by the platform on its policies regarding monetizing your content. The YouTube monetization policies are a series of rules that allow you to monetize your content on YouTube. They include YouTube's community guidelines, copyright, terms of service, and their Google AdSense policies. When you apply for the program, you will pass through a standard process. The process aims to verify if your channel meets the policies and guidelines of YouTube. It's only when your channel meets them that it will be accepted into the program.

YouTube will also constantly check your channel when in the program to ensure it continues to meet its policies and guidelines. Failure to comply with the policies will make you ineligible for monetization. For instance, if your channel has videos that showcase nudity and sexual content against YouTube's community guidelines, you will be deemed ineligible. You will be unable to apply for or continue in YPP.

2. You must live in a country or region where the YouTube Partner Program is available.

Not to worry, YPP is available in nearly every country.

3. You must have more than 1,000 subscribers and more than 4,000 valid public watch hours in the last 12 months.

This is a minimum threshold YouTube requires you to reach because when you reach this threshold, it usually means you have more content for YouTube to review and collect more information to check if your channel meets their guidelines. When you click the monetization tab in the YouTube studio, you see icons that display your progress towards reaching the minimum threshold. You can also decide to receive the notification by email when you have reached the threshold.

When you've made sure that your channel content meets all policy guidelines and you've reached the minimum threshold for channel subscribers and watch hours, you can now apply for YPP. To apply, follow the instructions outlined below:

- Sign in to YouTube.
- In the top right area, click on your display picture and then YouTube Studio.
- On the left menu, click monetization.

Initially, you will be expected to review and sign the partner program terms, essentially an agreement between you and YouTube that makes it possible to earn money. Click Start on the card that reads: "Review Partner Program terms" card. Once you've signed the term, they'll mark this step with a green "Done" sign on the "Review Partner Program terms" card.

Next, you have to sign up for or create a Google AdSense account and link it to your YouTube channel. This is the only way to get paid from ads on YouTube. Make sure you only have one AdSense account. To create an AdSense account, click on the Start icon found on the card that reads "Sign up for Google AdSense." However, if you have an account on Google AdSense that has been approved, you can go with it. Bear in mind that you can link many different channels to the same account on Google AdSense. Suppose you don't own a verified Google AdSense account. In that case, creating one is as easy as following the steps on the interface.

After this, YouTube will review your channel against their policies.

Congratulations! You have successfully applied for the YouTube partners program. When your channel has been reviewed and approved by YouTube, you can start earning money from ads and YouTube premium viewers watching your content.

This process does not happen straight away. Sometimes, it can take as much as a month to get your channel reviewed and approved, so be patient. If your channel content has met all the guidelines, you will definitely be approved for YPP. You can track your status progress on the monetization page in YouTube Studio. While waiting for your channel to be reviewed, focus on making more quality content to keep your audience engaged.

What if your channel isn't approved for YPP? If your channel isn't approved for YPP, it is probably because it doesn't meet some guidelines. Review your featured content against the policies, and take out videos that don't comply with the policies. Then you can reapply after a thirty day wait period.

Once you have been accepted into the YPP, you can now serve ads on your video content and earn money. You turn the ads on in the monetization tab of the YouTube studio. I advise you to select all the ad formats available as your default to maximize the ads served in your videos. You should, however, make sure that you're only serving ads on videos that comply with the YouTube advertiser-friendly content guidelines. I know, I know: more rules, more guidelines. Yes. This is a place of work. Sit up and work hard for your income. You can do it. Basically, you have to make sure the videos you serve ads don't feature sensitive content like drugs, hateful content, or sexually suggestive content. Be very careful to review the videos you're monetizing against these guidelines because YouTube reviews them and demonetizes any non-compliant video.

Once you've done this, ads will be displayed on every one of your available videos. The displayed ads are automatically chosen based on many factors, including your audience and video metadata. So, make sure to manage your audience well! YouTube will direct more ads targeted toward your audience if they notice your channel has good audience interaction.

You're all set up! Now, as long as you keep posting content within guidelines and improving audience interaction, you comfortably earn ad revenue from YouTube. YouTube can pay between \$2 and \$4 for every 1000 views you get on a video. Considering this, you can earn a pretty decent amount from ad revenue by consistently uploading engaging and interactive content. The higher your view counts, the better your chances of earning from YouTube. Make sure to work on improving your view ratings, making your content more engaging and interactive, ad growing your channel.

Good luck!

Monitoring your Earnings

Now that you know how to make money from ads let's look at how to monitor your earnings from YouTube. You mark your revenue performance against viewership and also watch time.

You can easily do this using YouTube Analytics. You do this by clicking your channel icon at the top right of the YouTube page. Then, click "Creator Studio." You can now click "Analytics," and then you choose "Reports" under "Revenue."

You can now pick a time frame for the period you are most interested in reviewing. It is simpler to review the data provided in the chart if you look at it weekly or monthly instead of daily. You can use the data provided to track your revenue flow for that period.

You can then use this data to review how much revenue you are making concerning your channel's number of views for a set period or with the total watch time of your channel. You can easily do this in YouTube analytics by clicking the "Compare metrics" tab and clicking one of the options provided. You'll see two superimposed line charts that compare your revenue to watch time or revenue to the number of views for the period that you've chosen.

If you see that the lines don't match up and you are doing more while earning less, there are certain factors to consider:

- Seasonality. Sometimes your video content doesn't appeal to your audience in that season. For instance, in December, Christmas-related content will be more audience-engaging and will pull more traffic to your account.
- Ad-friendly content. Suppose you've released any video with content that doesn't meet YouTube's ad-friendly guidelines. In that case, YouTube will demonetize that video, and that will affect your ad revenue earnings.
- Changed demographics. If your channel's nationality demographic changes, you might see an increase or decrease in ad revenue as some countries have higher ad rates than others.

These are some of the different factors to take into consideration. Carefully scrutinize the data to see what you can do to your channel to improve your earnings. There's so much you can do, and there's always room for channel growth. Don't forget that YouTube is a digital market, and like every market, there are trends. If you want to optimize the potentials of the YouTube market, utilize the trends to your advantage.

Conclusion

If you reach this page, it means you have successfully completed the book. I hope you found it interesting, easy to follow, and helpful in your quest to make it on the red planet of YouTube.

Warmest regards,

David Holland.

An eBook On Personal Branding Secrets

For Beginners. Winning Strategies to Create A Money Machine with Your Brand and Become A Top Player About Digital Networking

Introduction

We're constantly being flooded with information every other day. One of such information comes in the way of branding. Take a look around you, and you'll discover that the world has since turned into one giant billboard for different brands. On the clothes we buy, the shoes we wear, the food we eat, what we bath with; all have one form of branding. And although branding might appear like nothing more than a formal organizational signature, it goes beyond that.

Let's perform an exercise to see just how far branding has been incorporated in our day-to-day lives. When you hear the word "apple" what comes to mind? Sure, you might give the fruit a thought before your mind wanders to the technical giants that make the invaluable iPhone. The theme, blue and white, reminds you of Facebook. When you smell pizza, you think about Pizza Hut, Dominoes, etcetera. The thought of a search engine rings Google in your head. If you don't want an iOS phone, your next option without even thinking is the Android OS, even though there are lots of other operating systems out there.

Why do you think this way? What causes this behavior? It can all be traced back to branding. The concept of branding goes beyond a symbol of an organization. Think of it as a form of psychological programming. When strong, durable phones are mentioned, everyone remembers the petite Nokia phones of old. Those phones may long have been discontinued, but the branding that went into it lives long in the psychology of people. You think security, and the Blackberry comes to mind. Versatility and diversity, the Android. Even this is scratching the surface of branding because it goes deeper than that. Throw in colors and it's a different ball game altogether. The use of colors to program people into associating abstract qualities to a brand is one of the key roles of branding.

For instance, when the color green is used in antibiotics, we naturally assume the product to be healthy and environment friendly. A good example is Dettol. Blue gives us a sense of dependability and trust, as seen in Samsung, Nivea, Savlon, etcetera. Enough said about the psychology of branding. Now, how does it apply to you? Branding works indifferently of who uses it, and can be used to attract and program a target audience. What's more, the ease with which branding can be created is unimaginable. You need not be one of the big dogs in your industry to employ the power of branding. No. If you use social media, you should have come in contact with in-app marketplaces. And if you haven't, you probably know a person or two on your list of friends who trades on the platform. For one to successfully attract real customers on the internet and thrive in their trade, they must have painstakingly created and maintained a brand and reputation. And that's only on social media. What about off internet platforms—in the real world?

Learn more about branding in this amazing volume dedicated to teach you the nitty-gritty of the subject, and help you grow a reputable and trusted brand.

Chapter 1: What is Personal Branding and Why is it Important?

The term "personal branding" refers to a process of promoting and establishing yourself as well as the things you stand for. A personal brand is formed by combining elements like experiences, expertise, and personalities, which makes a person unique in and of themselves. When done efficiently, personal branding sets one apart from others in their respective industries. Personal branding sounds rather unusual, as people are more conversant with organizational branding. However, in this age of the internet where everything lives almost forever online, the concept might just be crucial now more than ever. Unlike corporate branding, a personal brand is etched into the minds of your target audience, as well as the market. Think of personal branding as a means of communicating and offering your value to the world. Let's consider another perspective on the concept. A personal brand is a means of promoting yourself. It is a distinct combination of elements that you want the world to see in you. It's the way you tell your story to your onlookers, and how that story is indicative of your words (spoken and unspoken), behavior, attitudes, and conduct.

From a professional standpoint, your personal brand is what people imagine when they think of or see you. It could be a culmination of how they perceive your personality in real life, or how the media conveys you. It could also be the impression you people gain from browsing the internet. The associative capacity of branding is as weird as it gets, but even that can be a selling point when utilized effectively. For instance, PewDiePie is in and of himself a personal brand. People think of him as the king of gamers or the biggest YouTube crusader alive. And that's just one person out of many who've gone on to excel at personal branding.

But beyond your personal heroics, a good personal brand also involves what others have to say about you as much as it is about what you think of yourself. The word as we know it is astutely focused on branding, so much so that the crucible of the concept is almost forgotten. Branding is a mere formality, a scratch of the surface in comparison to brand, which is more of an emotional attachment. For instance, just about anyone can take great pictures with a good phone and get top-notch designers to create brand webpages with stunning personal designs. However, all of that is shallow and the surface of what actually is. Personal branding differentiates you from others, but your brand is what constitutes everything you stand for. When done right, personal branding can factor into your business in several ways more than corporate branding. And then success is almost a given.

A flexible quality of personal branding is that you can choose to ignore it and let it grow organically. It's not a given this growth would be streamlined, chaotic likely, and it may span beyond your control. Alternatively, you can manage the growth of your personal brand to follow the path of path personality. Think Cristiano Ronaldo. From donning the number 7 shirt at Manchester United to becoming a force in it, he's gone on to incorporate it into his personal brand, CR7. His growth as a brand exploded from his tireless efforts on and off the pitch. Before the days of the internet, personal branding was down to a miniature business card. In those times if you weren't a high-profile individual discussed on mass media, or featured heavily in a popular advertising campaign, little to no person would have heard about you. However, the case is largely different in today's society, where the world is fast becoming a global, public, and interconnected place. The smallest of actions carried out in secrets is discussed on social media, and anonymity is a prize only a lucky few can afford.

Why is it important

Since we have progressed to the point where anonymity is rare and everything is available on the internet, being influential is a great bargaining chip. And if you must develop a strong personal brand, you best be ready to put yourself out there. Personal branding is the distinctive factor that tells you apart from all others, and you can use it to convey your expertise and knowledge in your areas of specialty. More often than not, a personal brand is the underlying factor behind how memorable people are. For instance, the Kardashian sisters are popular because of their family's branding, which served as the pedestal for their personal branding. In turn, their personal branding is how we can tell them apart or remember them even.

The millennial demographic especially, have little to no trust for advertising. And rightly so, too. According to studies, up to 84 percent of millennials have no trust for either advertisement campaigns or the brand behind those ads. Nonetheless, millennials are prepared to take the leap of faith for people they feel they know. Take a moment to digest that. A millennial would hurriedly hand their money to a brand if someone who they don't know half as much as their next-door neighbor is used in an as. Even if the brands behind the ads are ones that they hate. A good instance to consider is the debate over the use of masks in the wake of the pandemic. Some Americans were hugely against the use of masks, a substantial number of them Trump supporters. But the one minute the president donned a mask, they thought it looked cool and decided to jump on the bandwagon. And most of them aren't even millennials.

This behavior has made businesses stop and rethink their approach to marketing. As a matter of fact, this behavior is one of the leading reasons why influencer marketing has become a successful strategy in business in recent past years. Businesses are starting to incline towards personalizing high ranking social media influencers in their marketing strategies. For smaller businesses, it is even much easier to make this transition as there is little to no difference between the business and the sole trader. The challenges increase for bigger companies. However, there are those that deal with it correctly. If you didn't already know, Steve Jobs wasn't the only creator of Apple. There was someone else, name of Steve Wozniak who worked on creating the products, while Jobs focused on marketing and sales. But what made Jobs the face of Apple was his knowledge and use of personal branding even before the phrase became an industrial concept. In the same vein, the personal brand that is Elon Musk precedes the corporate brand that is his company, Tesla.

It is only sensible that the owner or manager of any business bonds with their target audiences or consumer bases on an individual level before trying to sell the company's message to them.

Understanding Personal Branding

Both professionally and personally, a personal brand is an important thing to own. Think of it as a CV that can be presented to potential or already existing clients. It is a sure way of ensuring that people perceive you in the light that you need them. The alternative to this is a more arbitrary, and somewhat detrimental perception. You don't want that. Personal branding serves as a platform for highlighting your strengths, passions, ethics, among others. It bridges the gap of being strangers, and people tend to feel they know you more. With it, you gain the trust of people who are otherwise strangers to you. And who people know, they trust, even if you haven't met any of them in person. A good example of this scenario is at play during the elections. Many people tend to be out for candidates with views on issues that resonate with them. For others, the process is rather tiring and they don't bother with it. Instead, they tend to vote for the candidate whose name they can recognize. Thus, it is no wonder why candidates with a strong personal brands tend to succeed more in the political landscape, regardless of the validity of their political and personal beliefs. I mean, Donald Trump is the president of the United States, because he has a personal brand. He'd been lurking around the political and business landscape long enough to get the attention of people. This helped him create a strong personal brand that attracted the vote of the masses.

Personal Branding Examples

When creating a personal brand, you need to do a lot of introspective and extensive self-reflection. Doing this helps you know yourself more, you'd be surprised at just how much of yourself you were ignorant of. For most people, it is rather difficult to describe yourself to others, and most would often find it much easier to explain themselves to others. Does it strike you as odd how you suddenly fall short of creativity when it's time to pick a username? That's no ordinary behavior. We l want to come off as the best at what we are, but sometimes we are unable to see ourselves beyond what we know. If your purpose of creating a personal brand is to boost the performance of your business, you are better off ensuring that you know and understand your target audience. It's best if your personal branding matches the audience you hope to reach.

To help you better understand how to do this, well consider some tips and tricks of personal branding. Take Hugh Hefner for example. The image he conveyed to his audience throughout his life was one and the same. The term personal branding might be alien to him even, yet he was able to be the face of the Playboy brand for years. He lived a lifestyle longed for by many, envied even. However, he would have been able to manage that if he was in charge of a more conservative brand and targeted customers that upheld political correctness. Hefner is a prime example of personal branding done right.

Another example is the infamous David Beckham, who is a retired footballer cum fashion aficionado. During his playing days, Beckham never had a hair out of place, and tried to look his best on and off the pitch. With that behavior, he was able to land the interest of top brands who wanted him to wear them. He was literally a walking fashion mannequin, appearing in designer clothes and representing brands. He sure was a good footballer, but not the best of his time. But his proficiency in good wears gave him a brand outside of football that he still uses to this day.

A final example to consider is Elon Musk, CEO of Tesla. Musk is a tech guru with an innovative mind, and he's never stopped to wow the world with just how great technology can get. This gets him invited to speak on subjects as unpredictable and broad as artificial intelligence. It makes him dream of putting men on other planets. He alone would not have been able to do this, meaning many others key into his dreams of a technologically advanced world. Musk is a personal brand—a statement in and of himself.

Chapter 2: Creating Your Signature Personal Brand

In this section, we'll talk about the intellectual part of personal branding. The elements that form a brand also serve as the actions that keep a brand alive. As such, since a personal brand doesn't take the form of a service or product, it is imperative to create a connection between the mind and heart. How can this be achieved? Your intellectual and emotional features are what spark this connection. When considering branding from this viewpoint, you will understand that the place of your brand in the minds of people links the feelings with which they are connected to it. Ensure to keep this fact in mind when thinking about your personal brand, and where you'd like it to be.

Mind Redesign: Thinking like a Brand

To create a signature brand, sometimes all you need do is follow in the footsteps of others who are ahead of you, and think like them. For that, let's see some factors that make successful brands stand out:

1. Identity

Everyone has one specific thing that helps to distinguish him/her from the crowd. It could be name, race, complexion or character. Same thing applies for branding.

One key component that sets a brand apart is the logo. Your logo is the first opinion of your brand. Due to its importance, many mistake it for the term "branding." The shapes, colors, fonts and any other attribute that makes up your logo must be a full representation of your beliefs or values.

2. Positioning

Your positioning explains your place in the business world. If you don't have clarity on the importance of your brand, it might be difficult to fit in perfectly in the market. The major responsibility of your brand is to serve people, and if you don't know your obligation, you will struggle to grow your brand. In addition to clarity, your position will help you standout from others no matter the amount of similarities you share.

3. Strategy

This is the area most brands neglect hence, their failure in business. Planning is essential. No matter how attractive your brand looks, you still need to properly plan how you want to run your business. And make sure that your plans affect every aspect of your business. In cases where you can put up a proper plan, you can hire a business strategist to help you do the needful.

4. Vision

This is quite similar to your position in the market. How do you want people to feel about your brand? What do you want people to know you for? You need to be known for something, That's the beauty of every brand. The vision of your brand is also an extension of your identity as it can help create a lasting impression on your customers. Also, in a bid to have a compelling vision, make sure it aligns with your values.

5. Mission

This brand element contains steps and procedures that will grow your brand. This is where you explain HOW you intend to increase your brand awareness. Add your priorities and strategies. Work with your plan as well. Those things your potential customers look for before they connect with you lies in your mission. Hence, you must be intentional about it.

6. Quality

Quality is the worth of something when compared to other things with similar attributes. Your brand worth is known through how knowledgeable you are or how effective your product or service is. Quality will not only help you stand out but will also distinguish your marketing strategy. In branding, always aim to be above the status quo. Sell your uniqueness via your product or service quality.

7. Value:

Value and quality trade blows in how important they are to a personal brand. Value refers to a process of appraisal in which the target audience makes a choice to associate with your brand. When all the important factors of personal branding are put together, value is arguably the most important of the lot. The usefulness or worth of your brand solely dwells on your target audience. It seems like such a huge responsibility, but the value of things increases with more attention. Remember the law of demand and supply? As such, every thought, experience, or feeling people have associated to the grand are contributing factors to its overall value.

Developing Your Unique Brand Story

The new trend among marketers everywhere in the world is brand storytelling. That makes sense in business, however, brand stories are not just narratives that talk about how a company has made money from fulfilling the needs of their clients. It's beyond that and stretches farther into the way a business captures the attention of the customers while also creating personal bonds with them.

You may have thoughts of creating a brand story that your audience can absorb. It's not that hard, you just have to know first, the meaning of the brand story.

It is not enough to just put out your company's history hoping it wins the attention and love of your customers. You need to include more than just facts about your company and go deeper into exposing your customers to the experience, principles, and convenience that you provide for them.

Creating a story about your brand is a deeper form of advertising. It is more than just writing and if properly done will resonate well with your current customers and prospective ones. Basically, you just have to infuse people with the spirit of your brand. There are lots of ways to create a compelling brand story. But following these steps will bring you to the point faster:

1. Outline your brand personality and mission

You cannot start great storytelling if you haven't a clear definition of what your business mission is. The interaction and communication with your customers should be built on your mission and values.

The moment you have clearly outlined your mission and values and figured out the uniqueness of your business, the next thing is to find out the voice and personality of your brand. While creating your brand story, make sure to always refer back to these details you have unearthed.

2. Make it engaging

Your story will be more engaging if you are able to infuse some humanity into it. Let your customers be shown the desires, motivations, emotions, and impulses that drive your business. Put out the challenges that the brand has overcome on the path to their present point. Let your customers and clients see that the experiences they have has also helped to grow the concept of the business.

3. Learn storytelling

It's not just about having a story to tell. You need to learn the art of telling it. When writing your brand story, it is important you know the similar narratives and how to place them. The center of your story should revolve around the main characters and then infuse details that glue the audience before opening up the revelation.

You will know you're doing it right if your story compels the readers to continue. Create the main characters and let them reflect on the values of your business. You don't have to panic if your real story is not based on a real character. Just create it and give the character a voice.

4. Include visuals

Your story needs to come live in the hearts of your customers if you want them to remember it at all. This is where visuals and images come in. That way, communication is effective while they also stick to remembering the information. If you feel you are not able to emphasize a point with your story, use visuals to aid your point.

5. Be consistent

Let your values be consistent as you claim. If you aren't your customers may see you as dishonest. So be careful not to contradict yourself while you try to win their hearts.

Also, ensure that your story is able to make a difference for your customers. When you have created your story, then you can unleash it.

Designing your brand strategy

A successful business cannot thrive if it does not have a firm brand strategy. Building a firm brand strategy takes time, effort, and commitment, and without a unified identity. Your business can suffer.

There's a saying that people do not purchase services and products instead they buy the stories, magic relating to them.

However, there are simple step-by-step processes that can help you create an effective, flexible brand strategy

1. Knowing who you truly are-What kind of person are you? What are your beliefs and values? Knowing

these will guide your decisions in ways that are useful to you and your business.

2. Be consistent in communicating your brand through every content you release to the public. The this, you're able to leave an imprint in the mind of your customers

3. Endeavour to lure the right customers. With this, you can create a long lasting and strong brand.

4. Place your brand in a position where you can compare the future and the present

Before we kick-start how to design your brand strategy, you have to understand what having a brand entail.

A brand is the perception people have towards your business. People are led by what they see.

Usually, when people talk about a "brand," they're referring to the physical mark, i.e. logo. A brand is more than a logo- It is an emotional experience that can be strengthened or weakened through every interaction with that business.

A brand strategy helps you understand who you are and acts as a blueprint to help you communicate it better.

Why is branding important?

Customers will identify with your brand for different reasons. A good product or service at a good price might be a reason, but what drives customers goes way beyond that.

When you don't know your mission, what you believe in, or what you're trying to achieve, your business definitely suffers. a lack of brand strategy causes problems at every level of any organization from customer communication issues to employee retention.

What are the things required in building your brand strategy?

Purpose: This explains the vision, mission, or values of your brand, so you should make marketing and business decisions that reflect them. Articulate your brand and carve out a discernable place in the market.

Consistency: Define what allows you to provide your services day in and day out. Some businesses don't have any documented marketing plan, they just hope that anything they do works. This mistake can cause your business to pack up in no time.

Emotional Impact: This is what helps form a bond or a connection between you and your customers. A brand strategy should develop an emotional impact and build upon it. Have a cohesive brand message; this helps you to attract people who share your values, either as employees or customers. Also, having a team that has the interest of your brand at heart will make it easy for employees to feel interested and engaged with your business.

In addition to these, determine your target audience, identify your competition, decide on a mix of products and services on which to focus, and establish a unique selling proposition.

Chapter 3: Reinventing Yourself

At some point in our lives, we realize that our current positions are not well suited for us. To prosper in certain places, we may need to make a change, and realizing that you need to reinvent your path is the moment you realize you need to make drastic changes in your personal life.

If you are looking to make a major change in your life, whether you want to start your own company or just make some personal changes, there are some principles will help you find the path you are meant to take:

Pushing past resistance

When coming to a point where you know a path must be created, obstacles, challenges, and blockages will arise. This puts your back against the wall and you will be forced to make decisions on whether the rewards you're seeking are worth the pain.

Sometimes, you know you need a reinvention due to past regrets, missed opportunities, and risks you've never taken. But you should consider these oppositions as fuel to trigger your ambition and drive. You have to recognize your vision and push past resistance, and the status quo. Know what you want out of life, what you want your life to be about. If you know what you want out of life, it's easier to go for it and more likely to achieve it.

Trust your guts and be a self-starter

No college course or certificate will prepare your mind for the transformation you are seeking in the real world. Take determined and optimistic approaches. Dig deep from within yourself and question what you are striving for. Embrace the moment and visualize that every day is an opportunity to reinvent you. Seek a mentor or a coach whom you can emulate or follow in their steps, but be careful to learn from their mistakes and not make them. Read books relating to your field of interest until you've built a mindset to move onto the next level of your craft. Leverage online resources, like podcasts, videos, articles, online courses, and programs.

Build and improve your skills and portfolio

Focus on relevancy and actionable results. Your portfolio speaks for itself. Whether you start a blog, create websites, or write articles for magazines, your content can speak volumes to and about your brand.

Look the part

This goes beyond the clothes you wear, it is about the confidence you exude. Throw yourself into your new identity with a lot of confidence. When you are confident in yourself, you also inspire the confident others to have in you. Until you get really comfortable with the new identity, pretend that you're already there and continue to act like it until it becomes a habit. This helps you to easily bridge the gap between the old and the new you.

Position yourself for the results you want

Always be ready, opportunities can come at any time. Make connections, you never can tell when you'll need them. It takes time to build yourself, but it's also an ever-changing landscape.

Take action

Avoid the regret others have suffered. Don't make other people's mistakes, rather, learn from them. Once an epiphany has presented itself in your mind, don't ponder on it, act immediately.

It is better to fail early and often and it is how you learn from your mistakes. Others around you can pinpoint small improvements, but you know the adjustments that you need to make. Action cures fear, hesitation, and doubt. You are granted the limited resource of energy and time in our existence, it is important to keep your mind focused on the end goal, which is your growth and progress.

How Your Personal Image Is Working Against You

A lot of people do not know this, but your brand comes to life in how you behave, promote yourself, and present yourself to others. This is what shapes your perception in the eyes of the public. It had to do with building your reputation, creating an image of yourself for the outside world, and marketing yourself as an individual. It is the story that's told about you in your absence.

Think about it. If you're walking down a lonely road at night and someone is walking towards you, you immediately and instinctively begin to formulate opinions and judgments about the person coming at you: Is this person to be trusted? Should I run? Can I feel safe with this person? Do they look friendly? These are more like quick judgments and not logical progressions of thoughts. They are based on the situation/environment and image of the person you're meeting. This is a bad image of yourself can speak terrible things about your brand.

If you go for a job interview, business meeting or you find yourself in any professional situation, you are judged first based on how you present yourself, even before you utter your first word. When people see you, they are inclined to think..."Do you take care of yourself, and will you take care of their project? Do you look the part of an executive at their company? What message are you trying to communicate with your outfit?"

At first, when you show up in person, you are judged by your non-verbal attributes, and the way you communicate creates an impression of who you are and what you value.

There's a saying that "it only takes one chance to make a good first impression." In the first few seconds after meeting you, someone has judged you, possibly as credible, confident and professional, interesting, valuable, and trustworthy or they can perceive you as lazy, disorganized, and insecure. Do you see why that first impression has so much impact on how you will be perceived by others?

Take an honest look at your physical appearance. Are your clothing and accessories appropriate for the audience you're trying to appeal to? You may think looks don't matter, but people still make quick judgments about you in the first moments of meeting you. What do you want their perception to be? If I perceive you as rude and unapproachable, I'm less likely to want to get to know you or to want to learn what you do and what you need. This can affect your business in so many ways and one such can be you missing an opportunity to have someone help you meet your goals.

Reinventing Your Personal Image And Brand

In determining the kind of image you'd like to project, consider these:

1. Note down the image you believe you have now and what you believe people perceive about you from your style. Consider if your dressing and presentation is putting out the right message about you. Do you have a cool and modern business but wear outdated clothing? Do you dress to look old when your audience are younger and give more lively vibes? Do you wear oversized clothing and look more big than you are? Take away any piece of clothing in your wardrobe that doesn't portray your personal brand and image.

2. Note down the image you want to be like and you want others to see you as. Do you think your confidence will be increased with a new suit? Will you feel more in charge and walk better with high heels? Do you think your feminine features will be highlighted with a skirt?

Do you feel that your work vibe will be stronger if you wear khaki slacks instead of jeans?

It's important that you are in charge of your wardrobe and image. It is important that you are dressed in clothing and accessories that boost the feelings of confidence, authenticity, and is consistent with the image you're putting out for others to see. It doesn't have to be bank breaking. Just go for really good quality products that you can afford. Just ensure that you're always dressed in a style that matches your personal brand. It becomes easier for you to enter the market and create a voice when your brand and your image fit perfectly.

3. Get professional snapshots. You just need photos that were taken in good lights, a calm and neutral background with you smiling. It shows you can be trusted.

4. Check your social media. What's it like? Hi through your social media profiles and what people perceive about you from there. For instance what does your Facebook profile show? If your profile is filled with complaints about the performance of your local team or a photo of you drunk with your friends at a bar. You may also post complaints about not being comfortable with the idea of starting work on Monday morning or you make posts about pets and animals.

Do you consider the flirty group selfies you took when you spent time with your friends? What image do you think that your prospective clients, investors, partners, employers will deduce from the updates and pictures?

This doesn't mean you can't have fun but rather, create a different Facebook page for your business and put limits on the current profile you have. That way your fun life can only be seen by your family.

5. Did you update your profile? Do you keep track of the kind of comment you comment on and like? What information is on your bio? You will not make a great impression if your profile is outdated, or inactive. Do you know what your prospective business partners and employers will think of you when they look up your online activities? If you're an employee, ensure that the words you use portray your most important duties in your job. Do this kind of assessment on all your social media profiles and do the necessary cleaning.

Reintroducing yourself to an ever-changing world

Now that you have transitioned and a revolution has happened within you, you need to find your new place in it. And to do that, you should be willing to show yourself.

Establish clear boundaries for yourself

You have spent a lot of time undoing years of behaviors you've learned, thought patterns, and emotional reactions. What this means is that you have made a lot of space for the new you to come in. It is therefore important now that you be wary of what you allow to permeate you. Only allow influences that serve and fuel you.

Limit the time you spend on things that do not let you grow and stay away from anyone who is not supportive of you changing your new life. Set clear mental boundaries. Choose what goes on in your space and the kind of people you allow in your space.

Let people know that you are exploring

Many people feel incompetent because they do not know how well to put themselves out there. In that position, just say the truth.

The first time you meet someone new, make it clear to them that creating new ideas is what you love and that you need to be certain that you're on the right path for

Some will cheer you on and some will try to shame you. Surround yourself with those who support, inspire, stimulate, and push you to find exactly what you need, they are your biggest fans.

Refine and practice

1. Invest in yourself: Take classes. You'll meet new people going through the same transition, and you'll be stimulated and inspired and together you'll grow. Volunteer in workplaces to gain more experiences

2. Work with a coach or a mentor: This way, you'll learn to gain confidence and also adopt new ways of thinking.

3. Empower yourself: If you are learning a new skill, practice it as much as possible. Educate yourself, listen to podcasts, reading publications curious around topics you are not naturally attracted to.

All of these will help you gain confidence, grow your new muscles, and most importantly lead you to exploration. You've shown courage, you've gone where very few dare to go and you're both self-realizing and self-actualizing both in improving yourself and your brand- That's something to be proud of. It is time to go and excel.

Chapter 4: Creating a Money Machine with Brand Positioning

Now that you have put in effort to shape and ensure you're embodying your own unique brand, the next milestone lies in figuring out how to gain maximum earnings from this venture. After all, the entire point of developing your brand is to have it gain influence and bring in profit.

To make this a reality, it is essential that you position your brand in such a way that it gets the right exposure.

Brand positioning has to do with the perception the public, and more importantly, potential customers/clients have of your brand, or the general feeling it evokes.

For instance, when hear the word 'Gucci', there is a good chance that your brain will conjure up images of luxury items made from quality material; something expensive and exclusive. Maybe, you even know some celebrities who often promote this brand by wearing their items and keeping up this air of products that are not for just anyone.

Now, think of what happens when something like 'Vaseline' is mentioned. This is far more common, isn't it? A household staple of sorts and something anyone might have access to.

What happened here? No photos or advertising were presented to you at this point, nor is it impossible to say that there are unimportant people who wear Gucci (some even patronise cloned products), or that wealthy people have no use for petroleum jelly. Rather, what this proves is that the way you position your brand is the way it will be seen by others, no matter what the reality might be.

Brand positioning is the place you occupy in people's minds when they are not actively learning new information about you. As Jeff Bezos, the multi billionaire and CEO of sensational online marketplace Amazon puts it, "Your brand is what people say about you when you're not in the room."

Since the brand in question here is a personal one, you must make certain you are being seen (and, in the right way at that), and that being seen is putting money in your pocket.

Looking at how best to go about this, ideal options would be to;

Sell Advertising – Ensure that your endorsement within the chosen industry (and even others) is seen as important by offering to publicise commercial brands for a price. If you have succeeded in modelling your brand properly, then you should have access to enough of an audience to market to. Now that you are in the public eye, everything you do, use or like becomes a form of advertising to your clients/customers; make this count.

All paid ads are not required to be personalised either, although these are preferable. Space on websites and pages can be made use of through Google Adsense. This is best for those just starting out however, since their per person rates are quite low, and you would have to attract quite the crowd to benefit from this.

Market Your Knowledge – As a personal brand in the limelight, the experience or skills you have to offer are assets waiting to be leveraged. Whether you choose to arrange mentorship classes or host seminar/webinars, it is vital you pass on your expertise in an exchange of intellectual value for money.

Another hard to ignore method is the writing and sale of books based on these skills or, should that prove too daunting at present, a paid newsletter.

Brand More, Sell More – Become less hinged on making each individual sale and get focused on making sure your general personality remains a cohesive whole. As generic as saying "look at the bigger picture" may seem, it is necessary that you focus on having a lasting impact on all those who try out your brand.

Create an Experience – This step is actually directly linked to the previous step. To become enough of a talking point that your specific presentation becomes a trademark of who you are, and by extension, something that other people will want to have their own taste of, you have to tailor make special experiences that set your brand apart from all others.

Keep in mind that you are marketing your person to sell you and your sponsors goods or services.

Don't Undersell Yourself – Starting out in a field (especially a niche one), there is a strong likelihood of you hearing a lot of criticism and ill-based advise to "be humble". Some older entities or businesses will place a lot of emphasis on your lack of experience and even suggest you engage in free labour or undercharge because of this. However, it is now becoming clear that this form of customer hunting is outdated and even a waste of time. You would find far more success in having confidence in your brand and being able to transfer that to your hopeful audience. As a matter of fact, some worthwhile agencies and individuals find this ploy more attractive.

Strategies for Comparative Advantage In A Visibility Driven World

As the world gets smaller and smaller through globalization and a widening offset of trends online, it becomes more difficult for you to really stand out from the crowd or do something nobody else is doing. While this is not to imply it can't be done, it may be expedient to prepare your mind for either scenario.

So, if 20 of you have the exact same idea to sell, what would inspire the average consumer to pick you over the rest? Yes! Brand positioning again.

Without further ado, here are some strategies to make sure you hold the advantage and remain visible.

Advertise – This is probably the most obvious step, but it also happens to be the most pivotal one. Telling people what it is you have to offer and getting them to tell more people is the age old method. While there is nothing wrong with it, this model can be improved on, and with the advent of social media marketing, this has become less of a task.

It would be far more effective to get into strategic advertising. Know specific places (real or virtual) that your target market is likely to frequent? Then, put more effort into getting your voice heard there. Make sure the "message" of who you are is being broadcast. And don't simply try to sell to it, have the sell for you.

Imagine the advantage someone seeking to sell vintage items who decides to join Facebook nostalgia groups and go reach out to older friends and acquaintances would have to the seller who simply prints flyers and pastes them around at random.

Build Credibility – A job well done the first time is worth the praise you'll garner when the brand is being passed on to the next potential client. Although client expectations may not always be realistic and in these cases there is only so much you can do, it is common to hear praise being doled out to businesses who delivered to the full.

You may bake the best baked goods in the state or distribute the highest quality shoes, but if you deliver a birthday cake by the time your customers birthday party is over or notice a scuff on a pair of leather shoes you're having sent out, will anyone really care to know? As industrialist an brain behind Ford Motors Harry Ford puts it, "You can't build a reputation on what you are *going* to do."

Make sure you are seen as trustworthy and use those references to your advantage.

Associate – Another step which may sound straightforward enough also warrants a mention. Make sure you're following, connecting with and supporting those in similar or connected fields. Going after mentors and those you draw inspiration from is all very well, but forming ties with other aspirants can also provide an unexpected boost.

Stay Simple – While a good part of creating a personal brand involves proving you have something special to offer, experts tend to recommend you do not get so carried away with this that you lose sight of the essence of what's at the core. Let your followers know at all times what it is that defines you.

Connect Personally – Every day, a large chunk of decisions are made or waived on account of familiarity. To truly become an influencer and gain an edge over similar brands, you must find a way to appeal to your target market on a deeper level. How you decide to go about this is dependent on the type of brand itself and the image you intend for the public to have of you. You may be the type that holds little get-togethers where fans can get closer to you or you may be the type who sends out the occasional tweet wishing all your supporters well (especially in times of national or global upheavals).

Show up – Seeing as brand positioning is about claiming your spot in the sun, it is in your best interest to participate; and as much as possible. Go to that event or summit for people in the same groups as you! Join in that Twitter conversation that concerns your field! Start conversations of your own! Just make sure that you stay relevant while also not becoming seen as too keen, and as always keep the fact that you represent a brand at the back of your mind.

Dazzle them – Make yourself a talking point for the right reasons by spoiling your loyal followers/customers. Create giveaways and hand out rewards and acknowledgements; let there be a sense of membership that makes those outside of this ring envious, or at the very least, curious.

Be Yourself – Many brands fail to truly connect with their target markets because they themselves do not truly know what they represent. Some people try to assimilate a personality they feel is marketable instead. If being outspoken is big, today they are outspoken. If showing political aptitude is admired in someone, tomorrow they are wildly concerned about party policy.

In short term sales, this may be enough to get by with, but if you really plan on going the extra mile and becoming a name to be noticed, there is every chance that you'll eventually get caught.

You will not only be called out for being a fake, but will also drive away present clients, and maybe future ones too.

Remember that no matter what kind of persona you are trying to market, there are those out there looking for just that. Be honest in your presentation and they will find you.

Intentional Communication as a Tool for Positioning in a Virtual Age

In an age so overwhelmed by competition in every sector, it is no longer enough to create a brand and hope it attracts the right attention. In fact, that is probably the best way to get completely overlooked, unless you are lucky enough to get discovered and publicised by someone noteworthy, and unfortunately, this is usually for the wrong reasons.

Intentional communication in positioning has to do with wilfully and consciously reaching out and overtly alerting the public of your intentions. It consists of being aware of your purpose and getting that purpose across to the public.

While the most obvious understanding and practice of this is advertising, it will take a bit more than that to influence the outlook your audience has of you and have that be a positive one.

Communication is the core concept behind getting your brand out into the public eye, but making this effective can be more complex.

It is advisable to:

Create a network – Those who patronise your services should be made to feel like they are an essential part of your process; which they are. To encourage this feeling it is necessary for you to form a platform on which you interact with them as closely as possible.

A lot of people can have their message heard, but you will find the most loyal fanbases are those who give testimonials about a brand like "they are unexpectedly down to earth" or "it really feels like they care about their customers". While a personal brand is still growing this seems simple enough, but the more momentum you gain, the more there is a tendency you'll start losing touch with the audience as individuals.

Listening intensively – Within this network, you should ensure that your brand not only provides space for people to express their views on your brand, but also takes stock of these opinions and puts them into action.

All feedback should be carefully examined and whatever useful information that can be gotten from these comments should be effected to improve on whatever it is you're currently doing. Know that you can never be one hundred percent right and that inspired advice can come from anywhere.

Evaluate – As a part of the cycle of feedback, you as the face behind the brand will be expected to respond to certain complaints and corrections. Here, it becomes important once again to recall that you represent a brand and no responses will be considered in isolation.

An unfortunate side effect of trying to take the advice of your customers can be overreaching and ending up piloting your brand in the wrong direction based off one person (or a group)'s point of view. A clothing designer who has a couple of people complain about some designs they have made and decides to completely remove that style in the future would be making a grave mistake, since there are most likely others out there who are fine with it. In contrast, a chef who gets a lot of complaints about how spicy their meals can be (assuming this wasn't their intention all along/isn't the goal of the restaurant) would do best to tune it down or risk losing customers.

Properly evaluate decisions before you make any, and make sure that the need to maintain cordial relationships is balanced with protecting the brand's stance.

No Bad Publicity: Effective Damage Control as a Tool for Brand Positioning

No press is bad press, we often hear it said. Especially with respect to those in show business or the entertainment industry.

It is true that any brand is hungry for and grateful for an opportunity at getting exposure, especially if it is very widespread. However, that phrase is not completely true since we all know of companies or public figures who have been levelled beyond repaired due to scandals. Don't let a callous set of words set you on the road to ruin.

A more accurate claim would be that no publicity is bad *if* you can properly handle this attempt on your brand's life.

So, how do you control the damage and make sure it leaves only a dent? Or, better yet, use it to your advantage for better positioning?

Early Handling – If you were to observe a typical argument between a brand and a consumer, you might notice differences in the methods businesses adopt to getting these scuffles under control. A customer causing a scene at being made to wait too long or not receiving the kind of service they would expect is a common sight. But, what about less trivial issues?

The age old mantra of 'the customer is always right' is quickly waning in this age of digital reputations that are being published for all to see, and likely to create permanent impressions. It's no longer viable to simply sit and hope a rumor or accusation will simply blow over, because they never will.

So, the first tip in PR you can get from this segment is to come out immediately and issue a (calmer) statement of your own.

Be Honest – In circumstances where you do in fact have a share in the blame, it is advisable to own up coming right out of the gate.

Like the child who's broken the flower vase, coming out and issuing an apology is a smarter course of action than waiting to be found out as this tends to attract backlash.

Highlight Positives – Negative press can also be overshadowed with the opposite.

Have a new product that's getting attention? Got a positive review from a trusted authority? Have satisfied clients from a similar experience/sale? Talk about it! Don't let an account or article about failure be the first result a search would pull up; even if it is the most common for some time.

All things being fair, highlighting your humanity and making your followers sympathise with you being fallible should slow your fall. If you couple this with a sincere attempt to make up for any mistakes or compensate a disgruntled customer, and readiness to bounce back from this setback, you should have a solid recipe for repositioning yourself in the right light.

Chapter 5. Winning Strategies for Personal Branding

Every goal has an array of steps on different paths that can be followed to achieve it. While all of them might get you there, some may take longer than others to deliver the expected results.

A phrase you might be familiar with industrial engineer Allen F. Morgenstern's quote "work harder, not faster". This may be seen a concise pointer at how strategic approach can reduce the amount of work which has to be done to yield results.

While it is to be assumed that you'll also discover your own secrets for success in selling your persona, incorporating these tactics into your game plan could really cut down your workload in getting established.

Evolution: Dynamism as a Personal Branding Strategy

Up to this point, a lot of emphasis has been placed on creating a rooted and recognisable front for your brand. However, all should not be set in stone.

This is actually one of the perks of having a personal brand as well as a business/company persona in that should you ever decide to incorporate new aspects into your business or completely rebrand, the reputation and followership you've built on just your name should be able to carry into these new ventures.

Connectivity: Building Relationships as a Personal Branding Strategy

What makes some brands connect so well with their target audiences? If you know what makes some people connect incredibly well with some individuals, then something could be learned about building brands for organizations. In many ways, organizations are like individuals as each has its specific fingerprint – i.e. character, strengths, and personality – that makes it recognizable and unique.

Think about it; that's how you know your friends and understand what it is about them that you like. We're in a world where there's hardly time for you to weigh all the available brand options. And this fingerprint acts as a shorthand that helps every one of us quickly sort through the maze. This is a remarkably real point of value at a time that is increasingly difficult or challenging to tell one service from another.

When an organization's brand fingerprint is clearly articulated and designed so that customers, partners, shareholders, distributors, and employees consistently feel they 'know' or 'recognize' the organization as well as what to expect from it, great magic happens.

It is at this critical point that high emotional engagement occurs, the period when 'raving fans' as well as customer loyalty are created. This is the period when establishments start to gain highly sustainable competitive advantage. Discovering as well as communicating this brand fingerprint, therefore, helps companies bring keen strategic focus to the power of their brand. This gives such brands a recognizable and meaningful shorthand that helps in cutting through the clutter and noise in order to connect with people.

The Brand 'Fingerprint' Process

There is a process that helps to unveil an organization's brand fingerprint quickly and ensures that the abstract attributes assigned to the brand – i.e. assets like innovation, integrity, etc. – are translated into a tangible, visual representation to which audiences can easily relate. This process has two phases which are:

- Strategy
- Visual translation

Here's how it works, broken down into quick steps for easy assimilation:

Phase 1: Strategy

Step 1: Determining your brand personality, values, and character

Step 2: Understanding the highly competitive landscape

Step 3: Find your position in the marketplace

Step 4: Building up your value proposition

Phase 2: Visual translation

Step 1: Intensify the brand mood

Step 2: Determining the crucial brand elements

Step 3: Broadening the brand roadmap

Phase 1 – Strategy

This phase can be compared to the conventional methods of brand development which is generally based on core values. The only difference here is that the activities employed in the facilitated sessions with the decision-makers in the company are designed to uncover brand attributes and values. They are also carried out in order to garner relevant information in such a way that it becomes incredibly applicable for the enhancement of the visual translation of the brand.

This is why it is essential to pair the decision-makers with the creative team right at the very beginning of brand strategy developments as it helps to gather input that will be crucial to visual translation.

This is of the utmost importance as experts say – after rigorous studies – that up to 80 percent of what we learn usually comes to us visually. Customers will, in most cases, likely to see brands long before they fully understand the strategy.

There are lots of benefits that come with considering how brands will be communicated visually at this stage. Some of these benefits include:

- Rehashing of intangible company attributes and assets into tangible representations that genuinely reflect the organization's core values
- Eschewing possible disconnects when websites, logos, and print materials are developed
- Long-term recall and in-depth understanding of brand messages by target audiences/customers
- Development of marketing materials that genuinely communicate key messages
- Consistency of brand messages over a specific period

Phase 2: Visual translation

This phase relies heavily on the previous phase as it takes all the information obtained therein and translates it into visual forms that people can see and easily relate with; this is the visible brand fingerprint.

An accurate and precise brand fingerprint can quickly communicate assets like zero defects, integrity, and even innovation in order to make them tangible, understandable, and visible. Target audiences will know – at a glance – 'who' that organization is, the message it has for them, why they should be moved, and why they should take positive steps to buy what is offered. It will be authentic, real, and it will satisfy requirements or make the cut because it is what people see that represents the logical thinking of the brand strategy.

Moreover, the benefits of developing highly visual components of the brand without deviation from strategy activities include:

- A brand mood that communicates with customers on an emotional level since the design is based primarily on reliable aspect's of the brand's personality and character
- Since the brand mood is a direct translation of the strategy that was jointly developed by the creative team and company decision-makers, there won't be any unpleasant surprises at the design stage.

- The prominent visual components of the brand will feel and look 'real,' thereby becoming the pillar on which other marketing materials will be built.
- There will be zero need for new visual approaches, themes, or deviations from the demonstrated visual translation. Brand equity usually builds with consistency. This is a cost-effective benefit that can never be ignored.

Brand communication

Being true or genuine to an organization's authentic brand is how trust, sustainable relationships, and loyalty are developed between the organization and its customers or target audiences. Great animation and cool graphics will not be effective as long as they don't accurately communicate the organization's brand or character. And something is definitely out of order if the company is not consistent and clear about how it is presenting itself in front of its target audience.

What is referred to as 'brand schizophrenia' occurs when an organization's brand and its image are not correctly aligned. This will significantly affect the level of trust and quality of the relationship with valued audiences which include both customers and employees. Both groups of individuals will lose confidence in such an organization as they do not know what to expect. No one likes to be kept in the dark about anything.

However, with brand strategy as well as clearly-articulated visuals in an exceptional brand fingerprint, an organization can quickly make a real connection with its target audience. And once this is established, the relationship enables the organization to communicate highly compelling value, stimulate long-term recall of brand messages, and foster the loyalty, trust as well as an emotional attachment that sustains relationships for a long time to come.

The Golden Rules of Personal Branding

Establishing or creating your personal brand is very crucial these days, even though it can be a daunting task. And the truth is there is no 'sounder' investment that you should consider above investing in your personal brand. Personal branding is all about how you market yourself to the rest of the world. And just as the advent of the internet created a level playing field for small businesses to compete favorably with the big ones in various industries, personal branding has become incredibly easier or simpler, thanks to the internet.

Nevertheless, just as almost every field of endeavor has some rules that one should abide by, the same can be said about personal branding. Therefore, here are the golden rules of personal branding in no particular order:

Have focus

You should never try to be everything to everyone at the same time. This will not only sap you of energy but will also lead you down the 'unfocused' lane in life. To build a personal brand, you have first of all to decide what your key message is, then do everything in your power to stick to it. The best personal brands out there are incredibly specific.

When you keep your message focused on your target audience, you will find it far easier to create relevant content around your personal brand. It will also make it far easier for others to define you and what you stand for.

Therefore, make sure you keep both your message as your content highly consistent within one niche topic in order to become very memorable within a specific or targeted community. The more focused or narrower your personal brand is, the easier it will be for people to remember you.

And you will be the go-to expert or authority the next time a speaker is will be hired to share your knowledge.

Be authentic, be genuine

The easiest way to have or build an original personal brand is to be authentic and genuine. These days, many people can easily see right through dishonest or cunning acts. And the internet has even made it easy for the audience to call out perpetrators of copycat brands.

Your personal brand should be a daily – and easy – filter that you can quickly create content and reach out to your demographics with. Therefore, you need to a master of your skillset, craft or industry before you even consider starting a personal brand. Your content will do the rest, and that is to amplify who you are and what you stand for at all times.

Research has shown that if you are highly skilled in one specific area, your reputation alone can help you to effectively and efficiently build the personal brand you want.

Tell a Story

Audiences, no matter the niche, love stories; that is how it is with the world as every one of us, are wired for stories. If your brand is not telling a compelling story that engenders a connection with your demographics, forget it; you have already lost at least half of your target and potential audience.

Effective branding strategies are focused on building authentic narratives. You may be shocked to find out that when you make noise about your personal brand on social media platforms, no one may hear you.

However, creating a story around your brand is another ball game entirely. You need to ensure that the story resonates with the target audience that you are eager to engage with. And one of the best ways to tell your story is via video or well-written content. Video is generally considered the most personal way to communicate online, and you don't even need high-tech equipment to make one or a few. Your smartphone will suffice; use it to create video messages for your target audience, prospective customers or clients in order to make that personal connection.

Create an image

What comes to mind when an image of Oprah Winfrey or Donald Trump or even Joyce Meyer floats across the TV screen? Each of these individuals has personal brands of their own, and they serve unique markets.

Just as the late Michael Jackson was synonymous to pop music – and was known as the King of Pop – you need to stand out. It has to do with developing your personal image to represent what you stand for in your niche adequately.

Be ready to fail

No one likes to fail because failure is pretty tough, and almost everyone would want to avoid it. It is human nature, and even animals that love hunting such as the lion, or cheetah don't like to fail when they sprint for prey, and it somehow eludes them.

However, having a personal brand that rises heads and shoulders above the rest is practically impossible if you don't fail. Many of the personal brand names out there failed at one time or the other before they eventually found their footing and waxed stronger in their respective niches. Having a good hard failure, according to Walt Disney, who failed a lot when he first started out making an animation brand, enables you to learn what can happen to you. What can happen is never as frightening as not even lifting a finger to try at all.

When you push past your comfort zones, you are bound to fail. But the key is getting back up each time failure smacks your candy ass down. You can never be your best until you have undergone a few trial and errors, failures, and mistakes which combined will build you up to perfection.

Create a positive impact

Your goal should be to continue building your brand over a period, and you can achieve this in two unique ways:

- Leap over others and burn your bridges, or
- Grow a community steadily around your brand

Bear in mind that you are your brand, irrespective of what your current job is or whatever project you are working on. The impact you leave on others is highly crucial and must not be taken for granted. Remember that all you have is your own reputation and that is your brand. Therefore, do your best to always be awesome and amazing to all and sundry.

In other words, when you keep a positive attitude while helping others, your personal brand will grow steadily and surely in the long run.

Follow successful examples

Since you are interested in personal branding, you should start marketing yourself like the influential individuals and celebrities that you look up to, day in, day out. To do this successfully, you should start working on how to cleverly dissect social analytics in order to establish the next big trend.

Yes, the next big trend can be within your grasp if you pay close attention to all social media platforms instead of focusing on only one.

Let others tell your story

The best PR, even when it comes to creating a personal brand in the public arena, is word of mouth. Once again, videos win the game here. You can create lively videos to tell your story, and soon enough, others will start telling your story even when you are not in the room.

According to the co-host of 'Malting On Movies,' Jessie Maltin, all you have in your life is your name as well as the reputation you have successfully garnered over the years.

Live your brand

Separating your personal life from your brand is one of the most challenging ways of building your personal brand. This may be possible, but it is far easier to create a personal brand when your brand, as well as your actual lifestyle, is the same.

What does it mean? It means that your personal life should reflect in everything you do and follow you everywhere you go. It must be a genuine manifestation of who you are and should also amplify what you believe.

Your personal brand, therefore, should reflect ideals like mentorship, giving back, thoughtful leadership as well as a series of job functions like marketing, finance, etc.

How to Create A Perfect Ecosystem with Social Media

Let's say you have a lot of knowledge, information, and skill to share while trying to put an ongoing program in place so that it will be maintained. How can you figure out the best social media platform to go for?

Surprising as it may sound, many businesses are still not on social media. They have their reasons which must be respected. However, most of us have since realized that a social media strategy is a must if we hope to generate interest in our respective businesses or ourselves. In order words, generating quality traffic is vital!

So, how do you choose the best platform to showcase your knowledge and talent? The answer is that it depends on the platform your target audience or prospective customers love to use. It is a waste of time if you put a lot of effort into a platform and only a small number of your customers use it.

It would be best if you also considered the medium, i.e. video, words, sound, graphics, pictures or images, and so on. Some organizations or businesses are more suited to a particular medium, e.g. think Pinterest vs. LinkedIn. The only thing you should consider here is that social media extends endlessly across all medium nowadays. You should always ask yourself: 'who is my client avatar?' 'Who is my target audience?' 'What does my target audience use?'

Re-purpose your content

The power of re-purposing is crucial in your social media strategy. This means that all the content you create should be used in different mediums and formats across multiple social media platforms.

Post your content or articles on your blog

It makes a lot of sense to own a website along with a blog. Then create a well-defined publishing schedule and consistently post articles on the topics you are interested in or want to share. You can even add relevant images to your posts in order to complement them.

Make sure you don't infringe any copyright when using images, so focus on using your own photos or those you have purchased.

Install share buttons on your website or blog

You should add share buttons on your blog or website to encourage your web visitors to share your content with their friends, families, and coworkers. You can ask for help from a technical person if you are not so sure how to go about this.

Set up weekly newsletter using an autoresponder

Since you are now writing and posting articles consistently on your blog, you should consider integrating your email list with RSS Newsletter. This automatically takes your most recent posts from your blog and sends them straight away to your list.

Of course, you need to build a list of dedicated followers and customers by using a landing page connected to an autoresponder like GetResponse or AWeber.

Video: the new game-changer

As discussed before, video has taken off tremendously. All you need to do is to start converting all your articles into videos. You may use a teleprompter after creating a video script and then share the video on your dedicated YouTube channel and its equivalent.

Podcasts

For every video that you create, take out the audio track and convert them into podcasts and post them on platforms like iTunes, etc.

Pictures or images

If you have original pictures or images, share them on Pinterest. Don't forget to link them back to your website or blog. However, you have to ensure that this platform is also relevant for your personal brand or business before using it.

How to Use Personal Branding on Social Media

By now, you already know that branding is not just for big organizations anymore. If you want to compete for the top spot in your niche, developing your personal brand is a must. And the second-best thing to do is build a strong or cult-like following of like-minded individuals on social media.

Gone are the days when social media was optional, when pseudonyms were the norm and reputation was not guarded jealously or painstakingly maintained as it is today. Fast forward a few years, and everything has changed: building as well as grooming your social media presence or personal brand is very important as it serves as an effective vehicle for presenting your professionalism and skillfulness to the world, among other aspects of your life.

This is a reputation-affirming effect that big organizations have capitalized on by pretending to be people on these social media platforms. And in the same vein, people have started behaving like brands through sharing a highly consistent story or narrative about themselves, based on specific themes.

If you want to use personal branding to succeed on social media, here are the steps to follow:

Revamp your social media accounts

This is the time when you have to take your social media strategy even more seriously. So, if you only post content here and there, maybe twice or three times a month, this is about to change, and for the better.

The first step to take, therefore is to start improving and modernizing your profiles in order to showcase your personal brand in the best light. Make sure your personal information is accurate and complete. Remove all unsavory posts and pictures that could work against your personal brand when unearthed.

Start beefing up your social media profile's appearance by using a welcoming and professional profile picture. Your profile must pop with interesting videos and images that will ultimately introduce people to your personality. And you will be loved for this since most people are visual.

Focus on and choose the best social media platform, then spread to others

Maintaining your social media presence can take a lot of energy and time, especially if it is part of your personal brand. And that is why it is practically impossible to give your best on all the active social media platforms at the same time.

Therefore, take enough time to determine which social media platform you will use quickly. This will depend significantly on the preferences of your target audience as well as what they use. It could also depend considerably on your industry as well as the type of content you want to start creating and sharing with your demographics.

For instance, visual content will do better on Instagram, while YouTube or Facebook would be great for videos. If you love researching and writing articles with in-depth content and case studies, LinkedIn is the perfect place to be.

Finally, your personal brand also plays a role in determining which social media platform you should stick to. If you feel you must be on all the social media platforms, you may have to hire a social media manager.

Create highly engaging content

Social media runs on content; the more original and interesting, the better. When people start engaging with the content that you have shared – a video, a blog post, an infographic, etc. – they will get a real sense of who you are and the expertise you bring to the table as well as your personality.

It is this interaction that ultimately draws people of like minds to your personal brand where they end up as loyal followers who will always return for more useful content.

If you are not too sure where to begin, start by taking a look at the unanswered questions your target audience is asking. What are the problems these individuals are contending with in your industry? Carry out your research on Twitter and Quora, a question-and-answer website. You may also invest in paid services or tools like BuzzSumo to enable you to discover the most popular pieces of content within your industry.

Leverage artificial intelligence

When you first got started with social posting and engagement, it was exciting since it was something new. But after a while, the novelty wore off; this is something you shouldn't allow when using personal branding on social media. And the best way to combat this occurrence is by leveraging artificial intelligence (AI).

There is a myriad of AI tools and apps such as Sprout Social and HubSpot that helps users to achieve and follow a regular posting schedule. These tools even curate relevant content for targeted audiences. You will also find a plethora of tools that you can utilize that will help you to engage with your demographics on your behalf efficiently.

These remarkable AI tools are great as they help you to set the pace effectively. Another tool known as HootSuite is used for social media planning as it is a management tool that helps to ensure that everything is timely and organized. These tools will help you take care of many tasks if you are too busy to handle them or don't have enough time to devote to social media.

Curate content

Although your personal branding should be the most powerful in terms of boosting your personal brand, posting curated content also has an incredibly valuable place. Curated content is content that was created by others which you have received the express permission to repost on your social media feeds.

You may be wondering what benefits come with curating content when you can always share your own content. Sharing someone else's content on social media is akin to nodding to the original creator of the content. And this currency is highly appreciated on social media. It helps you to network and also build relationships with real humans; people like you in your field. These relations, when nurtured carefully, may result in collaboration in the future.

Curating content also shows your demographics that all you want to do is to sincerely be of help to them, even by sharing content that is not your own. It helps your followers feel like you are one of them, and that you will always be there for them.

You should always and personally like any content that you repost. Go through it with a toothcomb so that you don't get associated with content that is not up to standard, which could damage your personal brand.

Join groups

Joining groups will help you experience that social media aspect of social media to the fullest. Facebook and LinkedIn have the highest number of groups geared to different industries. Locate the best ones in your industry and join them as they can help your personal brand in several ways, including:

- Getting ideas
- Getting highly valuable feedback
- Expanding your ideas
- Gaining confidence and experience
- Becoming a leader and a force to reckon with in your niche
- Helping others genuinely

The only way to reap these priceless benefits is by joining and engaging with others in the group. Post valuable content as often as you can while engaging with others. Comment on other members' posts and answer questions helpfully.

Always be positive

Social media profiles and even history are virtual resumes. Future collaborators and employers – as well as followers – may turn to these profiles in order to get a much better picture of who you indeed are and what you stand for.

Therefore, make sure your engagement and posting on social media platforms is always sincere. Be very careful when it comes to religious or political commentary. Always avoid comments that could instigate hate speeches or spats on social media.

Conclusion

As you can see, branding is much more critical today than it has ever been. Small and big organizations know this as well as thousands of networkers worldwide. Personal branding is how you efficiently secure for yourself a position in a market. You sell something that nobody else is selling or sell a standard product or service uniquely. This is done by selling the sizzle, not the steak.

The individuals who are the most successful with their personal brands these days are the filterers, the simplifiers as well as the synthesizers. These people are crystal-clear about who they are, what they represent, what they do best as well as how exactly they solve the most pressing problems of their target audiences. They are also able to effectively communicate their value and also embody their unique message, thereby making a successful and highly emotional connection with their target market. These individuals will find it easier to attract lots of clients and watch their businesses grow astronomically than those who don't focus on building their personal brands.

At the moment, you shouldn't really worry too much about what you are going to do. But be concerned about the significance of personal branding and how to make yourself into the person you should rely on the most. When you are true to yourself, practicing excellence and consistently playing to your strengths, you will eventually be able to create a unique and highly successful personal brand.

Personal branding offers you independence, flexibility, and security. It is an opportunity to choose your fate and make your own unique way in the world, blazing trails and conquering territories.

Therefore, until you understand the full meaning and significance of personal branding, you may not be able to take total advantage of this exceptional strategy to help you stand out and also make yourself count.

Passive Income 2021

For Beginners. Learn strategies and psychology to Earn money with Social Media in 2021 and Beyond

Introduction

This guidebook is meant to help the reader get the most out of several passive income sources that can be utilized these days. Many individuals are interested in getting a passive income going. They love dreaming about living on the beach and traveling to vacation hotspots in Gulfstream jets or yachts, doing anything they want to do at all times. But only a few realize the hard work that must go into creating a passive stream of income. The effort will be compounded if you must create several streams of passive income.

In this book, you will learn some of the numerous and different steps you may need to take in order to earn the best passive income possible. There are several options that you can choose from when it comes to earning income passively. But that can only be possible if you take certain steps that ensure you become very successful with it.

Therefore, in order to make the most out of this book, follow the steps outlined below:

1. Figure out what source of passive income you love and will be interested in working with. This will open your eyes in order to know the direction you should follow with the steps outlined in this book.
2. Work through each of these steps slowly, one at a time. This will make it far easier for you to give each

step the attention and time it needs instead of rushing through them.

3. Whatever advice you come across in this book, it is highly recommended that you take it seriously, not with a pinch of salt. It is essential that you work with each step in order to see the results you seek or want. Too many individuals have rushed through the processes of creating passive income, hoping to start making money within a few weeks. The steps outlined in this book will show you how to get it done.

4. Put everything together and be ready to put in some hard work and dedication. You will eventually be able to start earning the passive income that you have been dreaming about, which will remain elusive to many.

Although many people today want to earn their own passive income, it can be hard to work with. You will never be able to make any passive income if you don't put in any work or within a few weeks. But with the tips that will be shared in this book, you will be able to earn this kind of income and enjoy success within a short period.

Chapter 1: What is Passive Income?

Many people have heard of the words 'Passive income,' but only a few are curious enough to explore further. And sadly, even those who know what passive income is and how it can dramatically change their lives for the better will never experience it. Yes, they do love the idea of making a side income as a result of a side hustle while retaining their regular 9-5 jobs. Many even fantasize about going on vacations in the Bahamas or the Cayman Islands and generally enjoying life.

A lot comes with having a passive income because it is not just something that you turn your attention to when you feel like it. The truth of the matter is that you will need to work hard at first before the going becomes good, and that is if you have taken the right steps or done the right things. Over time, that hard work you put in when you started the journey will begin to pay off, and for many years to come, fetching you a good income weekly or monthly.

Therefore, what do you need to know about passive income? Here's what you need to know about creating a passive income and what it entails to build businesses that generate passive income

What is passive income?

Passive income can be a form of earning money that anyone can get and from any endeavor. It could be from a rental property or something else that does not require your active involvement day in, day out.

Passive income is taxable, just like regular active income, in the United States. However, the IRS treats this type of income a bit differently than other types of income. Nevertheless, it is an excellent way to make some income on real estate, investments as well as other kinds of endeavors without the need for you to have a direct relationship with each day.

To get a better understanding of passive income, it is essential to, first of all, take a look at the major types of income that are presently available. There are 3 of these that you can focus on building: portfolio income, active income, and passive income.

Passive income is a term that has changed a lot over the past few years. The way most people see it these days is far different from how it was in the past, which is a good thing. All that is required now is to learn more about it as much as you can, as well as how this kind of income works so that you can apply all you learn to make it work for you.

As a rule, a passive income is used to define any money you earn on a regular basis with very little – and sometimes – no effort on your part. It does sound like a dream come true; who wouldn't want to sit back and relax without having to do anything, yet money keeps trickling into your bank account.

There are different types of passive income that you can work with. The most popular or common options that are presently available include peer to peer, real estate, limited partnership, investing in dividend stocks, or any other enterprise.

If you see passive income as a good or positive thing, then you must be a booster of work at home. And you should be ready to lead a 'Be your own boss' kind of lifestyle. The types of earning you may earn at first may be small, but if you work hard, the income will eventually grow and become successful.

Why Should You Build Passive Income?

The greatest wealth-building tool is your income, which usually requires your active participation in the form of a full-time, 9-5 job. No matter how much you earn, working your 9-5 job, you won't say "No" to make some extra side income without too much sweat, blood, and time commitment.

Several benefits are associated with earning income passively. When you build a passive income, it does the following:

- Boosts your wealth-building plan
- Protects you from a sudden and complete loss of income if you lose your job
- Creates a rare opportunity to retire early
- It provides another stream of income, especially when you can no longer hold down a 9-5 job or outlast your retirement fund.

How Much Money Can You Make Passively?

What you need to know straight away is that passive income will not make you wealthy overnight. So, get rid of any get-rich-quick schemes or thoughts that may be passing through your mind.

However, if you follow the highly profitable passive income options that will be outlined later on in this uique book, you will be able to build a lot of serious money in the long run. You could make any amount from a few hundred dollars to hundreds of thousands of dollars, depending on the stream of income you opt for.

Types of Passive Income

Here are the types of passive income you need to know:

Property

Rental properties can be said to be passive income, though with a couple of exceptions. If you get involved in the real estate industry or become a professional in the industry, any rental income you make usually counts as an active income. If you own a space and rent it out to a partnership where you run your day-to-day business or corporation, it cannot be counted as a passive income source.

The only way it will count as passive income is if the lease was signed before 1988, which implies that you have virtually been grandfathered into having that income. According to the IRS Passive Activity and At-Risk Rules: 'It doesn't matter whether or not the use is under a service contract, a lease, or some other arrangement.'

Nevertheless, income generated from leasing land does not qualify as passive income. But then, as a landowner, you can benefit from passive income loss rules if that property nets a loss during the tax year. As for holding land for investment, all earnings are considered active.

Self-charged interest

When money is loaned to an S-corporation or a partnership that acts as a pass-through entity – i.e., a business that is designed to minimize the effects of double taxation – by the entity's owner, the interest generated on that loan to the portfolio income qualifies as passive income.

Certain self-charged deductions or interest income may be treated as passive activity deductions or passive activity gross income if the loan proceeds are used in a passive activity.

'No Material Participation' in a Business

Let's say you put $200,000 into a candy store after having an agreement with the owners that they will pay you a percentage of earnings, it will be considered passive income. But only if you do not directly participate in running the business in any meaningful way apart from placing the investment. The IRS states that if you help in managing the organization with the owners, your income will be perceived as active because you offered 'material participation.'

The IRS has set standards for material participation that include:

- If you have participated in up to 100 hours, which is as much as any other individual involved in the activity, it may be defined as material participation.

- If you have dedicated over 500 hours to an activity or business from which you are profiting, that is referred to as material participation.
- If your participation in an activity or business has been 'substantially all' of the involvement within that tax year, it is known as material participation.

Chapter 2: The 7 Streams of Income of Most Millionaires

Are you one of the numerous individuals out there with only one stream of income? Do you even know the average millionaire has more than 3 streams of income? Perhaps, that explains why they got rich so fast while you are still grinding at your daily or regular 9-to-5 job, barely making enough before the next payday. There is a lot much money out there to be made, but if you are not doing the right things to channel the money your way, you will remain the way you are for many years to come.

So, how many streams of legitimate income are you even aware of? The internet is rife with lots of get-rich-quick hype and glorification on how to become an overnight millionaire. But the truth is that many lots of people have grown comfortable living average lifestyles. Many have resigned to living mediocre lives, with no desire or drive to earn a great deal of money than they need to live fairly comfortably. It seems most people want to stop trading time for money or minimize the time they spend making some money.

To live comfortably holds different meanings to different people; some believe that living comfortably means they earn enough to get by, while others believe that becoming a millionaire is the only guarantee to live comfortably.

However, one thing that most people have, whether they were born with silver spoons – or wooden spoons as the case may be – is time. And every one goes through life trying to balance the time spent with family, the time spent working, and other aspects of life.

Here are the 7 income streams of millionaires:

1. Earned income

This is the money you earn when you spend your time or do something, i.e., the money you make in your day-to-day job, the salary you are paid when you work for an organization or someone.

This is where the quality of most salary earners suffers the most since they trade time for money. Jobs, in most cases, pay you just enough to stay above the 'broke' level. Perhaps that is why someone somewhere took every letter of the word 'job' and turned it into an acronym for 'Just Over Broke.'

The primary reason why most people hold down jobs is that they do not want to think beyond making money by trading their time because a job provides them with a reasonably comfortable income or zone. They love to remain in this comfort zone with the promise of earning some money when they reach their golden years.

But the problem with such a comfort zone is that it becomes your greatest enemy and will prevent you from reaching for an extraordinary life. The world is your oyster, but you may spend the productive years of your life in this income category. And you may never have enough money to lead a wealthy and extraordinary life.

If you can only come out from your comfort zone, defeating your life's biggest enemy, your life will improve drastically.

2. Interest income

This is the money you earn as a result of lending your money to a friend or colleague. For example, the extra money you make when you put your money in a bank, lend a colleague to launch a thriving business or government for purchasing Treasury Bills, etc. are interest income.

This is a great and excelent source of passive income in which your active involvement is not required as soon as the investment is made. Despite this, however, many people seriously doubt the efficacy of 'Interest Income' and its potential to generate wealth.

But its actual effect is felt when you consider the power of compounding. This is the perfect example of passive income as it involves minimum risk and even beats some of the income streams of most millionaires on this list hands down.

3. Profit income

This is the money you earn when you sell a product or item for more than it costs you to make or produce. For instance, most brick-and-mortar businesses sell products at a profit, at the wholesale or retail level. Manufacturers and distributors do the same thing. If you must earn profits, then you need to be an entrepreneur.

To start earning profit income, you may need a considerable investment as a start or launch a small business with a small investment. However, this could eat into your time, at least when you are still in the initial stages. But if you keep at it and learn to manage it incredibly well by automating some aspects of it, you will start earning remarkable profits. Entrepreneurship requires a different kind of mindset, which is not the same as those who love earned income via salaries, and so on.

Most people who are used to earning salaries usually find it pretty difficult to make a move to entrepreneurship, even if they want to at any stage of their illustrious career or life. The primary reason for this is the lack the courage to step out of their comfort zones and take steps into unchartered waters. And in most cases, this lack of guts may be relatively justified because of the family's needs and constraints.

To be a very successful entrepreneur, one who starts earning steady profits, the first thing you should do is identify a product or service. This product or service should be sellable, and you should be able to manage it as well as your clients.

Many people limit themselves to the 'Earned Income' and 'Profit Income' levels all their lives, forgetting that there are other serious ways of making money legitimately.

4. Dividend income

This is another stream of income that you should consider. Dividend Income is equally passive, and the additional benefit is that you will become a shareholder of an organization. This is the money you receive as a return or income on shares of an organization you own.

A perfect example is a dividend that most organizations announce or declare at the end of every year. Despite the efficacy of dividend income, many people today ignore this highly lucrative stream of income.

Take steps to invest smartly on the ex-dividend dates of highly successful blue-chip companies. The amount of money you will earn annually will far exceed that of

'Interest Income,' especially since you are now party to the Capital Gains that the share price undergoes. Therefore, it is one of the vital instruments that is highly recommended by millionaires for generating adequate and steady Cash Flow while getting a very good income.

5. Rental income

This is the money you make when you rent out an asset that belongs to you, such as a house or an entire building. This source of income is far better than others on this list, though there are a few drawbacks that must be mentioned.

First of all, the biggest drawback of this type of income is the amount of money required to purchase or create such an asset that will generate consistent rental income. The hugeness of that amount of money can make it impossible for you to develop or have such assets throughout your lifetime. The only way this could be possible, especially if you always limit yourself to the 'Earned Income' level, is to have other trusted sources of regular income.

For instance, you can start earning 'Dividend Income' or 'Income Interest' with an investment that starts from $500 or more. And when compound interest sets in, you are on your way to earning rental income with careful management on your part.

Another drawback has to do with the liquidity of the asset. It is often difficult to liquefy assets that generate Rental income quickly, especially when you move or change residence or in times of need or balance your portfolio mix.

6. Capital Gains

This is the money you receive when an asset that you own increases in value. For instance, when you purchase shares at $10 and sell it off at $12, the $2 is referred to as capital gains. The same can be applied when you buy a house at $150,000 and sell it for $200,000; the $20,000 is your capital gains.

Every country has different tax laws on capital gains, and you can even learn ways to come around taxes when the time comes.

7. Royalty income

You can only get this type of income when you allow someone else to use your ideas, products, or processes. That person makes all the revenue as well as all the hard work while you sit back and receive a small percentage of whatever that person earns.

For instance, let's say you have McDonald's Franchise; the royalty you sent to McDonald's for using their logo, marketing, processes, etc. is royalty income for them. If you write and sell books, you will get paid for every copy of the book that is sold.

The biggest challenge you may encounter or face when trying to get into this income level is to create something exceptionally unique and then make it repeatable. This will require special skills in order to create such an asset.

But the beautiful thing is that as soon as you create that asset, there is practically no limit to the amount of money that you can make or earn.

These are the 7 streams of income of most millionaires you see today. This is not to imply that all millionaires must have all of these 7 income streams. For instance, Warren Buffet is the billionaire that was quoted as saying, 'If you do not find a way to make money while you sleep, you will work all the days of your life.' Despite his status, he does not make most of his money from all the 7 streams of income outlined in this chapter. Buffet became a millionaire via Capital Gains and Dividend Income.

However, he did not get into Capital Gains on everything; in fact, he specialized in a tiny aspect, which is Capital Gains of organizations in the stock market. Then he honed his skills continually, year in, year out in valuing companies and re-investing in them until he eventually became a millionaire, and then a billionaire.

Bill Gates, who was once, the wealthiest individual in the world, generated most of his income via 'Royalty Income' and 'Profit Income.' The billionaire created an organization as well as an asset known as 'Windows.' He used the asset to change the way everyone interacts with computers today. Gates became so good by earning stupendous amounts of money through the income models discussed earlier. He climbed up the charts, appearing in Forbes magazine as one of the wealthiest individuals in the world.

There are several millionaires out there today who earned that status via the 'Profit Income' model. But then, they were pretty good at whatever it was they were doing. Perform enough research online, and you will come across individuals who became millionaires from Royalty Income.

Therefore, start paying more attention to what you can do right now from at least one of these streams of income outlined in this chapter. And from there, start taking steps to become the best you can be in a small but profitable niche.

'Earned Income' involves trading time for money, and this puts a severe limit on the amount of money you can make since there is a limit to the number of hours you can put in a day. All other income streams are not dependent on time; therefore, you can leverage time exceptionally well to generate wealth.

So, take enough time to choose your streams. You will be taking a substantial financial risk if you depend on only one source of income where you need to be actively involved. Get more details about each income stream so that you can understand them even more. Then take steps to try them out. This could be one of the most life-changing or earth-shaking decisions you could make, which will affect not only you but also generations after you.

Chapter 3: Top 20 Best Future Business Ideas for 2020-2030

The future that we craved for many years ago is here, and the future that is to come will be created by our actions today.

Therefore, if you really want to jump on the bandwagon and create businesses that will practically outlive you, the best time to start is now. You should know that small businesses are not going anywhere anytime soon and the same can be said of the internet.

Online marketing is getting set to become the most important thing for small businesses from 2020 to 2030. There are presently about 30 million small businesses in the United States alone. But that is not an indication that you shouldn't create yours because there is always space for more companies that offer value to its target market.

So, here are the top 55 best future business ideas for 2020 to 2030:

1. Internet Infrastructure

Businesses are presently restructuring and have increased their online interactions. And this massive reconstruction has created a growing need for advanced internet structure.

Internet infrastructure is projected to see an incredibly massive growth of 2.2 percent from 2020 to 2025. The expected generated revenue of this enormous business opportunity will be more than $37 million by the end of 2020.

Internet infrastructure connects internet users and allows them to interact with anyone in the world. Organizations are always looking for feasible solutions to deal with their internet demands and operate what is known as 'high-capacity backbones.'

High–capacity backbones are the process of connecting NAP (Network Access Protection) on a universal scale. This means that business owners can control the overall health of their computers and associated policies.

Here are several benefits for any business that chooses its own internet infrastructure:

- Security
- Efficient and scalable
- Location independence
- Cost-effective

More businesses will undoubtedly carry out daily transactions on the internet, thereby driving the demand for an effective and affordable solution like this one.

2. Amazon FBA Business

Amazon FBA (Fulfillment by Amazon) allows everyday people to source several physical products abroad and launch your unique brand. And the lovely thing about FBA is that you do not have to maintain inventory, deal or ship with returns yourself.

One common thing that FBA sellers do is to load up extra bonuses/items onto a suitable product in a bid to add even more value. For instance, selling a zucchini spiral spaghetti maker makes a lot of sense. However, you can add more value by adding a few cookbooks along with a skin peeler.

Building this business requires perseverance and a lot of patience. The primary factor that determines success is the product you pick. If you choose a product you don't connect with, you can quickly liquid your inventory by running paid Google or Facebook ads in order to recover your inventory expenses.

And as soon as the product ranks high on search engines and starts receiving a decent amount of good reviews from happy and satisfied customers, you have successfully built for yourself a piece of property on the web that will keep generating passive income for you for life which is a pretty good feeling.

The truth is that there are several moving parts to this business that you have to master. So, search for and invest in a good course that will show you how to go about it.

3. Chatbots

Chatbots are the rave of the moment nowadays, and that is because many organizations utilize them to handle minor customer service interactions personally and quickly. Research has shown that the outlook of these mini assistants is expected to reach a 136 percent growth rate over the next eighteen months.

You can invest in the design and implementation of a Chabot. It is imperative to hit up the perfect clientele to get optimal cash for your hard work. Therefore, you can readily get in touch with the following companies in order to get a high ROI on your investment:

- Bloggers
- Marketing agencies
- Gyms and fitness centers
- Authors
- Realtors
- Insurance agencies

Chatbots are potential passive income generators if you know what you are doing.

4. Drones

Starting a drone business is now more viable than ever, especially due to the many uses for drones in today's fast-paced market. Several industries use drones so much that researchers have projected the drone industry to be worth more than $100 billion by the end of 2020.

A variety of different models and prices exist today, which small businesses can capitalize on in order to create a nice stockpile of drones for use. Drones can be used for the following:

- Security
- Agriculture
- Search and rescue
- Surveying land

Corporations and governments continue to explore numerous ways to capture vital data and footage using drones.

5. Create an Online Course

Creating an online course is another digital product that has the potential to generate a steady stream of passive income. If you are an expert or possess a marketable skill, you can create a series of audio recordings or videos to impart your knowledge.

You may prefer to create eBooks, though this requires a lot of work upfront, especially if you are not conversant with creating courses. But if you eventually do, eBooks that get updated from time to time can turn to a profitable avenue for passive income.

There are several online platforms for course creators to use, such as Teachable, Udemy, Google Open Online Education, and Thinkific. There are profitable markets for different kinds of courses, from how to code to how to perform strength exercises.

Most people have skills and knowledge which they can turn into a course. But the #1 challenge centers more on finding the energy and time to start and finish creating the course and attracting the right audience or customers who will purchase the course.

6. Virtual Medical Appointment System

Do you know that the healthcare system – as a whole – has lost more than $150 billion within a calendar year as a result of appointment no-shows. You can imagine the devastating impact on independent clinics and hospitals.

You can fill this void by developing an interactive, affordable, and reliable online medical appointment system that can help these small clinics and hospitals fine-tune their patient notification and follow-up processes.

This is an extraordinary innovation that is incredibly high in demand and will continue to expand as the new decade progresses.

7. Biometric Sensor and Security Company

Effective, highly efficient, and secure are helpful aspects to performing business in 2020. And one that checks off all of the boxes is biometric sensors.

Biometric sensors are generally used to gather individuals' biological characteristics such as fingerprints, voice recognition, iris identification, facial images, and so on. Any behavioral or psychological characteristics will do the trick in ensuring that the biometric sensor readily identifies and verifies security and authenticity.

The biometrics market, which is 100 percent automated, is worth more than $16 billion and even projected to see a CAGE of approximately 35.5 percent from 2020-2025. However, there are both advantages and disadvantages that this system has. Here are the benefits and drawbacks of Biometric Security:

Pros

- Allows physical access to internal resources, buildings as well as computer systems without the risk of any security breach. It also strengthens existing security systems that utilize password-only measures.

- Automated calculation of employee hours minimizes manual and paper tracking systems that save companies both time and money.

Cons

- Initial set-up costs are significant
- Limited privacy for users
- There is still a risk of hackers or data breaches

8. DDoS Cyber Attack Prevention Security Company

DDoS (denial of service) attack is a desperately harmful or malicious endeavor designed to disrupt the traffic to your network or a computer server. The primary goal of a DDoS attack is to ensure your online service remains unavailable to your customers.

This comes about by flooding your service or network with lots of bogus requests, thereby impeding legitimate traffic from accessing your website. As you will agree, this is not nice and can even be very disruptive for business owners or startups.

DDoS attacks can be very costly to root, which will cost the company a lot of money to repair the damage and cost the firm its potential customers. The only way to stop these trouble-makers in their tracks is by hiring a DDoS cyber-attack prevention security company.

Research has shown that the DDoS protection and mitigation market is expected to reach up to $9.10 billion by 2025. And it is projected to have a CAGR of 24.9 percent from 2020 to 2025, which tells you that the perfect time to enter the industry is now.

The number of attacks keeps growing steadily, making more individuals and business owners proactively enlist the professional service and assistance of DDoS security companies. These security companies handle the following:

- Establish security infrastructure components
- Stop DDoS attacks within minutes, thereby minimizing any or all disruption to your businesses.
- Enhanced flexibility that blends third-party and in-house resources like dedicated and cloud server hosting
- Cleans up all the mess and quickly reroutes all legitimate traffic to your network.

9. Stem Cell Therapy

The revenue-generating potential of stem cell therapy is so enormous that it is somewhat surprising all the big boys are not in this industry.

Experts have predicted that stem cell therapy will continuously experience a massive growth with a CAGR of 27.99 percent over the next ten years. And the best part is that entrepreneurs without a scientific or medical background can reap the massive and growing income potential.

There are more than a few ways you can tap into this growing market. For instance, you can start a testing lab, a stem cell bank, or even use stem cells in health and beauty products. Or you may opt to invest heavily into any of these options stated below:

- Invest in stem cell stocks
- Become an affiliate or distributor for dedicated websites
- Open a 'for profit' stem cell unit or clinic or opt for the mobile route in order to minimize costs.

10.   Senior At-Home Care

It always matters a lot to ensure your loved ones retain their independence and comfort at all times. This will help to bypass concerns about the level of compassion and care your family member will receive.

For seniors who are still functional, at-home seniors are the best alternative for them as nursing home costs rise significantly high while homes are getting even more crowded these days. Trained staff and service providers assist seniors with appointments, medication as well as other household duties or activity. They are also highly skilled in handling different types of equipment a senior may require at any time of the day.

Hiring a home health assistant or aide is something that many families are willing to do because it saves them tons of money, especially after carrying out cost comparisons. Any business model that supports families of all backgrounds and situations is one worth investing in.

According to recent statistics, by 2030, one out of every 5 Americans will be 65 years or older, which opens a myriad of opportunities for senior at-home care businesses such as:

- Meal prep
- House cleaning and errands
- Non-medical in-home care
- Companion
- Personal care assistance
- Nutrition and fitness consulting
- Medical claims assistance
- Money management and financial planning
- Property management

You can maximize your earning potential when you launch this future business idea.

Chapter 4: Top 20 Best Future Business Ideas for 2020-2030 (Part II)

Continuing from where the last chapter ended...

1. Asteroid Mining

Do you know that precious material like silver, gold, diamonds, and platinum are found all over space? Space travel is still developing and is expected to become even more advanced. One of the first issues that corporations will address will have to do with mining asteroid for precious minerals like diamond and gold.

This is a serious and major undertaking that may not even be feasible until 2030. However, it is worth investing in, and many big companies are presently and extremely focused on this.

Research has shown that even a tiny section of space could be worth more than double the Earth's entire wealth. This means that the first set of individuals who manage to get a spacecraft to a resource-loaded asteroid could quickly become the world's wealthiest people.

Investing in asteroid mining could be capital-intensive as you may need to create robots and drones that will aid in drilling as well as mining asteroids. Whichever way you see it, this is an industry with a lot of incredible potentials and, of course, for people who are daring enough to try the impossible.

2. eCommerce

The world has virtually moved online, changing almost everything from the way things are purchased to delivery at your doorstep. Businesses that are not taking a leaf from the eCommerce industry run the risk of getting left behind.

This year alone, it has an estimated that consumers in the United States will spend more than $709 billion on eCommerce, representing a growth rate of 18 percent. This is slated to hit up to $4.9 trillion by 2021.

One thing is sure: eCommerce is the retail market tomorrow. And what makes eCommerce unique is that you do not even have to own or make the products you sell. All that you need to do is to utilize another aspect of eCommerce known as Dropshipping.

You can also choose to be an affiliate, a system of selling products which is explained later on. The truth is that the financial advantages of running an eCommerce business are staggering. Take a look at the following eCommerce highlights:

- Higher ROIs
- Elevated business reach
- Easy to track
- More search engine traffic
- Logistically solid
- Flexible, scalable, and profitable
- Automated product delivery systems

There is no better period to get online than now because, by 2030, the majority of shopping will be conducted online, i.e., digitally. Consumers will only use brick and mortar establishments as an experience. And such businesses will need to make considerable changes such as price reductions and specialization if they hope to stay in the game extensively.

3. Wallet Payment Solution

Wallet payment solutions have been somewhat slow to catch on in the U.S.A. Nevertheless, it is a market that is on its way to becoming a national corporation.

Wallet payment has to do with monetary transactions made with a virtual or digital wallet via a software program. It securely stores people's payment details and ensures purchases are super-easy.

This money-making concept is somewhat unknown in the United States because most people living in the country possess credit and debit cards, which are convenient, simple, and trusted means of payment.

Nevertheless, wallet payment solutions are taking some countries – such as China and India – by storm. Therefore, it is merely a question of time before the trend will take hold in the U.S. as well as other parts of the globe. It is currently projected to be worth an estimated and whopping $130 billion by the end of 2020.

This market has some established and hefty competition like Masterpass, ApplePay, and Chase Pay. However, it is just proof that there is a lot of money to be made in this industry since these brands are players there.

You can secure profitability in this industry that will soon change the entire trajectory of the world's future within a short time.

4. Virtual Interior Design Consulting

Interior design is all about placement and visuals, as well as the ability to transform a space into a comfortable and scenic sanctuary for clients.

The advent and rise of technology have made it possible for enthusiasts to launch an interior design business and run it from the sanctuary of their homes with nothing but a laptop, camera gear, tablet, software, and social media.

You will see the exterior and interior of a client's office space or property via the lens of your camera. Then, the next thing that you should do is to create stunning mockups for your clients, send them over, and consult regarding the next step to take.

As you well know, the marketing of your new remote interior design and consulting business will depend significantly on social media, your official website as well as getting in touch with your current connections within your network while working hard to create new ones.

5. Affiliate Marketing

Affiliate Marketing involves the promotion of someone else's products – using any means at your disposal – that you love or have tried and tested. And if someone purchases that product based on your promotion efforts and testimonials, you will receive a commission.

This is an online marketing model that you can leverage without doing the tough job of creating the product, handling customer complaints or support, and so on.

This is a business model that works incredibly well that up to 81 percent of businesses are currently taking advantage of this model in one way or the other. And if you set things up the right way, you can be making money passively or in your sleep for many years to come as long as your niche site remains live on the web.

6. IT Service and Support

The face of the corporate world will eventually be digital since more and more businesses, and individuals will continue to rely even more heavily on the internet as well as social media platforms. There will be a proliferation of software and hardware to contend favorably with this immense growth.

These vital tools will ultimately generate an influx in demand for both IT service and support enterprises. The projected growth rate for IT services is up to 22 percent in 2020 alone. Software development and other facets are seeing upwards of 32 percent growth rate, making it one of the best future business ideas to explore today.

Many business and individuals from around the world will need help with setup and maintenance and troubleshooting issues. This is because the most of the population in the United States is astonishingly clueless when it comes to tech stuff.

Remarkable advancements in technology around Cloud computing, Blockchain, AI, and even elevated automation will leave some of the most tech-savvy individuals and organizations seeking professional assistance. This is where you will come in as the messiah, especially if you love tech stuff or prefer to be called a tech nerd.

The options within the IT service and support niche are numerous, and this includes:

- IT Managers
- Database Admins
- Product Manager
- Software Inventory
- Blockchain Engineer
- Cloud Architect
- DevOps Designer
- Artificial Intelligence Engineer of AI Engineer

This is just a small section of an extensive list that you can explore to your satisfaction.

7. VR Live Events

Is there an annual conference that you can't make or want to enjoy your favorite band while still on tour? Do you even know that you can get a ticket for those events and experience them as if you were there in the flesh from your study or living room?

This is made possible thanks to VR, which helps individuals worldwide to readily access live events, helping the hosts generate mouth-watering and untold revenue.

At present, the revenue for virtual events is up to $78 billion, and projections currently suggest that this number will significantly grow to a breathtaking $774 billion by 2030.

Believe it or not, everything from conferences and exhibitions to music concerts is headed in the direction of virtual implementation. This implies that there won't be a limit to the sale of tickets based on the availability of space as it will now be possible to sell hundreds of millions of tickets to in-person and virtual spectators.

The adoption of VR for the modern world was not expected to take off as it did, but the scourge of the pandemic saw to it. The industry has been predicted to witness an unbelievable CAGR of 33.47 percent, which speaks volumes about its profitability for businesses in the space.

As it stands, the projected growth rate will even be much higher than this.

8. Virtual Event Planning Platform

Event planning has now taken on a new look and is presently leaning even more on online and virtual affairs.

Video streaming services have successfully eliminated geographical constraints, thereby allowing event planners to host exceptional virtual events to remote audiences. Embracing this virtual event to maintain cash flow and profitability is the best way for event planners to stay in business in these modern times.

To execute stellar events online, the following crucial fundamentals must be in place:

- Pick your platform
- Understand the needs as well as the expectations of your audience
- Develop or create your format and how you intend to make your event unique
- Determine the venue, day, and time
- Choose an MC or host that can captivate your audience and is highly entertaining.
- Always keep it simple, short, and to the point.

Event planners provide both a service and an experience. This is a business model that will continue to generate substantial profits with some creativity and the right infrastructure, as well as the willingness to shift to online solutions.

9. Tele and Video Conferencing

The pandemic has touched all aspects of the economy, especially face-to-face interactions and regular office work. It has resulted in the significant adoption of teleconferencing and video conferencing, and businesses like Zoom has climbed up Forbes' list, thanks to massive signups and subscriptions from multi-national organizations. The virtual meetings hosted by Zoom over the past few months cannot be quantified.

This can only mean one thing: video conferencing and teleconferencing are the new norms on how to conduct business transactions. From business communication and networking, teleconferencing provides individuals and associates worldwide the opportunity and ability to maintain highly productive or effective communication even amid the global pandemic.

The education industry has also taken a hit and has adopted teleconferencing and video conferencing as the best way to overcome the throes of COVID-19.

What if you had foreseen this circumstance and bought shares or even owned at least one of these teleconferencing and video conferencing conglomerates? That would have been cool, isn't it? Well, it is not too late because this business venture still has a futuristic appeal.

According to a well-researched publication, teleconferencing and video conferencing have been projected to see a growth rate of approximately 9.8 percent from 2020-2026. And it will purportedly reach a market value of more than $6 billion in the United States of America alone. This is too huge a pie to pass up, especially if you want to get in on the action in this growing industry that is reaching record highs and breaking barriers left, right, and center.

Teleconferencing, as well as video conferencing, efficiently delivers alternate options in order to maintain productivity, efficiency, and personalization.

10.   eSports

eSports offer a gamer's paradise with the competitive edge of live competitions. Organized tournaments in several sports –via video games – have started taking on a digital presence, as well as a lot of people around the world are taking notice.

And with the way the popularity of eSports is growing, it is presently estimated that viewership will see a CAGR of 9 percent from 2020-2023, and will purportedly fetch revenues that is more than 4646 million by the end of that stipulated time frame.

Game enthusiasts love the social component of eSports, and you will agree that we are a highly competitive bunch in any field. Live streaming, and social media platforms, are generally the driving forces behind the remarkable growth of this industry with no sign of slowing down.

And you can take a slice of this cake by jumping in on the action today. You can launch an eSports platform of your own as long as you are ready to adhere to the following recommendations:

- Choose your ideal target market and geographical area.
- Hone down the niche; pick one popular sport that you love and get after it.
- Organize your team and don't forget to include branding
- Put your infrastructure in place with the appropriate hardware. This should include a user-friendly eSports website.
- Secure sponsorships in order to fund this endeavor to enable you to compete at an elevated position.
- Remember to pick a location and aggressively promote your team.
- Fans, as well as additional recruitment options, is a must.

There is no doubt that eSports is presently revolutionizing virtual, competitive gaming and is considered one of the best future business ideas to adopt for 2020-2030. You can conduct in-depth research to ascertain what it takes to be incredibly successful in this 21st-century business.

In the next two chapters, we will be taking a look at Facebook Marketing and YouTube Marketing. Implementing these marketing strategies incredibly well has the potential of generating passive income for you.

Chapter 5: Facebook Marketing

In the first few years of social media networking, MySpace was the big boy. Between 2003 and 2006, it grew extraordinarily to 100 million users, and by June 2006, the website was even more visited than Google. Then came Facebook.

By 2008, Facebook had dramatically surpassed MySpace in global users and U.S. users about a year later. And as MySpace severely declined (it plummeted to about 25 million users as of June 2012), some businesses started to wonder about making significant advertising investments in Facebook. They feared it might also be displaced as MySpace was. But that was not the case.

In fact, globally, it's the biggest social media platform, with over 2.27 billion active users and almost 1.5 billion of whom are very active each day.

You will still find the best marketing opportunities on the world's biggest social network, and that is not going to change anytime soon. Spending time learning Facebook marketing is defintely worth the investment.

You are about to discover the basics or fundamentals of how to use Facebook to your utmost advantage. The book targets beginners or neophytes who want an introduction to marketing their numerous businesses on the world's #1 social media network.

What is Facebook marketing?

Facebook marketing refers to the creation—and active usage— of a Facebook page as a channel for communication, maintaining contact with and also attracting numerous users or potential clients. Facebook actively provides for this as it allows users to create individual profiles or business pages for organizations, firms, or any group attempting to develop a fan base for a product, service, or brand.

Who Can Utilize Facebook Marketing?

Every business should be using Facebook. It is as crucial as having a business website page—and much easier to create. Whether you represent an NGO or big brand or even a small startup that employs a handful of people, you can be sure that some portion of your customers is on Facebook. Commonly, Facebook marketing is used by:

- Brands. Electronics, food, home goods, and restaurants—nearly any kind of brand can be seriously promoted on Facebook, turning passive users or customers into active and raving fans who follow news of promotions and developments and share with friends on the platform.

- Personalities. Celebrities, musicians, authors, syndicated columnists—anybody who makes their legitimate money by being known- want to be known by as many individuals as possible on Facebook.
- Local businesses. Whether a business is a franchise of a larger company or family-owned, a Facebook Page can be used to transform a local customer base into a raving fan base that will frequently visit your store.
- Non-profit organizations. Charities, public service campaigns, and political groups can all leverage the natural sharing capabilities of Facebook.

Is your audience on Facebook?

Is your audience even on Facebook? The answer is, in all probability.

The most recent data shows that every age uses at least one social media network site, with younger users with higher percentages.

Moreover, both men and women use social media in approximately equal numbers.

And when it comes to which social media network many people use, Facebook dominates the list. As of January 2018, 68 percent of Americans used Facebook, with Instagram in distant second place with 35 percent.

Put differently, no matter what age group you are targeting, there will be more than enough of such users on Facebook.

Here's how to get little things set up and start promoting your products or services through Facebook;

Market with Facebook Pages

The first Facebook marketing tool for brands is Facebook Pages. Like a personal Facebook profile, a Page is the virtual hub of information for your brand, be it an organization, service, product, or even a celebrity or expert.

Facebook users can always "Like" a page they are interested in and also "Follow" it, which means they will automatically start receiving updates from that particular Page in their news feed.

But to see the posts every time they put up online, you need to click the option to view posts first. Otherwise, it is highly likely you won't see the updates because Facebook wants Pages to readily boost posts (by paying) for more visibility and reach.

So when you get Facebook users to like your Page, it is often considered a good idea to recommend they follow you so that they can see your posts first. It will save you lots of your hard-earned money if you do not have to boost posts as often or often.

There are a few major differences to take note of between Facebook Pages and Facebook Profiles. Connecting with someone as a personal profile will require both of you to confirm the friendship request.

When you have a Page, Facebook users can 'Like' and 'Follow' without your approval.

Another significant difference is that there are practically no limits to the number of users that can 'Like' your Facebook Page. If you have a personal/profile account, you cannot have more than 5,000 friends. But a Facebook Page can have thousands or even millions of people who 'like' it.

The best part of Pages is that they are free and very easy to set up. You can build a new Page in the next 15 minutes and make it look as professional as that of a Fortune 500 company.

The only downside is that—they can be tough to get off the ground. Unless you are a celebrity or notable brands like BMW or Coke, it takes a lot of work to get more people to 'like' your Page.

But if you are going to start with this, you will need to set up a professional page. Here is how to go about it:

How to set up the Ideal Facebook Page

It is quite unfortunate that many organizations do not use Facebook Pages to their full potential. Worse, some brands even use them very poorly and actually hurt their credibility.

The following guidelines will help you avoid making those silly mistakes;

Good Profile photo and cover image

Your profile photo should be your brand logo. The cover image, however, is a different story. This is because it is really up to you to decide what to put here. Some brands use photos of employees, while others use artwork and put their contact information in the cover image. M&Ms, for instance, does a great job blending their logo, characters, and product into their photos.

Pick and use a photo that will enhance your Page and catch the attention of your visitors.

The "About" section

The "About" section is placed immediately below your company logo. This is your best chance to tell anyone coming to your Page what your business does. It is short, so do not try to fit everything in. In the full 'About' section, make sure to add more details.

Explain what your organization or brand does, why you are unique, along with other interesting facts. Take your time to write it for your Facebook audience.

If you have a brick and mortar business, you can add a few more features like hours and locations. Remember to keep it as friendly as you can and as informal as possible. A casual tone works best on Facebook.

Post valuable info on your timeline

What you post to your timeline will show up in the news feeds of everyone who has "Liked" your Page, the same way it does when you post something to your personal profile.

So, make sure whatever you are posting is incredibly useful to your fans. Do not post continuous updates about the same thing. And do not post too often as this action may clog the news feeds of your fans.

Major brands like Apple usually post things they know will be very interesting to their fans, like product announcements or unique video ads.

Quick ideas for the type of information you should post to your wall include:

- New product announcements
- Links to articles related to your industry or company
- Links to your blog posts

- Links to useful online tools that your fans might find useful
- Coupon codes for followers to save on your products

Customized videos that will appeal to your target audience – You can use InVideo to make impactful and high-quality videos for Facebook

Again, make sure that your posts are interesting or helpful. Do not post more than a few times each day unless there is a special event going on.

One of the surest and dumbest ways to lose your followers is spam. If you don't do anything other than sending promotional blurbs about your brand without first of all add anything of value, you are going to have a tough time getting fans.

Before you post any update on your Facebook Page, ask yourself if it honestly adds value to the conversation.

Study your stats and results

Facebook Insights offers some excellent analytics for pages. Pay close attention to it. If you notice a big surge in fans (or even a significant drop off), take a look at what you may have posted recently to see if you can figure out a reason for the trend.

Then, start posting more of that kind of content (or less, if you're losing fans).

Using groups, the marketplace, and jobs

Over the last few years, Facebook has created several new features for different types of pages. Here is how to use them to each one to promote your company or brand.

How to Market with Facebook Groups

Facebook has had groups for some time. But they recently allow users to create brand-based groups associated with your Page.

First, you will need a Facebook Page for your brand. Then you can create a dedicated group to go with that Page. This allows you to have a little more control over the Facebook group since you can attach your company to it.

Facebook groups are very similar to dedicated discussion forums but with additional features that pages and profiles have (like a timeline). You can create groups that are related to your industry or product offerings in order to reach out to prospective customers.

The beautiful thing about Facebook Groups is that they're free, like Pages. They also have high levels of engagement. But the main downside is that they can be incredibly time-consuming.

To manage a Page, you may only need to check it once a day (or even less) to post something helpful and reply to comments.

With a Group, you'll want to monitor discussions continually, post relevant questions, and manage the members—perhaps several times a day.

How to Market Using Facebook Marketplace

If you have some products to sell, Facebook Marketplace might be the game-changer for you. It is very similar to Craigslist but built directly into the Facebook ecosystem.

Facebook's relatively newer feature is still revising, but it has enormous potential for eCommerce retailers as well as other types of product-based businesses.

When you list such products, they become searchable across Facebook, and other users can find them.

How to use Facebook Jobs

Finally, you can post jobs to Facebook. This is a newer feature, which was launched in the last few years or so.

Of course, this is not typical marketing like most people use on Facebook, but it can be beneficial if you are looking to hire someone.

Targeted Advertising

Facebook offers a highly targeted advertising platform.

You can create ads targeted that are specific to geographic areas, education levels, ages, and even the types of mobile devices used for browsing. Facebook also lets users hide ads that they do not like and "Like" a page right underneath an advertisement.

Because Facebook gathers a lot of demographic information about its users, the platform has one of the best and highly targeted ad programs online. You can target Facebook users based on virtually anything you might find in their profiles and track your success with every segment.

(It is also their most controversial feature, and one that has gotten them into some trouble recently. But let's set that aside in the meantime and focus on using these tools.)

Adverts can be run on a per-click or per-impression basis. Facebook shows marketers what bids are for ads that are similar to yours so that you know if your bid is in conformity with others within your industry. You can even set daily limits, so there is no risk of blowing your budget.

The advantage is that Facebook ads are compelling, and they are more likely to succeed than groups or pages since users can choose who sees the ads.

The downside is the cost. It is easy to run lots of Facebook ads without making anything back, so keep track of your budget.

Types of Facebook Ads

There are several ad sub-types you can choose from.

These include offers, video, leads, canvas, carousel, and many other types. Each one has a particular advantage and can be useful depending on the particular type of marketing you are embarking on.

One of the best methods to help you decide on the type of advert to run is to take a look at what your competitors are doing. You can go to the "Info and Ads" tab on any company page, and you can see what ads are active.

(You can also change the country if you like to see promotions in other regions.)

To create a new ad campaign, you will need to be the administrator of a page. From there, you can go into the Ad Manager.

It is a very complicated tool, but there is no need to start with all features

You should get used to the most important metrics and buttons for your brand and then build from there. You can always learn more a little later when you have used it for some time.

Powerful Targeting Options

Facebook has some of the most powerful, super-targeting tools of any online advertising program. You can target by anything on a user's profile. You might start with the location. You can specify the city, zip code, county, or even state.

This works incredibly well for local businesses. You can choose basic demographics, including age, relationship status, workplace, education (including both major and years of attendance), birthday, and much more.

You can target ads to Facebook users who have recently moved. So, if you own a gym in Hollywood and want to find all the individuals who recently moved to the neighborhood, you can easily target your ads and copy them.

You also can target users based on their interests. Say, for example, you have a new or unique product that is aimed at Cricket fans. You could enter Cricket in the 'Interests' field.

Or, maybe you have written a book, and you are sure that people who like another book in your genre will love yours. Enter the title of the book under 'Interests,' and you will specifically target only those users.

You can also target a private list of users. If you have an email list of of users that you want to target, you can easily use Facebook's Ads Manager to target those people.

Therefore, if you run a SaaS - Software as a service - business and have at least 200 people on your "prospect list," you can use their specific email addresses to target them with ads on Facebook.

Customize Your Ads

The other significant advantage of tightly targeted ads is that you can create different or several ads for different demographic groups. Highly targeted ads are going to garner much better results.

If you are targeting baseball fans, you might create individual ads for different popular teams. You could have one ad aimed explicitly at Cubs fans, one at Yankees fans, and another at Red Sox fans.

Then, you could have only those ads shown only to people who have previously indicated in their 'Interests' that they are raving fans of those baseball teams.

Or, let's say you have targeted people based on their love of a particular book, e.g., Harry Potter. You could mention that book in the advert itself in order to make it much more likely to catch their attention. Create different ads for different books in the genre and target accordingly.

Wrapping Up

Facebook isn't only powerful, but it's also flexible. No matter what type of establishment or organization you run, the social media platform has different marketing options to tailor your marketing efforts in order to fit your company, your budget, as well as your time constraints.

Yes, it can take a bit of time to get to know all of its features, but it's worth it. Facebook continues growing at a rapid pace, and every day it becomes a more indispensable part of social media marketing.

If Facebook is not presently part of your marketing campaign, it should be. Therefore, set aside some time to tinker around, launch a few test campaigns in order to see what happens.

Chapter 6: YouTube Marketing

YouTube is a social media platform where modern video culture was born. It has set trends and forms the demand for new video formats.

YouTube has given brands unprecedented opportunities to promote their products or services, create an image, and always keep up with the numerous requests of their target audiences.

Video content is presently ahead of other forms of advertising as outlined below:

- 59 percent of managers would rather watch a video than read a text;
- 64 percent of users are much more likely to purchase a product or service after watching a video about it;
- Most users stay on a page with the video almost 90 percent longer than on the page without it;
- Posts on social media networks with videos have 48 percent more views.

These figures suggest that creating original videos is not enough. The quality and content are what really matter. You need to develop an innovative video marketing strategy to capture the market.

In this chapter, the following shall be considered:

- Why YouTube marketing is a must-have for your marketing strategy
- How to create a highly successful YouTube marketing strategy in 2020
- The YouTube trends that will emerge
- The YouTube video formats you should focus on in the upcoming year.
- Video Content as a cutting-edge YouTube Marketing Strategy Foundation

Content marketing is something akin to a magic pill for many organizations. To present a product or service and make a prospective consumer want to buy it, a seller should totally influence the target audience. Podcasts, infographics, courses, texts, personal brand, etc. – i.e., everything is used.

But there is one promotion direction that completely overshadows the rest – and that is video marketing.

Video is the foundation of the YouTube marketing strategy, and here is how it becomes a robust tool of influence:

- Video easily simplifies user interaction with relevant information. Unlike texts or articles, videos don't force people to strain themselves to read.
- You can start the video and comprehend the information in the background.

- Videos combine both visual and sound effects to evoke emotions quickly and don't leave a user feeling somewhat indifferent.
- Video content is very easy to interact with – from smartphones, anytime and anywhere.

The most popular convenient platform for uploading and watching videos these days is YouTube, the third most-visited site after Google and Facebook. Up to 400 minutes of video are uploaded to YouTube every minute, and over 1 billion hours are viewed daily.

YouTube was initially designed for entertainment purposes, but today, it has grown significantly and is used for business promotion.

In 2019, almost 63 percent of brands used YouTube as a platform for the development of their business.

But how to make your compelling YouTube marketing strategy a real lead-generation machine in 2020 and beyond? At least, you should start applying the following YouTube trends and video formats.

YouTube Video Formats and Trends that You Must Use in 2020

A well-thought-out and carefully-planned YouTube marketing strategy should be based on the users' preferences, interests, and needs. Therefore, your task is to transform the commercial message into useful material, presented in one of the following YouTube formats:

- YouTube Live;
- Unboxing video;
- "How to" guides;
- Users decide;
- Videos around a particular routine;
- Trendy themes;
- 360-degree content;
- YouTube ads;
- Visual storytelling;
- YouTube as a search engine.

YouTube Live

This user interaction format is one of the most efficient marketing methods as it allows the viewer to interact with the speaker in real-time mode. The YouTube Live function has gradually replaced conventional, already-recorded videos; people spend eight times more time watching live videos on YouTube than watching ready-made or recorded videos.

Those who launch live broadcasts allow prospective consumers to influence the content: ask questions, clarify, and in such a way to feel more significant and valuable.

If you have never run YouTube live broadcasts before, it's high time you mastered this method.

Unboxing videos

Before making a purchase, eighty percent of users first watch a video tutorial or look for answers to their questions on YouTube. The platform has become a kind of unique search engine system where users can find answers to each of their requests. And how does YouTube affect users' buying experience? Several types of YouTube videos serve this particular purpose almost all at once:

Unpacking

Real-time shopping

Answers to questions – where and how to purchase a product.

Consumers choose brands when they feel some emotional connection. Thus, unboxing videos, which is one of the hottest YouTube trends, allows organizations to establish a positive experience with prospective clients and buyers. Video content is the most promising and shortest path to fall in mutual love with potential and existing customers.

A lovely idea is to address some influential YouTube bloggers to advertise your product through the unboxing video.

Users decide

One of the most promising trends you should add to your YouTube marketing strategy in 2020 and beyond is asking users for help. You can ask the viewers or subscribers what topic to deal with in the next video and their real interests.

For this, conduct surveys and polls, and urge users to leave their valued opinions in the comment section. All these will help you understand your subscribers' preferences and record great videos based on them. Thus, they are far more likely to achieve a well-defined business goal.

Videos around the routine

This type of video shows how celebrities and bloggers (or you) start their day, how they get super ready for bed at the end of the day, and so on. A similar format is in demand among YouTube subscribers. It helps them to efficiently organize the same daily tasks (morning coffee, makeup removal, house cleaning, training in the gym, etc.).

Plus, daily-actions-videos bring brands/bloggers closer to subscribers due to showing the stuff they have in common with users.

360-degree Content

YouTube video formats with 360-degree Content provide incredible immersion as well as unforgettable experiences for viewers. Users appear to be transferred to the picture they see, thereby reducing the distance between them and a product/brand.

360-Degree Content is one of the most efficient ways to present the product in detail and motivate buyers to purchase it. This transforms it into a lead-generation machine, especially when used in Facebook video ads.

YouTube Ads

Advertising on television is becoming less popular and profitable; it is replaced by advertising on YouTube. Over 75 percent of adults watch videos YouTube in prime time, which ultimately shortens the brands' reach for users. You can readily achieve high lead-generation results if you always implement the latest YouTube trends when running mobile advertising.

Visual storytelling

Users always want to be very close to the favorite celebrities and brands, so you should create videos that provide that feeling of proximity. Such videos may document events or personal stories, for example.

You can easily record amateur videos and upload one episode a week to make users eager for the next portion. This really boosts user engagement as well as retention. Try a visual storytelling technique in order to bring your brand closer to the target audience.

Conclusion

To wrap up, always beware when someone tells you there is no work involved in passive income. If passive income is your goal, you have to perform your due diligence, and that is work. Whatever investments you make requires constant management and checking up on the industries' progress where your investments are. And that, my dear friend, is work, too!

However, the good news is that both management and research will be a part-time endeavor. And you can do this work anywhere you are in the world.

Above all, do not forget to have fun as you research and implement the passive income plans that will enable you to live your dreams to the fullest. Making money every day, every week, and every month is fun, and testing your hands on the two most popular marketing strategies outlined in this book is fun as well.

So, go out there, implement what you have studied in this book, and take action!

CPSIA information can be obtained
at www.ICGtesting.com
Printed in the USA
BVHW061329150421
605035BV00001B/32